FREEWAY

Englisch für berufliche Schulen

Technik

von
Rosemary King
Wolfgang Rosenkranz
Graham Tucker

unter Mitwirkung von
Hellmut Imsel

Ernst Klett Verlag für Wissen und Bildung
Stuttgart · Dresden

FREEWAY – Ausgabe Technik
Englisch für berufliche Schulen

von

Rosemary King M.A., Fachlehrerin für Englisch an der Berufsbildenden Schule, Wesel;

Wolfgang Rosenkranz, Diplom-Handelslehrer, Oberstudienrat an der Freiherr-vom-Stein-Schule, Bad Oeynhausen;

Graham Tucker B.A., Fachleiter für Englisch an der Berufsbildenden Schule, Castrop-Rauxel

Beratung durch Hellmut Imsel, Studiendirektor, Fachleiter am Seminar für Schulpädagogik, Stuttgart

Dieses Werk folgt der reformierten Rechtschreibung und Zeichensetzung. Ausnahmen bilden Texte, bei denen künstlerische, philologische oder lizenzrechtliche Gründe einer Änderung entgegenstehen.

 Gedruckt auf Papier, das aus chlorfrei gebleichtem Zellstoff hergestellt wurde.

1. Auflage   1 ⁴ ³ ² | 1999 98 97

© Ernst Klett Verlag GmbH, Stuttgart 1995
Alle Rechte vorbehalten.

Redaktion: Volker Wendland
Grafik: Uta Böttcher
Einbandgestaltung und Computergrafik: Elmar Feuerbach
Druck: Grafos, Madrid. Printed in Spain

ISBN 3-12-809600-7

FREEWAY, das neue einbändige Lehrwerk für den Englischunterricht an berufsbildenden Schulen, führt aufbauend auf dem mittleren Bildungsabschluss zur Fachhochschulreife. Es entspricht den Richtlinien und Lehrplänen für berufliche Schulen der verschiedenen Bundesländer.

FREEWAY – Ausgabe Technik – ist insbesondere an gewerblich-technischen Fachoberschulen und Höheren Berufsfachschulen sowie in entsprechenden Kursen an Fachschulen und Berufsschulen einsetzbar.

FREEWAY – Ausgabe Technik – ist wie folgt aufgebaut:

Units 1–5 Basic Structures

Units 6–10 Advanced Structures

Further Reading

Units 11–15 Exam Preparation

Dem unterschiedlichen Kenntnisstand und den verschiedenen Voraussetzungen bei Schülerinnen und Schülern der angesprochenen Schultypen wurde durch eine flache Strukturprogression in den ersten fünf Units Rechnung getragen. Damit wird auch schwächeren Lernenden der Zugang zu den Themen erleichtert.

In den Units 6–10 werden Aufbaustrukturen in einem berufsbezogenen Kontext vermittelt. Es findet bereits hier eine intensive Vorbereitung auf die Anforderungen der schriftlichen Abschlussprüfungen statt.
Ein zusätzliches Textangebot (Further Reading) schließt den ersten Teil des Lehrbuches ab. Die Texte in diesem Teil sind auf einem gehobenen Niveau und decken die Themenbereiche Freizeit, Sport und Reise ab.

In den Units 11–15 werden schwerpunktmäßig technische Inhalte behandelt. Texte und Aufgaben entsprechen dem Prüfungsniveau, wobei insbesondere die Beschreibung von technischen Anlagen und Abläufen im Vordergrund steht. Die Grammatikschwerpunkte der vorherigen Units werden hier noch einmal wiederholt und gefestigt.

Im Anhang befinden sich neben einer ausführlichen Grammatikübersicht das Vokabular und die alphabetische Wortschatzliste mit dem Grund- und Lehrwerkswortschatz.

Die Hörverständnistexte der einzelnen Units sind ebenfalls am Ende des Lehrwerks abgedruckt.

FREEWAY – Ausgabe Technik – zeichnet sich durch folgende Merkmale aus:

Übersichtlichkeit und schnelle Orientierung

Die ersten zehn Units sind nach dem Doppelseitenprinzip aufgebaut:

Starter Motivation	Auf der mit Fotos und Zeichnungen illustrierten Motivationsseite findet eine erste Annäherung an das Thema statt. Bereits vorhandene Kenntnisse werden durch einfache Übungen aktiviert.

Teil A (Doppelseite)
Textarbeit   Anhand von Texten, Statistiken und Übersichten wird in das Thema der Unit eingeführt. Die Grammatikschwerpunkte werden kontextualisiert vorgestellt und imitativ bzw. reproduktiv geübt.

Teil B (Doppelseite)
Grammatik   Im B-Teil wird der Grammatikschwerpunkt der Unit trainiert. Die Übungen sind inhaltlich an die jeweilige Unit angelehnt, das Niveau des Wortschatzes wird hier aber bewusst niedrig angesetzt, um die Grammatik flexibel einsetzen zu können. Der B-Teil wird immer durch eine anspruchsvolle Aufgabe abgeschlossen, die mit "A" (= Advanced) gekennzeichnet ist.

Teil C (Doppelseite)
Textarbeit   Der C-Teil dient der Vertiefung des Unitthemas, wobei in der Regel ein längerer Text zu bearbeiten ist.

Teil D
Hörverständnis   Im D-Teil schließt jede Unit mit Übungen zum Hörverständnis ab. Dazu werden hier neben handlungsorientierten Aufgaben Sprechanlässe zur Verbesserung der Kommunikationsfähigkeit geschaffen.

Flexible Handhabung

Um den Vorkenntnissen und Interessen der Lernenden gerecht zu werden und um die Ziele der jeweiligen Schulform optimal zu erreichen, soll der Unterrichtende die Möglichkeit haben, flexibel mit **FREEWAY** zu planen.

Dabei sind z.B. folgende Varianten denkbar:

– Bei leistungsstarken Klassen könnte es sich z.B. bei den ersten fünf Units anbieten, nur die C-Teile zu bearbeiten (Vertiefung des Themas).

– Ebenfalls wäre es möglich, jeweils nur den A- und B-Teil (Einführung in das Thema und Grammatikschwerpunkt) zu behandeln.

– Soll verstärkt die Grammatik geübt werden, dann ist auch ein Schnelldurchgang möglich, indem lediglich der B-Teil durchgenommen wird.

– Die Hörverständnisübungen und weiteren Aufgaben im D-Teil können natürlich mit allen Varianten kombiniert werden.

Klare grammatikalische Strukturierung

Der Schwerpunkt der Grammatik liegt in den ersten Units auf der Wiederholung der wichtigsten *Tenses,* in den folgenden Units in den Bereichen *Conditional, Passive Voice, Reported Speech, Participle, Gerund* und *Infinitive.*

Um die Übersichtlichkeit im Lehrbuch zu erhöhen, wurden Übungen zu Nebenstrukturen in das Workbook ausgelagert. Eine benutzerfreundliche Grammatikübersicht mit Erklärungen befindet sich im Anhang. In den Grammatikteilen der Units wird jeweils auf die entsprechenden Seiten im Anhang verwiesen.

Intensive Prüfungsvorbereitung

Auf der Grundlage eines längeren Textes dient der C-Teil in den Units 6–10 der systematischen Vorbereitung auf die schriftlichen Prüfungen mit gezielter Hinführung zur Textproduktion.
Eine INFO-BOX zum schnellen Nachschlagen gibt eine Übersicht über die wichtigsten Schritte zur Bearbeitung von *Comprehension Questions*, *Summary*, *Comment*, *Translation* und *Description*.
In den Units 11–15 (Exam Preparation) liegt der Schwerpunkt der Prüfungsvorbereitung auf technischen Inhalten.

Weitere Merkmale

- Die Themen und der Wortschatz haben einen festen Bezug zur Arbeitswelt.

- Ein inhaltlicher und kommunikativer Schwerpunkt wurde auf die Bedeutung und Verwendung der englischen Sprache in einem zusammenwachsenden Europa gelegt.

- Unter Berücksichtigung des handlungsorientierten Ansatzes wurde versucht, die Lernenden anhand unterschiedlicher Situationen an adäquate Kommunikationsformen heranzuführen.

- Fester Bestandteil der ersten 10 Units ist die Schulung des Hörverständnisses unter Einsatz von Sprechern mit verschiedenen Akzenten (auch *non-native speakers*).

FREEWAY setzt circa 1 350 Wörter als Grundwortschatz voraus. Diese werden systematisch wiederholt und durch maßvolle Neueinführungen auf einen Gesamtwortschatz von circa 2 700 Wörtern erweitert.

Das Lehrwerk **FREEWAY** – **Ausgabe Technik** – umfasst das vorliegende

Lehrbuch, ein

Arbeitsbuch mit einem technischen Teil zu jeder Unit sowie weiteren schriftlichen Übungen zu Wortschatz und Grammatik, einen

Lehrerband mit didaktisch-methodischen Hinweisen und Hintergrundinformationen sowie dem Schlüssel zu allen Aufgaben des Schülerbuches und des Arbeitsbuches und eine

Cassette mit allen Hörverständnisübungen des Lehrbuches.

Wir wünschen Ihnen viel Spaß und Erfolg bei der Arbeit mit diesem Lehrwerk.

Autorin / Autoren und Redaktion

Basic Structures

Unit 1	**Training for work**	Page 9

Texts	Come to Leeds College
	Leeds and Dortmund: An exchange programme
Grammar	Present Simple
	Present Continuous
Skills	Giving your opinion

Unit 2	**Just the job**	Page 17

Texts	"Computers Unlimited"
	Workers – past and present
Grammar	Past Simple
	Present Perfect
Skills	Writing a letter of application

Unit 3	**Europe**	Page 25

Texts	A handful of Ecus
	The European Union – wider and wider?
Grammar	Past Simple
	Past Perfect
	Past Continuous
Skills	Interpreting charts

Unit 4	**Telecommunications/Advertising**	Page 33

Texts	The technological revolution
	50 billion dollars for advertising in Europe
Grammar	Future
	Adjectives
	Adverbs
Skills	Analyzing and writing advertisements

Unit 5	**Transport**	Page 41

Texts	The jam busters
	From jam to tram
Grammar	Relative Clauses
	Modal Auxiliaries
Skills	Analyzing and designing promotion material

Advanced Structures

Unit 6	Environment	Page 49

Texts	Everyone can help to save the world
	Vehicles go round again
Grammar	Reported Speech
Skills	Answering questions on a text

Unit 7	Energy	Page 57

Texts	More wealth – less energy
	New U.S. energy alternatives
Grammar	Conditionals
Skills	Writing a summary

Unit 8	Automation	Page 65

Texts	New production technologies
	The new industrial revolution
Grammar	Passive Voice
Skills	Describing a process

Unit 9	Changes in the British industry	Page 73

Texts	Newcastle takes off
	Jobs – from France to Scotland
Grammar	Infinitive
	Gerund
Skills	Writing a comment

Unit 10	Immigration in the United States	Page 81

Texts	Two faces of America
	Immigration and welfare
Grammar	Present Participle
	Past Participle
Skills	Writing a translation

Further Reading

1	Free time:	Computer games defended	Page 89
2	Sports:	The crying game	Page 90
3	Tourism:	Tourists resort to all the comforts of home	Page 91

Exam Preparation

| Unit 11 | Car technology | Page 92 |

Text	Back to the drawing board
Grammar revision	Mixed Tenses Passive Voice
Skills	Describing the internal combustion engine

| Unit 12 | Energy production | Page 96 |

Text	Energy from the wind
Grammar revision	Mixed Tenses Conditionals
Skills	Explaining electricity supply

| Unit 13 | Technology and pollution | Page 100 |

Text	A future for the earth?
Grammar revision	Mixed Tenses Gerund/Participle/Infinitive
Skills	Making decisions in waste management

| Unit 14 | CAD/CAM/CIM | Page 104 |

Text	Automating design
Grammar revision	Mixed Tenses Modal Auxiliaries
Skills	Describing industrial processes

| Unit 15 | Civil engineering | Page 108 |

Text	The Golden Gate Bridge
Grammar revision	Mixed Forms Reported Speech
Skills	Making decisions in civil engineering

Appendix

Grammar	Page 112
Vocabulary	Page 133
Word List (alphabetical)	Page 151
Tapescripts	Page 172

UNIT 1

Training for work

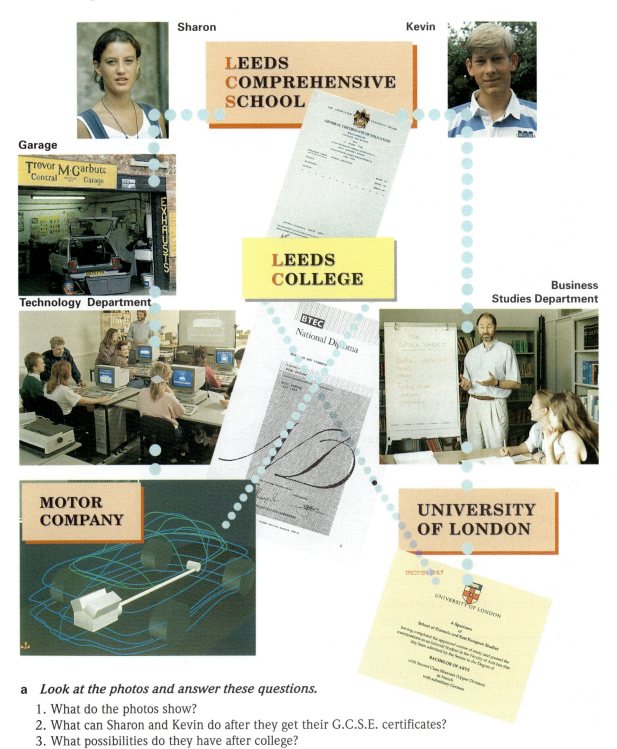

a *Look at the photos and answer these questions.*
   1. What do the photos show?
   2. What can Sharon and Kevin do after they get their G.C.S.E. certificates?
   3. What possibilities do they have after college?

b *Why are you at college?*

1 Come to Leeds College

LEEDS COLLEGE

Our college is one of the largest in the country. We employ over 400 teachers, both full-time and part-time. Our students are of all ages. About half of them are under 20, but we even have one who is 86 years old. The college runs over 200 courses at all levels. Most of the study programmes take place between nine and five, but we also offer evening and part-time courses.

B. Tec National Diploma courses

These full-time courses lead to higher job qualifications. Successful students can also go on to university. Changes are taking place in Europe. On these courses students can learn a lot about Europe and study a European language. This is a great start for a career in a modern Europe!

Costs:

The courses are free for students under 18. Students who live over 3 miles from the college receive a free bus pass. Students over 18 can get a grant from the Local Education Authority (LEA) to cover part of their costs for books and equipment.

For further details write to:

Leeds College
Shaftesbury Road
Leeds LS2 45
Telephone 0113/2449536

PROGRAMME OF STUDY

Engineering Studies
(Electrical, Mechanical or Civil)

First year subjects:
- Mathematics
- General Science
- Basic electrical/mechanical principles
- Computer studies
- English
- European language (French or German)

Second year subjects:
- Advanced principles
- Engineering applications of computer systems (CAD & CAM)
- Industrial control and instrumentation
- European language

Business Studies

First year subjects:
- Mathematics
- General office skills
- Basic accountancy
- Computer studies
- English
- European language (French or German)

Second year subjects:
- Advanced accountancy
- Statistics
- European Business and Finance
- European language

a *Answer the questions on the right. Start your answers with expressions like:*

> "In the text/brochure it says..."
> "In the second paragraph you can find out..."
> "On line... in the first/second... paragraph you can read..."

1. How do you know that Leeds College is very big?
2. How old are the students there?
3. When do most of the students have their lessons?
4. Why do the students learn a European language?
5. What can you get if you live far from the college?
6. How does the L.E.A. help older students and why?

b *Talk about your college. Think about:*

- size of the college
- teachers
- students
- courses
- your course
- costs

2 Two students meet in the college canteen.

Terry: Hello Sally. Long time no see. What are you doing here?
Sally: I'm doing a BTEC course.
Terry: And how are you finding it here?
Sally: Right now my big problem is mathematics. There are so many new formulas to learn. And then of course, there's the money.
Terry: I know what you mean. I've got a part-time job with my old firm. I work four hours in the evenings in the packing department. It's hard work, but it helps me pay for my flat.
Sally: Oh, it's easier for me. I still live with my parents. But I've got a weekend job in a restaurant. That gives me a little more pocket money. You know what I mean.
Terry: Which department are you in, by the way?
Sally: I'm in the Electrical Engineering department. First year. And you?
Terry: I'm in the Business Studies department. In my second year. We're studying accountancy, statistics and subjects like that at the moment.
Sally: What foreign language are you learning on your course?
Terry: This year I'm doing German for beginners – and that's my problem. There are so many new words to learn. Guten Tag. Ich … heiße Terry. … möchtest du …
Sally: Wow, look at the time. It's eleven o'clock. I've got a science lesson at five past. I have to rush. See you.
Terry: Bye. … eine Tasse Kaffee?

a *Complete the information sheet about the two students.*

	Student 1 (female)	Student 2 (male)
Name?		Terry
Course?		
Department?		
Home?		
Problems?		

b *Now write about the two students using the information above.*

c *Use the expressions in the dialogue above and make a new dialogue between these two students.*

Mike
- 1st year BTEC course in mechanical engineering
- bedsitter (one-room apartment)
- weekend job as a tennis coach
- problems with French/money

Linda
- 2nd year BTEC course in social studies
- house with three other students
- evening job as a waitress at a local club
- problems with statistics/money

d *Now write about your college, home and any work you do.*

UNIT 1 **B** PRESENT SIMPLE   PRESENT CONTINUOUS   SEE PAGES 121/122   PRESENT SIMPLE   PRESENT

1 Jill is a student.

This is what she says about herself:

"I'm eighteen and I go to Leeds College. I don't have any brothers or sisters. I live in Leeds with my parents. My parents give me £100 a month. I spend most of the money on books and things for college. In the evening I work at Pete's Pizza Palace. I need the money, because I buy quite a lot of clothes. In my free time I don't go out very often.

I usually go to college by bus. Sometimes a friend takes me there in his car. At college we have a lot of subjects. I'm in the second year. I like English and mathematics best, but I don't like French. We don't have German. Very often I do my homework with a friend. Normally we both work hard for our course. It leads to higher qualifications and I hope to find a good job afterwards."

a *Now talk about Jill.*

> **Example:** "Jill is eighteen and she goes to Leeds College. She doesn't have any brothers or sisters. She..."

b *Do you remember? Ask your partner(s) questions about Jill. Do not look at the text above.*

> **Example:** Where – Jill – live?   Where does Jill live?   Jill lives in Leeds.
> Who – live – with her parents?   Who lives with her parents?   Jill lives with her parents.

1. Where – Jill – go to college?
2. Who – give – her – £100 a month?
3. What – Jill – do – in the evening?
4. Why – she – work?
5. How – she – get – to college?
6. Which subjects – Jill – like best?
7. Who – do – homework – together with her?
8. How – they – work – for their course?
9. Which subject – they – not – have?
10. What – Jill – hope to find?

2 In the cafeteria

a *Guess what the students in the picture are doing.*

> **Example:** Tracy's writing.

b *What do you think? Ask your friends questions about the students in the cafeteria. What are they doing exactly?*

Use:

| What | How many | Where |
| What... about | Who... to | |

> **Example:** What is Tracy writing?
> I think she's writing a letter.

Michael   Dick   Terry   Tracy
Pete   Sam   Mary
                    David   Jenny
                Jill

JOUS SEE PAGES 121/122 PRESENT SIMPLE PRESENT CONTINUOUS SEE PAGES 121/122   **B**   UNIT 1

3 People at Leeds College

John is a student and Lucy is a secretary.

- Talk about *John and Lucy.*

  1. What do they normally do?
  2. What are they doing at the moment?

– usually
– normally
– on weekdays
– from Monday to Friday
– every day
– often

today...
right now...
at the moment...

– do homework
– organize meetings
– help visitors
– listen to teachers
– take a lot of calls
– do tests

4 On the phone

- *Fill in the right tense.*

Sally: Hi, Tom. Are you busy at the moment?
Tom: Yes, sure. Why?
Sally: What **1.** (do) you?
Tom: I **2.** (do) my homework, of course.
Sally: What again? You never **3.** (do) anything else, Tom. Why you **4.** (stay) home all the time?
Tom: You know that I **5.** (prepare) for my exams and right now I **6.** (try) to do my mathematics. Our teacher **7.** (give) us more than 20 exercises every day.
Sally: And what about me? I **8.** (wait) for your call every evening.
Tom: I'm really sorry about that. Why you **9.** (not go out) with Susan sometimes?
Sally: I **10.** (not see) her very often, because she **11.** (study) for a different exam this year. And Peggy **12.** (live) in France at the moment, because she **13.** (work) on her French project. I'm so unhappy...

5 Money problems

"Is your daughter having a good time at college?"

"You know, students are always complaining about money but every third student owns a car."

"Nowadays a lot of students are thinking seriously about their future and things are getting more expensive. And as you know, money makes the world go round."

- *Fill in the right tense.*

  "As you **1.** (know) life **2.** (get) so expensive these days, especially for poor students like us.
  I always **3.** (tell) Jack – why **4.** (go) you shopping at the corner shop?
  Things **5.** (cost) much less at the supermarket near the college.
  It **6.** (annoy) me because I **7.** (get) the feeling that he **8.** (not listen) to what I **9.** (say).
  It's terrible. We always **10.** (have) arguments about things like that.
  Sometimes I **11.** (think) he just **12.** (be) lazy.
  On the other hand there are other things where Jack **13.** (think) we can save.
  We **14.** (own) a little car for example. Jack **15.** (say) we **16.** (not need) it.
  He **17.** (be) quite right. And so we **18.** (think) of selling it.
  We **19.** (have) to do something. Money **20.** (not grow) on trees."

1 Leeds and Dortmund: An exchange programme

a *Look at the picture which goes with the newspaper article below. Who do you think the people are?*

b *Read the article and check if you are right.*

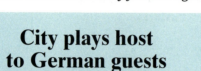

City plays host to German guests
by Marigold Prince

"For these young people it's quite an adventure" says head of department Willi Schmitz from the Berufsbildende Schulen in Dortmund, Germany. His group of 16 students are just getting to know their English host partners at a reception at Leeds College.

"For many of them it's their first visit to Britain and their first chance to put their English to the test." Indeed, the group of 18–20 year old students don't know very much about each other before their first meeting. Usually students in both groups receive a passport photo of his or her partner and a short introduction form before the exchange. This form gives them information about their partner's leisure interests, plans for the future and their favourite food and music.

"I hope mine's not a smoker who's only into heavy metal!" remarks one young Leeds student to his friend as he passes me with some coffee and biscuits for the visitors.

As well as the new situation with their partners and the language, for one week the group has to cope with the different way of life in an English family. "But," adds Willi Schmitz, who is on his fourth visit to Leeds, "after they get to know each other on the first evening, they usually all get on like a house on fire."

This week their programme includes visits to a number of local firms, trips out to the Yorkshire Moors and the Lake District as well as a joint project in the College workshops. "This year both groups are working together on a business studies/technology project on local environment problems," says Peter Stewart, Leeds College's exchange organizer.

"We find that working together on a project is certainly one of the best ways of making really good friends. Many of the students from past exchanges still visit their partners or go on holiday with them and every year there are always one or two students who are especially unhappy when it is time to leave," Peter tells me.

As I leave the staffroom at the College, the German students are collecting their luggage and leaving for the first night with their partner and his or her family. Already it seems to me that some of their earlier ideas about Britain and the British are changing. I hear a couple of comments from some of the German students. One of them says, if I understand his German correctly, "they seem really friendly." "Yes, and it's not raining, either," replies his friend and smiles. Maybe travel really can broaden the mind!

426 words

c *Use information from the text and make a list of:*
1. four things on the programme in Leeds this week.
2. four people the students expect to meet during the week.
3. four things the students may worry about before they leave Germany.

d *Which of these statements are true and which are false? Use information from the text to support your answer.*

1. The first exchange visit to another country is always an exciting experience.
2. Exchange students are well-informed about each other before the visit.
3. One of the Leeds students wants a smoker as a partner.
4. After one meeting, the exchange students generally like each other very much.
5. There are visits to local sights on the week's programme.
6. Students who work together get to know each other well.
7. There are two projects this year, one for the business students and one for the technology students.
8. Students who take part in these exchanges do not often see each other again.
9. Before they go to their partner's houses, the German students pick up their bags.
10. After the first evening, the Dortmund students already have different ideas about the British.

e *Which four of the true statements in exercise "d" represent the main ideas in the text?*

f *In these sentences from the text, who or what do the words in bold type refer to?*
1. ...**it**'s quite an adventure... (line 1) — An exchange programme
2. For many of **them** it's their first visit to Britain... (line 7) — German students
3. ...**he** passes me with some coffee and biscuits... (line 19) — Willi
4. ...who's on **his** fourth visit to Leeds... (line 24/25) — A young Leeds student
5. As **I** leave the staffroom... (line 43)
6. ...**they** seem really friendly... (line 50/51)

g *Find in the text the opposites of these words:* guest; work; same; last; arrive; alone

h *Here are some words from the text and their dictionary definitions. Find the matching pairs.*

1. host d)
2. to get to know e)
3. leisure h)
4. to cope with g)
5. exchange b)
6. joint (project) a)
7. to broaden c)
8. adventure f)

a) something people do together
b) when things or people change places
c) to make something wider or bigger
d) person who has guests
e) to meet someone for the first time
f) something difficult or dangerous
g) to manage a situation well
h) free time

i *Now answer these questions. What do you think?*
1. Why is an exchange visit such an adventure?
2. Why is Willi Schmitz sure that his students can have a good time in Leeds?
3. Why is it important for the students to work together on a joint project?
4. Why do students from past exchanges still visit each other?
5. Why does one student say "Yes, and it's not raining, either"?

j *Translate lines 43 to 53. (City plays host to German guests)*

2 An informal letter

You are taking part in an exchange scheme that your college is organizing. You already have some information about your partner and now you want to write to him or her to introduce yourself.

- Write an informal letter in English.
  Begin with 'Dear...' and end with 'Yours...' or 'with love from...'

Include these points:	Use these expressions:
yourself and your family	I am... /in my family we usually...
your interests	I am interested in...
what you like/dislike	I like/love/can't stand...
your personality and what you look like	Some people say I am.../I look...
your town	There's.../we've got... in our town
the weather in your area	it's sometimes.../often... here

15

1 An exchange visit

 a *Listen to the cassette and then answer these questions.*

1. Who are the speakers?
2. Who is talking about what? The pictures below may help you.

b *Listen to the cassette again and correct these statements.*

1. The exchange students are working on the environment project at the end of the week.
2. John thinks that visits to local firms and factories are boring.
3. Klaus thinks you learn more about the British as a tourist.
4. John's mother is not very enthusiastic about the exchange.
5. John believes that the Germans are all serious and hard-working.
6. Klaus finds living in an English family strange.

c *Complete the sentences below with the phrases in the box.*

> I suppose   I think   I believe   I'm sure   in my view
> I agree   in my opinion   I'm quite certain   I don't think
> for example   for instance   I mean

1. …it's really great that we have the chance to see places like that.
2. …, that's why these exchanges are such a good idea.
3. Oh yes, … with you.
4. …that tourists learn half as much.
5. They don't have enough contact with the locals, …
6. They still think, …, that all the Germans are serious.
7. …, isn't it a bit strange for you, Klaus, living in a foreign family?
8. …, you're all so friendly to me.

2 Giving your opinion

a *Now try to find more arguments for exchanges.*
Use the expressions in the box above for your arguments.

b *Comment on the following statement using the expressions in the box above.*

"Learning a foreign language at college is a waste of time."

UNIT 2 UNIT 2 UNIT 2 UNIT 2 UNIT 2 UNIT 2 UNIT 2 UNIT 2 UNIT 2 UNIT 2 UNIT 2

Just the job

Are people always asking you what you want to be when you leave school? Try our special chart to help you discover which is the job!

- *Work out the best job for your partner. He/she should answer 'yes' or 'no' to the questions. It's more interesting if your partner closes his/her book. When you reach one of the symbols, look at the list below for a suitable job.*

 You're creative and like people and talking. The job for you: something creative like a singer, dancer, journalist or hairdresser.

 You're active and practical. The job for you: something active like a sportsman/woman, police officer or mechanic.

 You're helpful and friendly. The job for you: one where you can help people like a nurse, air steward/stewardess or receptionist.

 You're practical and creative. The job for you: something like an office worker, tourist guide, salesman/woman or designer.

 You're clever and independent. The job for you: one which has something to do with books like a language teacher or writer.

 You're logical and like to learn. The job for you: one where you must solve problems and is well-paid like a computer specialist or advertising manager.

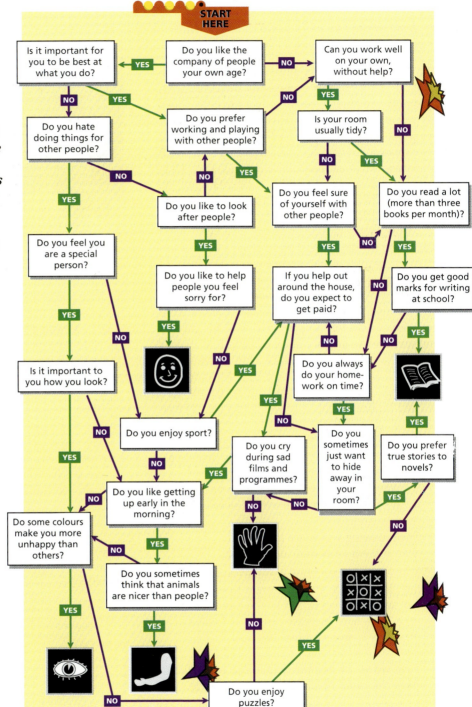

© *Jacqui Deevoy, London*

1 "Computers Unlimited"

a *Look at the two photos and describe what you can see.*

Me

My boss

The American dream is alive and living in North London. John Sanson started his own business, Sanson Computers, 6 years ago in a small flat above his parents' butcher's shop. However, in the last few
5 years his sales have increased so enormously that his company now has a turnover of £13.5m. At 28 Mr Sanson has already become a very rich man. Only 2 weeks before he opened his computer shop, he graduated from Nottingham University with a de-
10 gree in Electrical and Computer Engineering. "A lot of people in my family were self-employed and I wanted to do the same. I have always been interested in computers and while I was at University I saw the possibilities of a growing market in personal
15 computers. So, when I left University , I decided to take the risk," John explains. However, there were not a lot of risks for him; he lived with his parents and was used to life on a student's grant. Moreover he only had a staff of one, so he didn't have a high
20 wage bill. Sanson's firm is now called 'Computers Unlimited'. He employs more than 80 people who sell and service PC software and hardware. "Nowa-days you can go out and buy a computer like a TV or video recorder," says Sanson. As a result his business has expanded enormously . In his first year he 25
made a profit of only £11,000. In the meantime his profits have reached £ 2.3m a year. Naturally enough, he has moved from his small shop in North London and has now rented a large store in a business park just outside London. He sums up his success story 30
like this: "Of course it has been hard work. But the secret is that I still enjoy the work and my boss likes me, too."
302 words

© Roger Trapp, The Independent, London (adapted)

b *Answer the following questions.*

1. Where did John Sanson open his first shop?
2. What did John study at university?
3. Why did he decide to start his own business?
4. Why didn't John have a lot of risks at first?
5. How has his business developed?
6. Where has he now moved to?
7. Why, do you think, has he moved?

c The following words are in the text. *Match them with their definitions.*

1. to employ (line 21) – 2. electrical engineering (line 10) – 3. student's grant (line 18) – 4. self-employed (line 11) – 5. enormously (line 25) – 6. to increase (line 5) – 7. alive (line 1) – 8. success (line 30)

A. the technology of electricity (n.)
B. active (adj.)
C. to give work to. They ... 150 workers in that factory (vt)
D. money that students receive during their studies from the government.(n.)
E. to a great extent (adv.)
F. (good fortune) to have great ... in life. (n.)
G. to make or become bigger in size or number (vt)
H. having your own firm or company (adj.)

d *Find words or expressions in the text which have the same meaning as the following.*

1. company   2. little   3. grown   4. left university with a degree   5. workers   6. computer equipment   7. even to this time   8. employer

e *Say whether the words you have found are nouns, adjectives, adverbs or verbs.*

f *Use the words to talk about John Sanson.*

2 A radio interview

"Young people in Southampton" is a popular programme on Radio Solent, the local radio station. Des Jacky is talking to Roberta Crumb.

DJ: Welcome to "Young people in Southampton". Today we have Roberta Crumb with us in the studio. Roberta, you are 24 and you ran a small video production service here in Southampton. Now could you tell our listeners a little about what has happened to you and your business?

RC: Well, it all started when I saw an advert in the local paper. At that time I was employed at a large electronics firm near here.

DJ: And what was the advert for?

RC: "Starting your own business." The local bank offered to give advice to young people who wanted to start up their own business. At first I didn't take it all that seriously. But the more I thought about it, the more interested I became. I talked to my parents and my boyfriend about it. They said I should do what I really wanted to do, namely, to start up a small video production service. So, after some time I went to the bank and had a talk with the bank manager. He explained all the advantages and also the risks of being self-employed.

DJ: What happened then?

RC: Well, after a lot of thought I made up my mind to start up the business. We recorded customers' weddings, birthday parties – anything like that, but I didn't earn as much as in my old job.

DJ: And what happened then?

RC: Well, I still had to pay back a lot of money to the bank for the video equipment, and advertising cost me a lot, too. I couldn't live on the income from my work. So I decided to close down the business. I think my main mistake was that I didn't watch the market development carefully enough. People nowadays have their own video cameras and don't need a professional service.

DJ: And where are you working now, Roberta?

RC: I've got a job in a photographer's shop. The pay's not bad, but the problem is I have to pay back the money to the bank. I haven't had a holiday for 2 years now. I just can't afford one.

a *True or false?* 1. Roberta worked in a photographer's shop. 2. The local bank put an advert in the newspaper. 3. Roberta earned enough money from her business. 4. The bank manager gave her some advice on starting her own business.

b *Complete these sentences. Choose from the nouns and verbs in the boxes. Use the same tenses as in the dialogue.*

1. Roberta... a video production...
2. She... an... in the local newspaper.
3. She... a talk with the...
4. Roberta... up the business.
5. She (not)... the market... closely enough.
6. Roberta (not)... enough customers.
7. She... down her business.
8. She... in a... shop.

have (2) – see – run – start – watch – work – close

advert – development – service – business – bank manager – photographer's

c *Join the sentences with the following linking words.*

Example: 1. In the interview we hear that Roberta ran a video production service 2. First she...

In the interview we hear that... Then...   After that...   However... As a result...   So...   Now...   First...

UNIT 2 B PAST SIMPLE   PRESENT PERFECT   SEE PAGES 122–125   PAST SIMPLE   PRESENT PERFECT

1 Softright Systems

Jane Topper moved to Glasgow seven years ago. There she met Harry Coe who didn't like his old job in an import company. As they both were interested in computers they **1.**(decide) to start a small software company. First they only **2.**(write) computer programs for Harry's old import company, but soon they **3.**(see) that a lot of other companies also **4.**(need) special software. So they **5.**(hire) some young programmers who **6.**(work) in small teams and **7.**(develop) a lot of new ideas. The company **8.**(be) profitable from the start. Although other companies **9.**(have) their problems Softright **10.**(not lose) money. In their third year in business they **11.**(make) a profit of £150,000. Then they **12.**(try) some advertising and it **13.**(work). That is why they **14.**(spend) more on marketing in the following years. At the beginning Jane and Harry only **15.**(have) two small rooms for their work. After some time they **16.**(rent) offices in several different buildings. But last year they **17.**(buy) a warehouse in central Glasgow. The move **18.**(not be) easy and it **19.**(take) more than two months. "We **20.**(lose) quite a lot of money when we **21.**(move)," Jane said. "But we **22.**(not want) to work in different places any more. That **23.**(be) a good decision!"

a *Complete the sentences in the past tense.*

b *Find the missing parts in the following statements about Jane and Harry's company. Ask a classmate about it. He/she should give you an answer with the help of the information in the cloud.*

Example: 1. When did Harry's parents move to Glasgow? They moved to Glasgow in 1966.   2. Where…

1. Harry's parents moved to Glasgow in…
2. After college in Glasgow Harry worked at…
3. The company imported…
4. He enjoyed his… very much.
5. But one day Harry left because…
6. He met… on a computer course.
7. She told him…
8. Of course, they needed… for their new company.
9. So they went to…

> some money   a bank
> that she wanted to start her own business, too   he wanted to be his own boss
> his partner   1966   his father's company
> electronic parts   work

2 Times have changed

- *Describe what has happened to the following two companies in the last few years.*

Example: Evans & Sons have been in Sheffield since 1990. Linda Graves has…

	be in Sheffield	sell	make a loss	expand	buy a company abroad
Evans & Sons	since 1990	120 million cassettes so far	never	three times	already
Linda Graves	for five years	about 1000 cars up to now	once	just	not yet

20

ES 122–125 PAST SIMPLE PRESENT PERFECT SEE PAGES 122–125 PAST SIMPLE PRESENT UNIT 2

3 An Interview

Mary Wilson has applied for a job in the export department of **Kwik-Fit**. In an interview she talks about her life and career.

a *Take her role. Use the following verbs.*

| be pass get live go study travel work | **Example:** "I was born in Leeds in 1972. I went to school from…" |

```
1972   1977   1988   1990   1992   1994   today
 *                            *      *
 born                        exam   married

              in Leeds              in Sheffield

         to school  as a me-  at      at Clarks'  self-
                    chanic    college  Ltd.       employed

                            interested in foreign languages

                         *    *   *    *
                         abroad four times
```

b *Ask your classmates about:*

| date of birth, schools, college, important exams, address, trips abroad, experience in English, experience at work, hobbies |

c *Complete the following report about KWIK-FIT. Put the verbs into the simple past or present perfect tense.*

Example: 25 years ago Tom Farmer opened two garages in Edinburgh. In 1974 he…

Kwik-Fit

25 years ago Tom Farmer (open) two garages in Edinburgh. In 1974 he (sell) to G.A. Robinson. Shortly afterwards Robinson (get) into difficulties. Then Farmer (buy) the company again. Since then the company's name (be) Kwik-Fit. In the beginning most of the business (be) with private cars, but in 1987 Kwik-Fit (begin) a service for companies. In the last few years customers (include) ICI, Avis and British Petroleum. Up to now Kwik-Fit (keep growing).

4 How long …?

a *Answer the following questions.*

1. How long have you been working with this book?   for … weeks/since …
2. How long have you known about this college?   for … years
3. How long have you been learning English?   for … months/since …
4. How often have you visited England?   once, twice, … times, never

b *Translate the following sentences. Watch out for the correct tenses.*

1. Peter arbeitet seit Januar bei Seafood Limited.   2. Er kennt den Manager seit einigen Jahren.
3. Sie planen seit drei Monaten ein neues Projekt.   4. Peters Frau hat sich dreimal um eine Stelle beworben.   5. Sie wartet schon seit langem auf eine Antwort.   6. Sie sind schon lange nicht mehr zusammen im Urlaub gewesen.

1 Workers – past and present

a *In one sentence say what subject these texts have in common.*

For the people who lived in the East End of London in the middle of the nineteenth century, life was hard. Often a whole family lived in one room and even 12 year-old children went out to work. Working days were long, often from five in the morning until nine at night. There were no holidays until 1871 when the government introduced the first Bank Holidays. At this time 77% of the population of Britain belonged to the working class and so had to live in such conditions. Even to buy the most basic food could cost a man three days' pay. When a man lost his job, which could happen at the end of the week, the day or even the hour, or when he became sick, he had nothing except his family and friends to help him.

Europe's workers – underpaid but happy!

This is the result of a survey which a London firm has just completed for the managers of a number of multinational companies who have employees all over Europe. The survey shows companies what they can expect from the workers in each country. More than 500,000 workers answered the questions about attitudes to pay, workmates and benefits.

The survey shows that in general Europe's workers enjoy what they do, get on well with their workmates and identify with the company they work for.

However, attitudes to pay are less positive. Although 57% of workers in the Netherlands are satisfied with their wages, in Switzerland only 44% of the workers are happy with their pay. In Britain the number is much lower, 35%. Moreover, the Dutch also feel happiest about their working conditions and benefits. Workers there receive paid sick leave after two days at 70% of their pay for one year.

Working hours within Europe vary quite a lot. In Luxembourg the maximum is 48 hours and in Denmark it is much lower, 37 hours. Britain, however, has no laws about the maximum number of working hours.

There are also no laws in Britain about the amount of paid holiday a worker can have. The average is usually 23 days. Greek workers on the other hand can expect four weeks minimum holiday after one year's work.

Finally, on the question of job satisfaction, the survey's results are positive. Most of Europe's workers are happy with their workmates as well as with the job they do.

The European, London (adapted)   255 words

Are you happy with your pay?

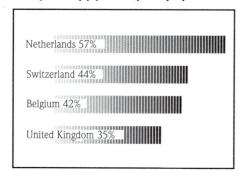

Are you satisfied with your job?

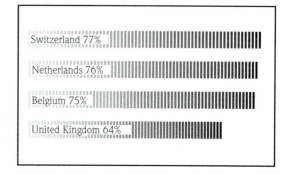

b *Which of these pictures show conditions of work which are mentioned in the texts? Name them.*

c *The following numbers appear in the texts. What information do they give?*

> 500,000; twelve; 2;
> thirty-five; 5; twenty-three.

d *Answer these questions.*
1. When did 77% of the British population belong to the working class?
2. How many hours per day did people often work in the past?
3. What help did workers in the past receive when they became ill?
4. Why did the London firm carry out its survey?
5. The survey shows that most workers in Europe agree about some conditions of their work. Which ones?
6. Which two conditions of their work are the Dutch the happiest about?
7. Which conditions of their work do you think the British are unhappy about?
8. Job satisfaction depends on pay. Do you agree? Use the charts to help you with your answer.

e *How has the situation of workers in Europe changed in the last one hundred years?*

f *Translate lines 1 to 8 (Europe's Workers – underpaid but happy!)*

2 What about you?

a *Talk about your experiences.*
1. Have you ever worked full-time or in your free time?
2. Have you ever had a job you enjoyed?
3. Is it important for you to enjoy your job?

b *Choose five things in this list which you think are important.*

	workmates	pay	travel	holidays	working hours	to help other people	to be independent	to have a secure job
important								
not important								

c *Give reasons for your choice.*

In my job	I want to… it's important to me to… I would like to… I hope that…	because… in order to… so that…

Job advertisements

A leading European engineering company requires a
Technical Assistant
for its sales department in Manchester.

The successful candidate must be aged 21–30, have a B. Tec National Diploma or similar qualifications and some experience in engineering. A good knowledge of English and German is essential.

We offer a 4 year contract (renewable) with a top salary and excellent working conditions for the right person.

Apply in English and enclose your CV and copies of certificates to Mr Len Linscott
      Top Tools Ltd.
      105 Oldham Road
      Manchester M13 9PL
      England

Export Assistant
Euromove, a leading Import/Export company is looking for a responsible person, aged 21-30, to work in its expanding export department. The new assistant should be willing to travel overseas and be able to speak at least one foreign language. Applicants should have professional qualifications in Business Studies and some commercial experience. The company offers an interesting job with an attractive salary and company car.

Applications with full CV to

Ms Penny Skinner
Euromove
93 Marsh Green Road
Exeter EX4 6EW
England

a *Answer the following questions.* 1. What are the firms looking for? 2. What qualifications must the applicants have? 3. What advantages can you find in the jobs?

b *Apply for one of the jobs above. Complete the missing information in the letter below. Use your own personal details, where possible.*

---

name and address
of employer above

your address
date

Dear Sir/Madam/Mr.../Ms...,

With reference to your advert in today's newspaper, I would like to apply for the vacancy of (job). I am (age) and of (...) nationality. I have attended (college in....) since (date). In (date) I hope to pass my examination in (department). Before college I was employed at (name of firm) from (date) to (date) as a (job). In my job there I (tasks). I am applying for the job as (name of job) in your company because (reasons for applying). Enclosed please find my CV and copies of certificates. I look forward to hearing from you soon.

Yours faithfully/Yours sincerely
(name)

---

c After you have written the letter of application, the next step is to write a curriculum vitae (CV). *Write your own CV including the following information:*

> personal data, education
> qualifications, job experience
> interests, references

d Mr Linscott is interviewing two candidates for the job of Technical Assistant. *Find out:*
1. names of the candidates
2. their favourite subjects at school/college
3. their present jobs
4. why they have applied

e *Decide who you would choose for the job. Give reasons.*

UNIT 3

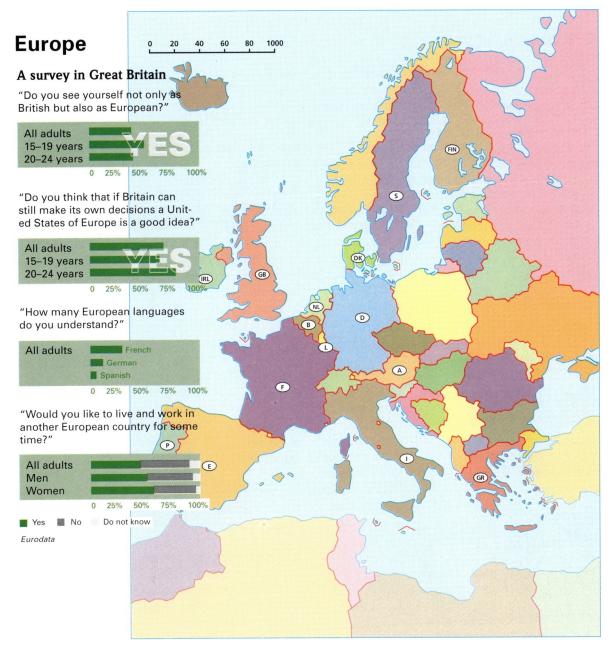

Europe

A survey in Great Britain

"Do you see yourself not only as British but also as European?"

"Do you think that if Britain can still make its own decisions a United States of Europe is a good idea?"

"How many European languages do you understand?"

"Would you like to live and work in another European country for some time?"

■ Yes ■ No ■ Do not know

Eurodata

a *Put the letters of these words in the right order to find the names of some European countries.*
canfre; dianler; laity; yemnarg; desnew; umigleb; cegeer

b *Answer the following questions.*
  1. Which letters on the map show which countries?
  2. What is the capital city of each country?
  3. What are the most important languages in Europe?
  4. Which of the countries on the map are now in the European Union?

c *Look at the chart and make a survey for your class. Replace British/Britain with your own nationality.*

1 A handful of Ecus

The Ecu is the new single currency of a united Europe, or is it really? Are the European Union nations ready for this coin on the road to unity? In order to answer these questions our journalists in Brussels, Marseille and London decided to go shopping with Ecus in their pockets. However, they quickly found out that people were still very suspicious of the new Ecus.

Donald Watson

For one moment I thought I had made history. I had bought a book and had paid with a 100 Ecu coin. The only problem was the change. The bookshop assistant first apologized that she didn't have any Ecus. But after she had looked up the exchange rate, she gave me a handful of Belgian francs with a smile. But then things started to get difficult. I decided to go to a second bookshop and try my luck again. I offered the manager another 100 Ecu coin for that week's edition of the "European".

While he was examining the coin, I started to explain the advantages of the new currency. He agreed with me. However, after he had examined both sides of the coin, he gave it back to me. "I'm afraid I can't accept this. I have no idea how to give you your change," he explained. The same thing happened in three other shops. I soon realized that the day of the Ecu had not arrived yet.

David Payne

I had some problems with my Ecus while I was working in the South of France. When I offered a taxi-driver in Aix en Provence the Ecus he simply got very angry and demanded his fare in francs. In the same city the receptionist of the Hotel Mercure thought that the coin looked nice, but didn't accept it. "A little souvenir, perhaps? But it's not real money, is it?" she remarked. In Marseille, on my way to the airport, another taxi-driver whom I had offered Ecus for the journey looked impressed. He had never seen them before. "They look nice. I can put them on a gold chain and give it to my wife," he said and put it in his pocket. Up until now I have not had much success with my new Ecus. I have still got most of them.

Maria Phillips

While I was staying in London, I decided to go to the famous Harrods department store. With the new European currency in my hand I tried to buy a watch for £49. The shop assistant looked very surprised when I gave her the Ecu coin. She turned it over and tried to decide what it could possibly be. In the end she refused to accept it and called the manager. After he had looked at the coin several times, he said "We take 16 different currencies in our store, even lira and Scottish pound notes, but I have never seen anything like this before." Nevertheless, after he had checked with the bank, he decided that he could accept it. And of course, I received pounds sterling for change.

The European, London (adapted)   505 words

a *Find examples of the following in the text:*
1. countries   2. cities   3. shops   4. jobs   5. European currencies

b *Answer the following questions.*
1. Why did Donald Watson think that he had made history?
2. Why didn't the shop-assistant in the first bookshop give Donald his change in Ecus?
3. What did Donald do while the manager in the second shop was looking at the Ecu?
4. How did the French taxi-drivers react when David Payne offered them the Ecus?
5. Why didn't the French receptionist accept the Ecus?
6. Why did Maria Phillips go shopping?
7. When did the manager accept Maria's Ecus?

c *Find the verbs or adjectives in the text which go with these nouns. Say where you have found them.*

Example: I have found the verb 'pay' on line 6 in the sentence "I had bought a book and had paid with a 100 Ecu coin."

noun: payment – decision – examination – explanation – agreement
verb: ? ? ? ? ?

noun: surprise – difference – impression – difficulty – anger
adjective: ? ? ? ? ?

d *Use the nouns above to complete these sentences.*

1. To Donald's... the taxi-driver accepted his Ecus.
2. At first he had great... in understanding the taxi-driver.
3. However, David tried to explain the... between an Ecu coin and French franc.
4. In the end they came to an...
5. The taxi-driver agreed that the... to introduce a single currency was a good one.

e *Answer the following questions.*

1. Do you think that people are now more willing to accept Ecus?
2. What advantages can a single European currency have?

2 The European Union*

European unity has been a slow and sometimes difficult process. After the 2nd World War most people in Europe dreamed of a United States of Europe: democratic, peaceful and wealthy.

However, many governments put their own political and national interests first. These factors have often slowed down the building of European unity.
Below you can read about some of the important steps on the road to a united Europe.

1957 Belgium, France, Germany, Italy, Luxembourg and the Netherlands...
1958 The European Community...
1960 Great Britain first...
1963 General de Gaulle, President of France...
1969 De Gaulle...
1973 Denmark, Ireland and Great Britain...
1979 First direct elections for the European Parliament...
1981 Greece...
1986 Portugal and Spain...EC
1991 Twelve member states...
1993 These twelve members...
1995 Sweden, Finland and Austria...

join the European Community
applies for membership
sign the Treaty of Rome
become members of the EC
vetoes the British application
comes into operation
joins the EC
sign the Maastricht Treaty for the European Political and Economic Union
resigns as President of France
take place
introduce the Single European Market (The European Union)
enter the EU.

a *Complete the sentences above with the information in the box.*

b *Give a report on the history of the EU. Now use the past tense. Use the linking words on page 19 to join the sentences.*

c *What happened in the EU after 1995?*

* In November 1993 the EC became the EU.

UNIT 3 **B** PAST SIMPLE PAST PERFECT PAST CONTINUOUS SEE PAGES 122–125 PAST SIMPLE PAST PERFE

1 Travelling in Europe

Last summer Robert Page, a computer salesman, travelled around France by train.
Here are his travel notes.

a *Answer these questions.*

1. What time did he arrive in Paris?
2. When did he go to the hotel?
3. What sights did he see in Paris?
4. Where did he meet John Walters for lunch?
5. What did he do on Wednesday morning?
6. Who did he meet on the train to Marseilles?
7. When did he visit the old port?
8. What did he do on Friday morning?

b *Make complete sentences with the following words:*

> **Example:** after/arrive/Paris/go to/hotel
> After he had arrived in Paris he went to the hotel.

1. after/be to/Eiffel Tower/meet/John Walters
2. after/meet John Walters/have/lunch
3. catch/train to Marseilles/after/do/some shopping
4. after/get on/train to Marseilles/meet two workmates
5. after/arrive/in Marseilles/visit/the old port
6. have/a meeting with Martin Turner/after/see/the old port
7. after/have/breakfast/spend/day on beach
8. catch/plane to Manchester/after/spend/day on beach.

JULY

12 MONDAY 18.00 Paris Gare du Nord
evening hotel – Montmartre

13 TUESDAY morning Eiffel Tower, Notre Dame 13.15 John Walters – business lunch Café des Artistes

14 WEDNESDAY morning shopping 13.10 train to Marseilles (Dan and Mike – workmates)

15 THURSDAY morning old port (very hot) 14.00 meeting – Martin Turner

16 FRIDAY 11.00 breakfast – Hôtel de Roi rest of day on beach 18.30 flight to Manchester

17

2 Some business trips do not go as well as others

Andy Williams met Robert Page and told him about what had gone wrong on his trip.

- *Use past perfect in one clause and simple past in the other. Use the words in brackets to join your sentences.*

> **Example:** arrive at station – ticket office close already (when)   When I arrived at the station the ticket office had already closed.

1. get to platform
   train – leave already   (when)
2. the next train – be late
   the engine – break down   (because)
3. at the hotel – find
   leave my case on bus   (that)
4. get to bus station
   it – shut already   (by the time)
5. ask a friend to
   meet me at youth hostel
   he – not arrive   (although)
6. later – remember
   give my friend the wrong address   (that)
7. leave the hotel to go for a meal
   lose credit card   (after)
8. return to hotel
   someone else – take my room   (by the time)

3 At the airport

a Mr Jones, a businessman from Cardiff, went to the airport last week to get his plane to Brussels.

Make sentences about these situations.

> **Example:** drive to airport/start to rain;
> As/While he was driving to the airport it started to rain.

1. show ticket at airport/passport fall out of pocket, 2. look around bookshop/meet a friend,
3. plastic bag break/he and friend go upstairs, 4. friend get coffee/he sit down at table,
5. they call his flight to Brussels/he and friend drink coffee

b Jason Norman is a journalist for the "Evening News" in Manchester. Two weeks ago he travelled to Frankfurt. At the airport he went to the bank to change some money.

Put the verbs in these sentences into simple past or past continuous. Be careful, some sentences have both verbs in the simple past. Join your sentences with one of these words: "while", "as", "when" or "and".

> **Example:** A lot of passengers wait at the counter – Jason Norman walk into bank
> A lot of passengers were waiting at the counter when Jason Norman walked into the bank.
> Jason put down his case – he take out his newspaper
> Jason put down his case and he took out his newspaper.

1. he look at the exchange rates – man behind him ask to borrow a pen
2. he stand in line – he count his money
3. he get to counter – Jason hand the money to the assistant
4. he talk to the assistant – there be an announcement
5. Jason listen to the announcement – the assistant leave the counter
6. she return – she give him a form
7. she count his money – Jason sign the form
8. she give him the money – he put it into his pocket

4 On the boat

- *Put the verbs in brackets into the correct form of the past tense (past simple, past perfect, or past continuous).*

While Tim Smith **1.** (stand) and **2.** (look) over the side of the boat which **3.** (take) him to Ostend, he **4.** (try) to imagine the people who **5.** (travel) below him in the Channel Tunnel. Although the tunnel **6.** (open) some time before and he **7.** (have) enough time to get used to the idea, he still **8.** (find) it difficult to imagine the journey to the Continent by rail and not by boat. Before they **9.** (complete) the tunnel, Britain **10.** (always be) an island and many people still **11.** (want) it that way.

1 The European Union – wider and wider?

Is it possible for the European Union to accept new members and, at the same time, to become an efficient and democratic political union?

YES says **Dominic Moisi**, assistant director of the French Institute for International Relations

It is an illusion to believe that we can live on an island of wealth and peace in western Europe while
5 the rest of the continent still has political and economic difficulties. The countries in the east also belong to Europe and so we must open the EU to them.

They have won freedom, but their political and
10 economic situation has not become stable yet. In order to become healthy and stable democracies these countries hope to join the EU in the near future.

After Greece, Spain and Portugal had become
15 democracies again, the EU accepted them as new members. Therefore we should now accept the new democratic eastern states in the same way.

In my opinion this can help both
20 the EU and the new members to open up new markets for their products. Another advantage is that the peoples of Europe can work and live together more
25 freely and so develop a democratic Europe. To do this we must then give the European Parliament more power.

NO says **Alman Metten**, Dutch MEP and Labour Party spokesman on European affairs

As the countries of eastern Europe are looking to the 30 West, politicians are talking about opening up the EU so that it becomes a community for all Europeans. But is this really a help for these countries? 35

The fact is that the present EU-members have not reached total European union. New members can only slow down this process. The present EU still suffers from one main problem: It is often difficult to make decisions quickly because at the moment there 40 are too many institutions and the member countries often only defend their national interests. In a real democratic union the European Parliament must have the power to make the decisions.

Is it at present possible for the EU 45 to accept new members and, at the same time, to increase its democracy and efficiency? In my view, the answer is "no" because with each new member the chances of agree- 50 ment become less. Before we accept new members the present members must give up their national positions and start to think and act as true Europeans. This is 55 the only way to reach an economic and political union.   354 words

The European, London (adapted)

a *Describe the cartoon.*
What is the cartoonist trying to say?

b *Which of the following arguments are given in the statements?*
1. We must help other countries to become stable democracies.
2. After the countries in Southern Europe had become democracies, we helped them immediately, and so we must help other countries, too.
3. Decision-making takes too much time in the present EU.
4. The old members must solve their problems first.

5. All European countries should belong to the EU so that Europe can become a strong political world power.
6. The present EU countries and the future members can sell their goods more easily to each other.
7. Although many people had argued against the membership of Spain, Portugal and Greece they joined the EC and Europe has profited from it.
8. With new members it will be more difficult to reach European union.
9. Many politicians in Europe still think about their national interests too much.
10. We shouldn't accept eastern European countries in the next 20 years because their economies are not strong enough.
11. If the EU wants to be No 1 in the world economy, it must be open for new members.

c *Say which of these arguments are for and which of them are against a wider EU.*

d *Answer the following questions on the newspaper articles in complete sentences.*

1. What did the EU do when Greece, Portugal and Spain wanted to join?
2. Why, according to Mr Moisi, should the EU accept new member countries from eastern Europe now?
3. Why is the way to European union so difficult?
4. In Mr Metten's opinion why can a true European union be even more difficult to reach if more countries enter the EU?
5. Should the EU accept new members? State your point of view.

e *Translate lines 36 to 57.*
   (The European Union – wider and wider?)

2 Why they joined the EC/EU

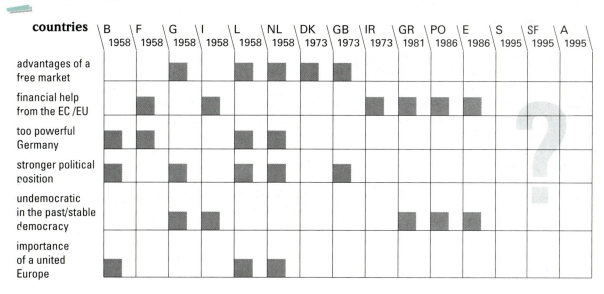

a *Give the main reasons for joining the EC/EU in complete sentences. These words may help you:*

b *Give your opinion.*
   Why did Sweden, Finland and Austria join the EU in 1995? Why did Norway vote against joining the EU?

…joined the EC/EU	because / in order to
see want (to) realize become receive be interested in remain be afraid of always believe in enjoy	

31

UNIT 3 UNIT 3 UNIT 3 UNIT 3 UNIT 3 UNIT 3 UNIT 3 UNIT 3 UNIT 3 UNIT 3 UNIT 3 UNIT 3 UNIT 3

1 Voting systems

 a *First listen to these two European politicians who are talking about their own political careers and find out about the following points:*

1. Name
2. Country
3. Political party
4. Special interests
5. Constituency
6. Former job
7. Member of Parliament since

b *Now describe the two politicians in complete sentences.*

c *Listen to the first politician's talk again. He went on to talk about the following statistics. What do you think he said?*

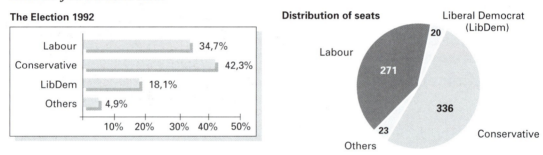

2 The British parliamentary system

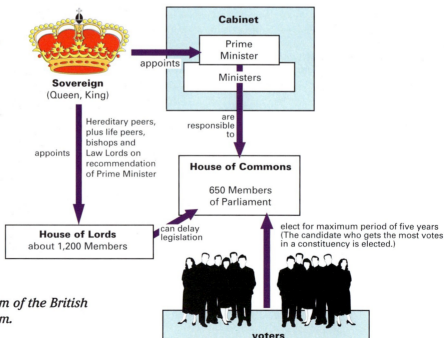

- *Describe the diagram of the British parliamentary system.*

UNIT 4

Telecommunications / Advertising

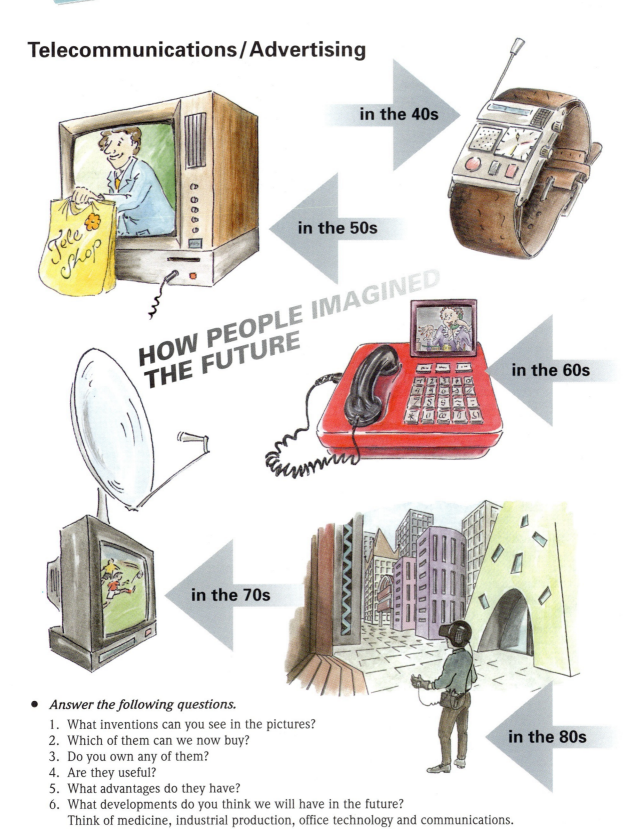

HOW PEOPLE IMAGINED THE FUTURE

- *Answer the following questions.*
    1. What inventions can you see in the pictures?
    2. Which of them can we now buy?
    3. Do you own any of them?
    4. Are they useful?
    5. What advantages do they have?
    6. What developments do you think we will have in the future?
       Think of medicine, industrial production, office technology and communications.

1 The technological revolution

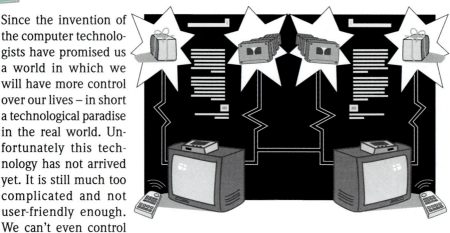

Since the invention of the computer technologists have promised us a world in which we will have more control over our lives – in short a technological paradise in the real world. Unfortunately this technology has not arrived yet. It is still much too complicated and not user-friendly enough. We can't even control the technology in our own homes; that is why our video recorders are still blinking 12.00... 12.00... 12.00...

But now a new trend in user-friendly technology is coming as engineers combine computers, consumer electronics and the media. The new super appliances and services will change all our lives. Firstly, powerful computers are becoming smaller and smaller. Secondly, information transmission is going digital. In this way a new world of easy-to-use communication with high speed data networks will open up for us all. It will be possible to send and receive "multimedia" documents that combine texts, sound waves and pictures. This computer revolution will be even bigger than the PC revolution of the 80s. Why? The computer revolution of the 80s reached only about 15% of homes, mainly because people don't really need expensive and complex machines to store addresses and telephone numbers, for example. The next revolution will introduce computer technology into most products that consumers already have. The big difference will be that people will actually be able to use devices because they will be more user-friendly. We will be able to communicate with them, and in future we will be able to communicate with other users in the form of electronic networks.

A typical example will be the new digital TV sets. They won't just have better pictures. The computers inside them will enable us to have our own private video store. All you have to do is to call up a special computer program. "TechnoTown" appears on the screen. There are shops, banks, schools, a cinema, a museum and much more. In addition to this, "TechnoTown" users will actually be able to talk to each other through microphones on the remote control. People can meet in digital schools or watch a football match together and even speak to each other while they watch.

So we will all get the technology – and the future which we always wanted. It still won't solve the big problems, such as war and poverty. But at least we will have powerful devices that we will be able to use and not ones we do not really understand.

407 words

a *Match the words in the bubble.*

b *Answer the following questions.*

1. Do we live in a "technological paradise"? Why (not)?
2. Which two developments are leading to the new computer revolution?
3. What do we mean by "multi-media documents"?
4. Why will this new development be more important than the PC revolution of the 80s?
5. How does "TechnoTown" work?
6. What big problems won't this technology solve?
7. In your opinion, what else could people use computers in their homes for?

video – networks – multi-media – recorders – transmission – remote – documents – data – control – information

c *Find the words or expressions in the text from these definitions and then make five new sentences in which they appear.*

1. a device which records pictures and sound
2. apparatus for receiving and showing television transmissions
3. a complex system which connects and transmits information
4. vibrations in the air by which noises are carried
5. an appliance which controls another device from a distance through electronic signals

d *From the information in the text explain the technological revolution in your own words.*

2 Who owns the hardware?

(1990)

The bar graph shows the percentage of home electronic devices in five European countries.

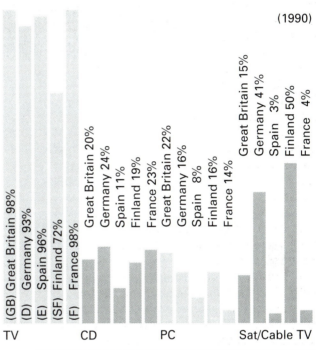

households with   TV   CD   PC   Sat/Cable TV

(GB) Great Britain 98%, (D) Germany 93%, (E) Spain 96%, (SF) Finland 72%, (F) France 98%

TV: Great Britain 98%, Germany 93%, Spain 96%, Finland 72%, France 98%
CD: Great Britain 20%, Germany 24%, Spain 11%, Finland 19%, France 23%
PC: Great Britain 22%, Germany 16%, Spain 8%, Finland 16%, France 14%
Sat/Cable TV: Great Britain 15%, Germany 41%, Spain 3%, Finland 50%, France 4%

a *Compare countries in the following way. Use the phrases in the box on the right.*

> **Example:** 1. The graph shows that the number of TVs in GB is higher than it is in Finland.

1. TV – GB/SF
2. CD – D/E
3. PC – E/GB
4. Sat/cable TV – GB/SF
5. Sat/cable TV – D/F

The graph shows The figures show We can see from the statistics	(device) owners households who have a (device)
that	is higher is lower
the number of the percentage of	in (country A) than it is in (country B).

b *What could be the reasons for these differences? Use the following phrases.*

> I'm pretty sure that...   That may be because...   A possible reason is that...   I'm sorry, but I've no idea why...

1 Life in the future – what will it be like?

a *Ask your classmates what they think about the following ideas about the future. The words in the box on the right can help you.*

> **Example:** unemployment / increase
> What do you think, will unemployment increase?
> I think unemployment will increase.

> I'm of the opinion;
> I think/don't think;
> I expect; I suppose

1. people / read / books any more
2. computers / control lighting, heating and cooking
3. we / have / more wars
4. television and computer games / replace / sport
5. There / be / more pollution
6. All houses / use / alternative energy

b *Now answer the questions in short form and give reasons.*

> **Example:** What do you think, will unemployment increase? Yes, it will because computers will do all the work.

2 In the office of the "Daily News"

- *Make sentences like this:*

> **Example:** The phone is ringing. A secretary is walking towards it. She is **going to** answer the phone.

1. Jim Price has sat down at his computer. His notes for a story are in front of him.
2. Sally Jones is looking at her address book. She picks up the phone.
3. Two secretaries have left their desks and are putting money in the coffee machine.
4. Sam Smith, the head reporter, has invited a local politician to the office. He is preparing some questions.
5. It is eleven o'clock in the morning. Jim is taking some biscuits out of his bag.
6. The receptionist and her friend are in the restaurant. They have chosen their food and are standing at the till.

3 Fast Fax Electronics

Sam Smith wants to write an article about developments in the modern media for the "Daily News".
He has invited James Bradshaw, manager of "Fast Fax Electronics", for an interview. Here is part of their conversation.

- *Put the verbs into the correct form of the future.*

Sam Smith: Come in, Mr Bradshaw, sit down. **I'll take** your coat and I expect **Janet will** bring us some coffee in a minute.

James Bradshaw:	Thank you, Mr Smith.	
Sam Smith:	Now, as I said on the phone **I'm going** to do an article on media developments and I'd like to ask you a few questions. Don't worry about that noise, by the way, it's our fax machine. **It's going** to break down any minute.	
James Bradshaw:	Oh dear, I hope it's not one of ours.	
Sam Smith:	Oh no, of course not. Now, Mr Bradshaw, how is business? Do you think this year **1.** (be) as successful for you as last year?	
James Bradshaw:	Well, I certainly hope so. I have our most recent sales report here and the figures show that the firm **2.** (do) very well again this year.	
Sam Smith:	Of course, the market is growing all the time, isn't it? In the next few years I expect we **3.** (see) an even bigger increase in the use of communications technology. But do you think this **4.** (be) a good thing?	
James Bradshaw:	Well, for me and my company certainly!	
Sam Smith:	But what about the customers? It's an expensive business, isn't it? I've certainly decided that I **5.** (not spend) any more money on the latest developments.	
James Bradshaw:	Well, just a minute. I **6.** (show) you our brochure…	

4 The trainee journalists

Two new trainee journalists have started work at the Daily News newspaper in London. They are on a one month test period. Ken Brown, the head of the foreign news department, has to write a report on them. He has used the following system:

++ = excellent
+ = good
- = bad
- - = terrible

	Duncan	Tina
General work	++	+
Typing	+	-
Shorthand	-	+
French	++	-
Communication skills	- -	++

a *First make sentences about Duncan. Use the verbs in the box.*

> speak – type – communicate – write – work

> **Example:** Duncan's general work is excellent. He works excellently.

b *Form adverbs from the following adjectives.*
careful, slow, fast, accurate, polite, quick, correct, hard, wonderful

c *Now choose from these adverbs to compare the trainee journalists in the following way:*

> **Example:** – general work
> Duncan works more carefully than Tina does.
> Tina doesn't work as carefully as Duncan does.

5 A report

- Look at the adjectives and adverbs. Then complete Ken's report on two other trainees.

> On the whole I can say Phillip's work in the office has been **fairly good**. **Unfortunately**, he types **terribly**. On the other hand, his French appears to be **very good**. In comparison Charlotte has worked **extremely well** over the last four weeks. Although she speaks French (real) (bad), her shorthand is (extreme) (good). Nevertheless, she seems to be the (good) of all our trainees. (General), she keeps (calm) in a crisis and doesn't get (nervous). All in all, I think she will (probable) make an (excellent) journalist. But she must learn to speak more (polite) on the phone. I (certain) cannot say the same about …

50 billion dollars for advertising in Europe

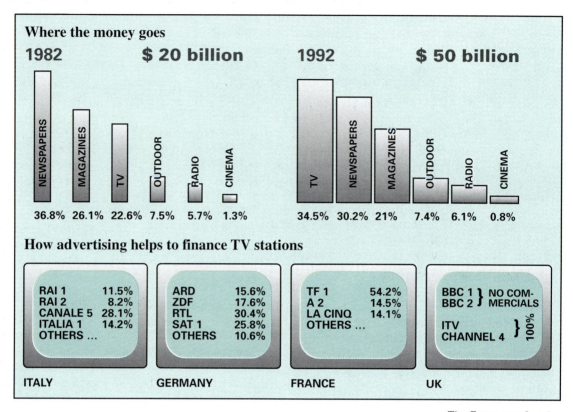

The European, London

a *Compare the figures for advertising.*

1. How has the total amount of money spent on advertising changed?
2. Which of the media had a much bigger share of the advertising market in 1992 than it did in 1982?
3. Whose share of the advertising market fell between 1982 and 1992?
4. Which TV stations do not show any adverts?
5. Which German stations depend most on advertising?
   What do you think the reasons are?

b *Read the text below and answer the following questions.*

1. Which of the media in the chart above are mentioned?
2. What could the headline of the following text be?

... ?

If you see a big yellow M on TV, will you recognize it and – more importantly – will you know what product it stands for? Most people will recognize it, according to an international survey. They believed that the M was one of the best known logos in TV advertising.

For the companies that had spent millions on the production of commercials and on airtime the results of the survey were quite important. The companies whose products came first were pleased. But the problem is that compared to every commercial that becomes popular 100 others fail.

Indeed, according to the survey, one of the main disadvantages of TV advertising is that only a third of commercials receive our full attention. One in five plays to empty rooms, while people are making tea or going to the toilet. Two in five act as background while people are eating, reading or even sleeping. With the help of "hidden" video cameras in a number of homes, the survey showed what surprising things people actually do during the break – one man even practised his tennis serve.

According to the survey even people who stay in the room during commercials do not always watch them. A new generation of viewers has arrived – people who watch with remote control in hand and switch to another channel when the commercials come on. Reports from America, where this habit is much older, say that in this way companies waste a quarter of the money which they spend on TV advertising.

Of course, it was not the TV companies which paid for this international survey, it was the newspapers. They used it for a £8 million advertising campaign. The message was simple: Advertisers overestimate the value of TV commercials. The reason why newspapers started their campaign is also easy to see; their share in the advertising market has been decreasing worldwide, and is down to about 15% in Britain.

Newspapers and TV stations have different viewpoints on advertising. On the one hand, Bert Hardy, who is the manager of the newspapers' campaign, argues: "The most expensive time in TV advertising – the break in 'News at Ten' on ITV – costs around £60,000 a minute, whereas a full page in a national newspaper only costs £20,000 and lasts all day. The companies could use some of the money that they waste on TV advertising to increase their profits and cut prices." On the other hand ITV manager Malcolm Wall points out the fact that newspapers themselves spend millions on TV advertising.

Today many advertising managers are sure that a mix of the advertising media will be the best way to reach consumers. Some companies have already changed their advertising campaigns. Many more are planning the same and are going to advertise not only on TV in the future but also on the radio and in newspapers. 474 words

The Telegraph plc, London 1991

c *Find the expressions with the same meaning in the text.*
1. 20 per cent 2. 25 per cent 3. 33 per cent 4. 40 per cent

d *Try to make some more expressions in the same way.*
1. 66 per cent 2. 75 per cent 3. 10 per cent 4. 80 per cent

e *Read the text again and answer the following questions in complete sentences.*
1. Are all companies happy with the results of their TV advertising? Why (not)?
2. What percentage of the commercials on TV do viewers really watch?
3. What do people do during the commercial break?
4. Who paid for the international survey on TV commercials? And why?
5. What financial advantage do firms have when they advertise in newspapers?
6. What media will many companies use to advertise in the future?

f *Give your opinion.*
If advertising on TV is so expensive, why are firms willing to spend so much money on it?

g *Translate lines 40 to 52 (... ?).*

1 Radio advertising

 a *Listen to the cassette and find out:*

1. the product
2. the name of the product
3. the price
4. the name of the shop that sells it

b *Listen to the cassette again and find adjectives from the ones below which describe the products. Say which of the products they describe.*

> careful – cheap – superfast – superb – modern – safe – excellent – popular – polite – wonderful – light – accurate – good – quick – easy to use – comfortable

2 Analyzing advertisements

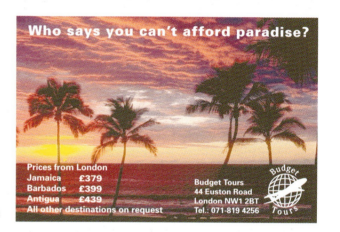

a *Try to analyze the advertisement on the right.*

1. Say what this advert is for.
2. Identify
   - the slogan/key words.
   - the logo/brand name/name of the company.
3. Say what other information is given in this advert.
4. Describe what the picture shows.
5. Say what ideas and life-style you associate with this picture.
6. What target group could the advert be aimed at?

b *With reference to what you have found out above do you think this advert could be successful?*

3 Writing an advertisement

a *Look at the photo on the left and think of a product/service you could sell with it. Choose a suitable target group.*

b *Now write a short advertisement for your product/service. Refer to the points in D2.*

c *Present your advertisement to the class. Say why you have designed it in this way.*

UNIT 5

Transport

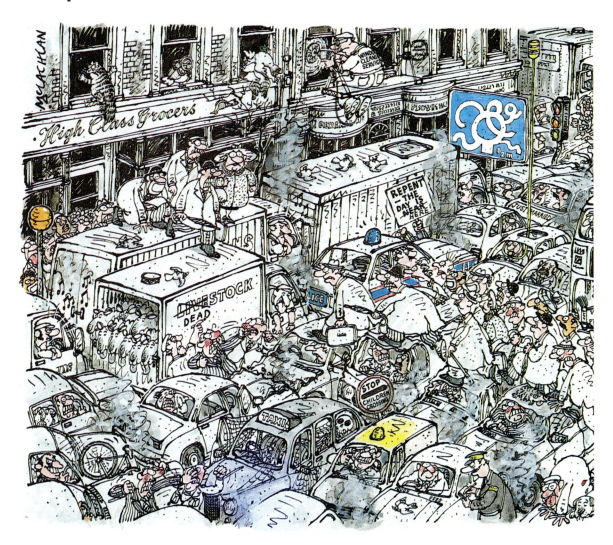

a Describe the situation in the cartoon.

b Look at the people's faces. How do they feel?

c Decide which of the following comments in your opinion best describe the situation in the cartoon and say why.
   1. People in cities don't need their cars.
   2. Private transport will be the death of us.
   3. If you want to reduce your stress level, leave your car at home.
   4. It's quicker on foot.

d What is your view of the traffic situation in our towns and cities?

1 Traffic

Every day we can hear reports of cities which are congested by traffic and this situation is getting worse day by day. Town centre thrombosis and the congestion of motorways cause major problems for drivers
5 and the environment. These problems have grown with the development of private transport. We have got used to a life-style we find hard to change. More and more people who own cars are not able to imagine a life without them. The question is how to find
10 a solution people would accept. Some people believe public transport should be the answer. Others are looking into technological innovations such as electronic navigation systems.

a *Match the following words with their definitions.*

1. congestion
2. environment
3. (town centre) thrombosis
4. public transport

A. the world around us
B. a way to travel for people in large groups, e.g. bus, tram, train
C. the state of being too full or overcrowded, especially on roads
D. thickening of blood, e.g. in the heart

b Here are some statements we heard at a transport planning meeting.
Complete these statements with the words used above.

1. "During the rush-hour the... on the M25 leads to long traffic jams every day."

2. "The fumes from cars pollute the..."

3. "Moreover most European town centres are so congested with traffic that they soon will experience a... , where traffic comes to a complete standstill."

4. "I believe we should use... and leave our cars at home."

2 The jam busters

Can electronic route planners help drivers? Sue Baker tests two of the latest devices.

Recently I have been driving, equipped with two of the latest high-tec aids for congestion-free jour-
5 neys and punctual arrival. One of these aids works out your route and tells you where to go. The other shows you where not to go. Each device can run on its own batteries or you can plug them into the car's electrical supply from the dashboard.
10 The portable Columbus Navigation System looks and works like a Gameboy for drivers. Switch the device on and then type in your starting point and destination. You can also type in any points you want

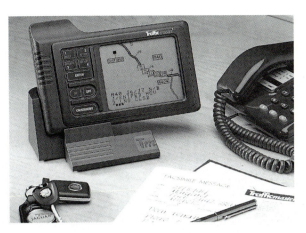

a traffic jam on the way, the Columbus has a traffic re-route function which suggests a diversion.

The other device I tested was the Trafficmaster System. This is not so expensive for the driver as it only shows the position of traffic jams and slow moving traffic on motorways. But how does the Trafficmaster receive this information? More than 800 infrared sensors which are installed every two miles on the motorways monitor the traffic flow. These sensors transmit this information to the drivers who have the Trafficmaster in their cars. They have a small screen fixed to the dashboard of their cars. The screen shows a map of the motorway network. Any congestion appears on it and it tells them also the speed of any slow moving traffic (under 30 mph) on the motorways. So the Trafficmaster drivers can quickly choose an alternative route if they want to avoid any delay in their journey.

to avoid. The Columbus then tells you the total mileage, journey cost and your fuel consumption. After that it displays a series of route instructions to guide you through your journey. If there is an accident or

302 words

© Sue Baker, The Observer, London 1993 (adapted)

a *True or false? Give reasons.*

1. The two devices Sue tested only run on the electrical power of your car.
2. The Trafficmaster System shows you how fast all traffic on the motorways is moving.
3. The monitor of the Trafficmaster System displays maps of the major cities.
4. The Columbus Navigation System works out how much petrol you will use on your journey.
5. The Columbus Navigation System can show you a different route if an accident has happened ahead of you on the motorway.

b *Here are some radio travel news announcements. Find nouns in the text to complete them.*

1. Traffic... on the M1 near Nottingham is causing problems for drivers. Try to avoid the M1 near Nottingham if possible.
2. Due to an accident on the A30 near Exeter there is 3 miles of... So take care when driving on the A30 near Exeter.
3. Road works on the A58 south of Rochdale. The police advise drivers to follow the... signs.
4. Due to motorway repairs on the M4 there is a 5-mile... in both directions near Bristol.
5. Fog on the M62! Drivers should reduce their...

c *Rewrite lines 10 to 19 of the text "The jam busters" and replace some of the expressions with those in the cloud. Start like this:*

> **Example:** The handy Columbus Navigation...

d *Try to answer the following questions in your own words as far as possible.*

1. How does the Trafficmaster System work?
2. How is it different from the Columbus Navigation System?

> length of your journey – handy – turn on – trip – help – petrol needed – appliance – put in – shows – places – a number – gives – the place you want to go to

43

UNIT 5 DEFINING / NON-DEFINING RELATIVE CLAUSES – MODAL AUXILIARIES SEE PAGES 119/120

1 Getting around

a *Look at these pictures and the information below. Then make sentences like this:*

Example: 1. The girl who is standing at the bus stop is going to college. 2. The bus which…

be on his way to his office
go to West End
transport computers
go to college
work at the garage

b *Now describe the other parts of the pictures in the same way.*

Example: 1. The girl who is cycling…

2 Travelling home

• *Complete the following story. Fill in "who" or "which" where necessary.*

At 5.30 Henry arrived at the station — he knew so well. He showed his ticket to the man **who** was standing at the gate. Then he got on the train **which** was waiting at platform 7. He politely greeted the woman **(1)** was sitting next to the door. She put down the book **(2)** she was reading. They both smiled and then he walked to the seat **(3)** he always chose. He sat down and filled the pipe **(4)** he had taken out of his jacket. This was the time of day **(5)** he liked best. After some minutes he started to read the paper **(6)** he had bought at the station. The couple **(7)** were sitting next to him were talking about the plans **(8)** they had for the weekend. He listened for a while and then he looked out of the window at the countryside **(9)** was passing by. What a nice day it was! Henry started to think about the work **(10)** he had done at the bank. He smiled. He remembered all the years **(11)** had passed and all the people **(12)** had worked with him. When the train arrived at the station he at once saw the woman **(13)** was waiting for him. He walked up to her and kissed her.
It was the first time his wife had met him at the station. She had bought him the flowers **(14)** he liked so much and he knew it would never be the same again.
This had been his last day at work after 48 years.

3 A guessing game

a *Guess who or what it is.*

1. It's a person who makes a journey for pleasure.   2. It's a place where trains arrive and leave.
3. It's a person whose job it is to serve passengers in planes.   4. It's a piece of paper you buy when you want to travel by train or bus.   5. It's an electronic appliance which helps you to find your destination.   6. It's a big road vehicle you can transport goods in.

b *Now describe other persons, places, vehicles etc. in the same way.*
Don't mention their names. Your classmates should find out who/what they are.

G/ NON-DEFINING RELATIVE CLAUSES – MODAL AUXILIARIES   SEE PAGES 119/120   DEFINING    UNIT 5

4 Changes in travelling

- *Compare travelling today, in the past, and in the future. Make sentences like this:*

Example: Lots of people must/have to wait in traffic jams today. 100 years ago most people had to walk. In 100 years' time I think people will …

Today…	100 years ago…	In 100 years' time I think…
lots of people/wait/ in traffic jams (must/have to)	most people/ walk	people/use/public transport in cities
passengers/travel/to America in a few hours (can/be able to)	passengers/get/to America in a week	passengers/travel/ around the world in minutes
drivers/stop/at most European borders (needn't/not have to)	drivers/have/a driving licence	drivers/stop/at any borders
travellers/enter/some countries without showing their passports (can/be allowed to)	travellers/take/their cats and dogs into Britain	travellers/enter/ all countries freely
man/fly/to Venus (can't/be not able to)	man/fly/to the moon	man/fly/to the stars
people/drive/ faster than 70 mph on British motorways (mustn't/ be not allowed to)	people/drive/without a person carrying a red flag in front of their vehicles	people/drive/cars in city centres

5 A day in the life of Harry S.

Harry **(1)** works in London. But he lives in Bacon End **(2)**. Every day he has to travel one and a half hours to the computer firm **(3)**. At 7.30 when he leaves his house, he gets into the car and drives to the station **(4)**. Harry arrives there at about 8 o'clock and he gets on the train **(5)**. On the train he reads the newspaper **(6)**. Sometimes he talks to the passengers **(7)**. When he arrives in London he takes the underground line **(8)**. Sometimes he meets his colleague **(9)** and together they walk to work. On his way home **(10)** he usually listens to his personal CD player. His girlfriend **(11)** meets him at the station. Sometimes they go to the restaurant **(12)**. Or they go to the sports centre **(13)**. Both like the cinema and when they're showing a film **(14)** they spend their evening there…

- *Complete the text about Harry S. with the information below. Use relative clauses. Decide if the relative clause is necessary or not and find out if you can replace "who" or "which" by "that".*

Example: Harry, who is 24, works in London. But he lives in Bacon End, which is 35 miles away. Every day he has to travel one and a half hours to the computer firm he writes programs for. At 7.30…

Some more information on Harry S.:
a) They both like this restaurant best.
b) The journey home also takes about one and a half hours.
c) The line goes to Cannon Street Station.
d) Harry is 24.
e) They are both interested in action films.
f) He writes programs for the computer firm.
g) He usually buys a newspaper at the station.
h) Bacon End is 35 miles from London.
i) The passengers are sitting next to him.
j) His colleague also works at the computer firm.
k) His girlfriend works in a boutique in Harlow.
l) The sports centre offers squash, fitness training, etc.
m) The station is in Harlow.
n) The train leaves at 8.05.

1 From jam to tram

A year ago Peter Wood took an hour to reach his office in Manchester by bus. Now, thanks to the town's new tram system, his journey only takes 16 minutes. "It's a very good service," says Wood. Other
5 passengers are happy too. One of them, Mike Pulman, adds "I stopped using my car simply because the tram is so convenient."

Their views of the tram are quite different to the ones people in Britain had after the war. At that time
10 people thought that the trams were noisy and slow and so they got rid of them. In the 1920s, Britain had over 14,000 trams in more than 100 towns, but by the 1960s the tram remained in only one town. At that time the attractive alternatives were the bus and
15 the car. The bus because it provided a more flexible alternative to the fixed-route tram and the car because of the freedom it gave to the individual driver. Of course, in those car-crazy days, "nobody thought about the congestion and pollution which all those petrol
20 engines would produce," says Don Roach, who is head of London's traffic department. Today however, environmentalists and city planners are welcoming back the electrically-driven, new-style tram or 'light-rail system' as they now call it. They see it as an efficient and
25 ecological solution to inner city traffic chaos.

Today's trams are most profitable in cities which have populations of half a million or less and no more than 20,000 passengers an hour at peak times. Although one alternative – an underground system, may
30 be a good solution to the traffic problems of large cities, Mary Browning, a British environmentalist says "it doesn't make sense for medium-sized cities and is much more expensive to build than a tram system." In fact, a team of traffic experts has esti-
35 mated that building one kilometer of underground costs 11 times more than building the same length of tramway. "The main reason trams are coming back is not just because they are good for the environment," says Browning, "it's because they are cheaper
40 and more efficient."

However, the fact that there are two good arguments for trams doesn't mean that they are easy to introduce. Public transport of any sort is unpopular with car drivers and the car industry so that gov-
45 ernments do not always support it. As a result, it is difficult for town planners to put tramway projects into practice. In Britain for example, you are only allowed to build a tramway system when Parliament allows it. This fact helped to slow down the open-
50 ing of Manchester's system by nine years and is now also slowing down progress on a similar project in South London. However, since statistics show that there will be twice as much road traffic by the year 2025, sooner or later governments will have to look
55 at light rail systems as one possible solution to the transport problems which European cities will face in the 21st century.

492 words

a *Find the forms of transport mentioned in the text.*

b *Match four of these headings with the paragraphs in the text.*

Trams – an old idea made new
Trams reduce journey time
Trams save money for medium-sized towns
Trams – a danger to private transport?
Trams – too noisy and dirty

c *Now do these tasks.*
1. Describe the difference which Manchester's tram system has made to passengers.
2. Say why trams were unpopular in Britain after the war.
3. Explain the advantages which today's modern 'light-rail systems' have.
4. Compare the costs of a tram system with an underground system.
5. Give reasons why it is often still difficult to introduce tram systems.

d *Complete these sentences with information from the text. Use your own words.*

1. As a result of Manchester's new tram system passengers…
2. Traffic planners are in favour of the tram because…
3. Although Britain had 14,000 trams in the 1920s…
4. Buses became more popular than trams because…
5. Although there are two good arguments for trams…
6. As a result of the increase in road traffic in the future…

e *Translate lines 8 to 25 (From jam to tram).*

2 Solutions to traffic problems

Two traffic experts are talking about possible solutions to traffic problems:

– But **don't you think the best thing would be to** improve the public transport system?
– Certainly, but that's not enough. People will never give up private transport completely. They would lose their freedom and industry would suffer. **I think the answer to the problems of** congestion for example, is technology. Why not make car computers cheaper, then everyone could have one?
– Yes, but that doesn't solve the problem of pollution, does it? **One solution to that problem could be** a tram system. It's the quickest and most convenient means of transport and **I would definitely suggest it** for a medium-sized town.

- *Discuss the other solutions you can see in the pictures below in the same way.*
  Use the expressions in the dialogue or similar ones.

1 Travel announcements

 a *Listen to the cassette. Where could you hear these announcements?*

b *Listen to the cassette again and answer the following questions.*

1. Where is the train to Liverpool?
2. Where does it stop?
3. What must passengers do who want to travel to Leeds?
4. Where is the plane with flight number BA98 flying to?
5. Which gate should the passengers go to?
6. What was the reason for the delay?
7. Why is there trouble on the M4?
8. How long is the traffic jam?
9. According to the police, what should the motorists do?

2 Welcome to Wakefield

Since the great coaching days of the 18th century Wakefield has always been at the "crossroads of the north". This fact is now even more important in a world where fast and easy communications are a must.

In any part of the Wakefield district you are only minutes away from a motorway, the M62 to the two main ports of Hull and Liverpool, and the M1 to London which is only a three hour drive away.

Moreover, you can reach Wakefield by rail from all parts of the country. Regular train services operate from most cities in England, Scotland and Wales. Again London is only two hours away.

On top of all this, Wakefield has two major airports nearby: Manchester (only an hour's drive on the M62) and Leeds (only minutes away via the M1). These fast growing airports provide links with four major intercontinental airports – London, Amsterdam, Paris and Dublin.

An ideal base. Discover Wakefield yourself. It could work for you.

For further information write to
Wakefield Tourist Information Centre
Town Hall
Wood Street
Wakefield WF1 2HQ

a *With the help of the text and the map answer these questions about Wakefield.*

1. Why do you think Wakefield is called the "crossroads of the north"?
2. How can you get to continental Europe from Wakefield?
3. Why are the Manchester and Leeds airports so important for Wakefield?
4. Why do you think Wakefield has produced this promotion brochure?

b *Design a promotion brochure in English for your town. Concentrate on road/rail/air/sea connections.*

UNIT 6

Environment

Looking for a home

In one year the average family of four throws away 112 pounds of metal, 90 pounds of plastics and an amount of paper equal to six trees. Of the 18 million tonnes of waste we produce each year, as much as 80% could be...

a Describe what you can see in the picture.

b Answer the following questions.
   1. What kind of waste do you think they are transporting?
   2. Where, in your opinion, does this waste come from?
   3. Where are they probably taking the waste?
   4. Do you agree with the Greenpeace protest? Give reasons.

c Describe the chart on the left.

Development of household waste (in kg/per capita)				
	1975	1980	1985	1989
D	335	348	318	318
F	228	260	272	303
I	257	252	263	301
NL	–	489	426	465
UK	323	312	341	357
USA	648	703	744	864
JAP	341	355	344	394

Eurostat 1992

1 Everyone can help to save the world

We are all environmentalists now. We all know about acid rain and the ozone hole. But what are we doing about these problems? As consumers we have the power to make decisions which will contribute to a better world. For example, when we walk into a supermarket we can choose to buy environmentally-friendly products and refuse products which damage our planet. In this way we also have the power to influence retailers to sell us these so-called 'green' products.

The supermarkets have understood the message and are now trying to improve their environmental image. They are turning to less wasteful and recyclable packaging. The range of 'green' products will continue to expand to meet the growing demand. This message has also reached the manufacturers. Companies are now developing environmentally-friendly products which mean no decrease in quality or increase in price. They have realized that protecting the environment may start as an advertising campaign but in the hands of intelligent people it can become a very profitable business.

We also know there are other areas where all of us can make a positive contribution to a cleaner, healthier and safer environment. We can all reduce energy consumption at home and so cut the emissions from power stations. There are a number of ways we can do this.

For example, we now know how important it is to insulate our houses well. In the use of electrical appliances and lighting we should choose the best energy-efficient technology, such as modern light bulbs which can reduce electricity consumption by 80% over the older ones. Rubbish is another area where we can act. We all produce tonnes of rubbish and so waste disposal is becoming a big problem. As an environmentally conscious consumer we should buy products which do not have so much packaging. At all costs we should avoid non-returnable goods such as plastic bottles and cans.

In conclusion it is important to emphasize once again the rise of consumer power. We must realize that we are all part of the problem. Nevertheless we must also realize that we have the responsibility to be part of the solution.

355 words

a The text above has four paragraphs. *Find headings for each paragraph in the following bubbles.*

- The influence of consumers on supermarket products
- The use of public transport
- The introduction of 'green' products and price increases
- The problems of acid rain and the ozone hole
- Other ways to protect the environment
- Everybody's duty to contribute to a cleaner world
- The reaction of retailers and manufacturers to environmental problems

b *Answer the questions on the text.*

1. Which decisions can a consumer make in a supermarket?
2. How have supermarkets reacted to these decisions?
3. Why have manufacturers become more interested in environmentally-friendly products?
4. How can we reduce our consumption of energy?
5. How can we help to avoid waste?

c *Give your opinion.*

1. What is the message of the text?
2. In what other ways can you protect the environment?
3. What other examples of 'green' products can you think of?

d Look at the following nouns and find the verbs in the text. Say which line in the text.

1. choice 2. reduction 3. insulation
4. production 5. emphasis 6. sales

e Now find the nouns from the following verbs in the same way.

1. to consume 2. to demand 3. to decide
4. to contribute 5. to waste 6. to solve

f Find synonyms in the text for the following words.

1. shop owners 2. 'green' products 3. waste 4. to manufacture 5. to cut 6. to make better

2 Pollution

1   2   3   4

a Read the statements and then match each statement with the photos.

A Emma Shaw, chemist: "I have just read a book about acid rain. Did you know it was a Scottish chemist, Robert Angus Smith, who invented the expression 'acid rain' in an 1852 article on the air and rain in Manchester? Moreover, according to him air pollution damages buildings and forests more quickly in countries where people use more fuel than elsewhere."

B Paul Jenkins, environmentalist: "It is true that this government is doing a lot to reduce the level of air pollution here in Britain. However, in my opinion, we consumers have the power to make the biggest improvement. We should buy cars which don't pollute the environment so badly or we should use public transport."

C Jill Kemp, journalist: "As I see it, we, the people of Britain have been using our rivers as waste disposal channels for hundreds of years. I am convinced that our government must act. Furthermore, we need better pollution control over companies, farmers and even local government."

D Richard Palmer, politician: "I think the ozone hole is the greatest danger to our planet. It is not true that we can afford to wait. The ozone hole will cause serious dangers to our health. In addition all over the world people must stop making household products with CFCs* in them."

* chlorofluorocarbon

b Why did you make those decisions? Answer in the following way:

Example: I chose the photo of... for text A because Emma Shaw says/tells us...

- Report what each person says and introduce each reported sentence with a different verb. Use the table on the right.

	Direct speech	Reporting verbs
OPINION	"In my opinion…" "As I see it…" "I think/believe… "	be of the opinion take the view think/believe
EMPHASIS	"I am convinced…" "We should/ought to/must…"	maintain emphasize
AGREEMENT/ DISAGREEMENT	"It is true…" "It is not true…"	agree not agree
ADDITIONAL INFORMATION	"Moreover…" "Furthermore…" "In addition…"	point out go on to mention add

UNIT 6 **B** REPORTED SPEECH SEE PAGE 128 REPORTED SPEECH SEE PAGE 128 REPORTED SPEECH SEE PA

1 Protect your environment

For a project on the protection of the environment, the consumer magazine 'What?' interviewed some people in Birmingham. Here are some of the answers they got.

1. "We are fighting for more cycle paths here." Joe Straw, member of Green party.
2. "I'm joining the WWF tomorrow. People don't give enough money to help with their work." Roger Williams, bank clerk.
3. "I don't buy cans." Mrs Black, mother of two children.
4. "I ride my bike to school every day." John Smith, teacher.
5. "We are closing some streets to traffic in the city centre next year." Ray Peters, town planner.
6. "My husband doesn't wash his car here in the street any longer." Mrs Rivers, housewife.
7. "We always buy bottles we can return to the shop." Fred and Jim, college students.
8. "Well, I'm just taking my old newspapers to the container like I usually do on Saturdays." Peter Bone, old man.
9. "We don't buy goods which aren't environmentally-friendly." Anna and Rob Nelson, young married couple.
10. "We must all save a lot more energy in the home. We're buying an energy-efficient heating system tomorrow." Mr Field, farmer.

- *Report the answers like this:*

> **Example:** 1. Joe Straw, a member of the Green party, said that they were fighting for more cycle paths there. 2. Roger Williams, a bank clerk, said that he was joining the WWF the next day. People didn't give enough money to help with their work.

2 Retailers and the environment

The manager of a large supermarket group gave the following statement to 'What?' magazine about retailers and the environment:

> "We opened our first supermarket just ten years ago and we have had a lot of success since then. We have always kept our prices low and our quality high. We will of course continue to do this in the future.
> However, and I know you are interested in this, we have always had a special interest in environmental matters. Right at the beginning we sold goods with as little packaging as possible and placed bottle banks and containers in all our car parks.
> As from next month we won't hand out free plastic bags any more and we will stop selling all drinks in plastic containers.
> Over the last few years we have introduced more and more 'green' products and we certainly haven't felt sorry about this.
> Two years ago, when we started to plan our second store here in this area, there wasn't a bus service. But after we wrote to the council they agreed to introduce one.
> All in all I think I can say that we are really doing our best for the environment."

Chris Hawkings, who reported this statement for the magazine, began his article like this:

> **Example:** The manager of Dippy Supermarkets spoke to me yesterday … He told me that they had opened their first supermarket ten years before and that they had had a lot of success since then. He went on to say… that they had always… and that they would of course…

- *Complete his article.*

UNIT 6

3 Interview with "Whiz Bang Electronics"

Chris Hawkings' next job was to interview the head of "Whiz Bang Electronics" about their new washing machine, which they want to sell as an environmentally-friendly model. Here is his list of questions.

1. Do you plan to replace all your old models with environmentally-friendly ones?
2. How many models will you produce per year?
3. Why do you call it environmentally-friendly?
4. Do you think the new model will sell well?
5. When did you begin to develop this model?
6. How many litres of water does it use?
7. What is the energy consumption like?
8. What plans have you made to recycle these washing machines?

Later at lunch, the head of "Whiz Bang" told one of his colleagues about the interview and that the reporter had wanted to know a lot about their new model.

> **Example:** 1. He wanted to find out if we planned to replace all our old models with environmentally-friendly ones.   2. He also wanted to know how many...

- *Now you go on.*

4 The inner city traffic situation

Last night there was a meeting in the town hall to discuss the inner city traffic situation. Here is part of this discussion:

Town planner: ...and so in my opinion, the only solution is to close the centre to traffic completely.
Shop owner: What will happen to our trade? No one will want to come into town at all then. And we already have enough competition from these big out-of-town superstores.
Town planner: But we have already introduced a number of highly successful park and ride schemes and I'm sure people will prefer shopping without all the noise and exhaust fumes from cars.
Shopper: That may be true, but we don't like carrying heavy bags of shopping for miles and miles before we can get them into the car.
Shop owner: You see, we must discuss the problem in more detail. Do you realise the problems we will have with deliveries?
Town planner: We do, Mr Black, and as long as lorries can deliver before 10 in the morning, there won't be a problem.
Shopper: I suppose shopping is more pleasant with no traffic. I will certainly feel better about bringing my children into town then. In some cities they even have special play areas for children. Can't we have something like that here, too?

- *Now report this discussion. Use as many different reporting verbs as possible.*

Vehicles go round again

The three R's of waste management

Randy Newbury, manager at an international car company, has a dream. "In thirty years our company will be 100% environmentally friendly. On the one hand we will not pollute air or water any more during the production process, on the other hand we will only produce cars from recycled material. And I hope we will then be able to recycle these cars completely." This sounds unlikely? Not to Newbury, who is responsible for such environmental problems. What is more, lots of other international companies are actively trying to find solutions to make this dream come true. While they are already re-using waste heat and raw materials, they are reducing the amount of waste in the production process. Moreover, they are trying to increase the number of parts they can re-use. And of course the products themselves must be recyclable. To be more precise, these companies are employing the new 3 R's to protect the environment: reduce, re-use, recycle.

The 3 R's were not always part of the companies' vocabulary. In fact, until the late 1980s, companies wishing to go 'green', installed filters in the factories and then tried to get rid of the waste they had collected there. "People were just shifting their pollution from one place to another," states Ron Humber for Friends of the Earth in London. "What we need is a completely new approach to waste management."

"I'm dreaming of a factory," says Randy Newbury, "in which scrap vehicles enter through the back door for 100 per cent recycling and leave as new cars through the front door."

"At the moment this is only a dream," he quickly adds, "but we must do something now. We estimate that in the near future up to 12 million cars in Europe alone will go to the scrap dealers every year."

"Up to now industry has only been able to recycle the metal parts. But after they have taken them out, they still have up to 250 kg of mixed waste – plastics, glass, rubber and engine oil. The scrap dealers have to pay £50 a tonne now to dump this waste – and the costs are rising. In our view special firms should collect and dismantle old vehicles and they should return as many parts as possible to the car manufacturers.

The next step is to sort and sell all other materials for recycling. We have already started to code the plastic parts of each car. So it will be easier to separate similar material for recycling. In this way we can reduce the amount of mixed waste to 60kg which we cannot recycle at the moment.

But of course, our engineers and suppliers are working on it and they are trying to find substitute materials for the rest. For example, they are thinking about new dashboards now. At present our dashboards consist of metal, foam, plastics and textiles. We think our people can make them from one family of material. This will add £60 to the cost of a new car. But of course, we will be able to save money if we can re-use or recycle the parts.

This means that one day we will produce a car which is 100% recyclable, which allows us to use the same materials over and over again. As we see it every new vehicle we design in this way helps us to solve tomorrow's problems today."

564 words

a *Before answering the following questions on the text, look at the "steps" on the opposite page.*
1. What is the manager for environmental problems dreaming of?
2. How are other firms attacking the waste problem?
3. In what way did companies try to solve the problems of pollution in the 80s?
4. How can special firms improve the work of the scrap dealers?
5. How can car companies help to solve problems of pollution when they are designing new cars?

UNIT 6 ANSWERING QUESTIONS ON A TEXT  UNIT 6

Follow these steps	Example (Question 1)
1. Read the text carefully.	
2. Find the lines in the text which contain the information necessary to answer the questions.	*lines 29–32*
3. Look up all the words (in a dictionary or below) you must understand to answer a question.	*scrap = metal from…*

dealer (n)
1. A **dealer** is a person who buys and sells things.
2. A **dealer** in a game of cards is the person who gives out the cards to the other players.

dismantle (v)
If you **dismantle** a machine, you carefully take it to pieces.

dump (n)
A **dump** is a place where rubbish is left.

dump (v)
1. If you **dump** something, you throw it away carelessly.
2. If a company **dumps** goods, it sells large quantities at very low prices, usually in another country.

recycle (v)
If you **recycle** things that have already been used, such as bottles or paper, you process them so that people can use them again.

reduce (v)
To **reduce** something means to make it smaller in number, size, price etc.

re-use (v)
When you **re-use** something, you do not throw it away. You use it again.

scrap (n)
1. A **scrap** of paper is a very small piece of it. Usually you do not want it any more.
2. **Scrap** or **scrap** metal is metal from old or damaged machines, cars, etc. which is melted so that it can be used again.

shift (n)
A **shift** is a change from one position to another.

shift (v)
If you **shift** something, you move it or change its position.

substitute (n)
A **substitute** is a person or thing that takes the place of another.

substitute (v)
If you **substitute** a thing, you put the new thing in the place where the old thing was.

4. Use part of the question as an introduction to your answer, if possible.	*The manager for environmental problems…*
5. Use synonyms and paraphrases.	*The manager for environmental problems has a vision of…*
6. Write your answer in complete sentences. Be careful with the tenses and use the phrases below.	*It says in the text that the manager for environmental problems has a vision of a factory in which old cars become fully recycled new cars.*

> In the first (second,…) paragraph the author mentions that…/On line one (two…,) we read that…/It says in the text that…

b *Translate lines 52 to 65 (Vehicles go round again).*

INFO-BOX: HOW TO ANSWER QUESTIONS ON A TEXT

1. Read the text carefully.
2. Find the information necessary to answer the questions.
3. Look up all unknown words which are important for your answers.
4. Now answer the questions.
   - If possible, use the question as an introduction to your answer.
   - Use the main facts that you have found in the text.
   - Write your answers in complete sentences.
   - Use your own words.

1 Ecology or economics?

 a *Listen to the news report on Radio 4 and find the correct answers.*

1. The news report is about
   a. a North Sea oil project
   b. a zinc ore mining project
   c. a coal mining project
2. The reporter mentions the effect of the project on
   a. the tourist industry
   b. the air
   c. the countryside
3. The people against the project are
   a. technologists
   b. hotel owners
   c. environmentalists

b *Now listen to the recording again and find out more about the following points:*

1. where the company has found the zinc ore deposits
2. why this area is especially interesting for the company
3. how many jobs the project will create
4. what this development will probably mean for nature in this area
5. the fears of the hotel owners

c *Use your answers to write a short summary of the radio report.*

2 Zinc UK project: A public enquiry

Zinc UK, a mining company, have found large deposits of zinc ore in the attractive coastal area of Cornwall. The ore is rich in zinc and is near the surface. This means mining will be relatively easy and therefore profitable. The project will create new jobs for the area.
The problems:
This is a particularly beautiful area and it is the home to many wild plants and animals. It is also a tourist attraction for the visitors to the small seaside resorts along the coast. The seaside resorts are small because of the poor road communications and there is no railway. The mining company has promised to build a new major road which will go directly to the motorway 25 miles away.
Unemployment in the area is high. Most of the jobs are on local farms and in the seaside resorts. However, in the last few years the seaside resorts have had fewer visitors. Local taxes for houseowners are high and the local government wants to keep tax increases as low as possible in the future. Zinc UK would contribute to the income of the area. The small town of St. Agnes has a new housing estate, but it only has a few shops, a coffee bar, a pub and a primary school. There is no public library, sports centre or cinema in the area.

a *What advantages/disadvantages do you think the project could bring to the area.*

b The local MP for North Cornwall has decided to hold a public enquiry to hear the views of the people concerned. The enquiry will help to decide whether Zinc UK should be allowed to start their mining project or not. The following people are at the meeting:

1. managers of the mining company
2. teenagers from the area
3. members of the local environmental group
4. hotel owners from the area
5. unemployed houseowners from the area

Imagine you are one of these people.

1. List the advantages and disadvantages that the mining project might have for you personally.
2. Play your role at the meeting. Use expressions like "In my opinion" etc. to introduce your arguments.

c *After you have discussed the issue write a report of the meeting. Use reported speech.*

Energy

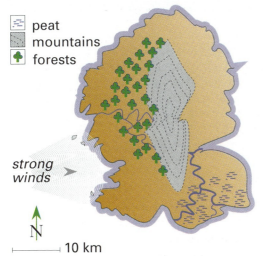

peat
mountains
forests

strong winds

10 km

This is an island off the west coast of America. The island has strong winds from the west, high mountains with fast running rivers, thick forests along the west coast and peat bogs in the south east. There are no resources of coal, oil or natural gas on or near the island. At present only a few people live there.

- You are in a project team which wants to develop the island.
  Think about and discuss these ideas.
  1. What material would you use to build homes on the island?
  2. Which two materials could help you to produce heat to cook food?
  3. What could you use to produce electricity to run machinery etc.?
  4. Where would you build houses on the island? Give reasons.
  5. What environmental problems will you cause when you use the natural resources on the island?
  6. What conclusion do you draw from your study?

1 More wealth – less energy

Low prices and high technology have led to a situation in which most people feel relaxed about energy. The prices have created the impression that we have plenty of energy, the technology has made us believe that there will always be an answer to future problems. But we have little reason to feel secure.

More than half of the world's population (mostly in the developing countries) lives without a commercial supply of energy. The total energy consumption per head in areas such as South Asia is only 5% of that in the United States. By 2020 the number of people in the world will rise to about 8 billion (compared with 5 1/2 billion today) and 85% of mankind will live in poor countries. Either billions of people will continue to live in poverty, or the demand for energy will grow enormously. Governments and companies will invest trillions of dollars in the next twenty or thirty years – more than ever – in the developing countries. And if they do so, economic growth will mean much higher consumption of energy in the Third World.

Although the availability of fossil fuels is limited, experts predict that in the 21st century the world will still depend on them, especially coal which is plentiful in India and China – countries with the highest populations. The problem is that developing countries care far more about the standard of living of their citizens today than they do about pollution and global warming. That is why they use the little money they have to increase the production of goods. If they had enough money, they would be able to produce and use energy in an environmentally-friendly way.

On the other hand many wealthy industrialized countries are introducing methods to save energy and they are developing technologies which provide new sources of renewable energy such as solar power. Of course, it is not an easy job to transfer these expensive technologies to the poorer parts of the world. But if we help the developing countries, they will be able to increase their energy efficiency. In this way the countries of the Third World will manage to raise the standard of living significantly. At the same time they will consume only little more energy than today and the production of this energy will not harm the environment so much.

The time to take action is now. The West is beginning to learn from the mistakes it has made. Surely it is important to help the developing countries so that they can avoid the same mistakes. If we do not act now, what will life be like in 2020?

© *The Economist, London (2 October, 1993) (adapted)*   436 words

a *Refer to the text and correct the following statements.*
1. We must start to help the developing countries in the year 2020.
2. The number of people in the world is falling.
3. Today the United States consumes 5 times more energy per head than developing countries in South Asia.
4. In many developing countries people have developed methods to save energy.
5. The developing countries do not buy new energy technologies because they do not want to save energy.
6. The prices of energy are relatively high today.

b *Find the nouns in the text.*
1. grow
2. consume
3. pollute
4. supply
5. demand
6. produce
7. poor
8. efficient
9. wealthy

c *Find antonyms in the text.*
1. less
2. poor
3. high
4. a lot
5. past
6. industrialized (countries)
7. difficult
8. slightly
9. cheap
10. (the number will) fall

d *Answer the following questions.*

1. Which are the sources of energy mentioned in the text?
2. Which of them is a fossil fuel and which is a renewable source of energy?
3. Which of the following are fossil fuels, which are renewable sources: gas, water, wind, oil, peat?
4. Which advantages and disadvantages do fossil fuels and renewable sources of energy have? Think about these points: geographical position, availability, costs, pollution.

2 Talking about graphs

a *Study chart 1 and its description.*

b *Now describe chart 2. Use the words in the boxes below.*

Chart 1: Development of world temperatures

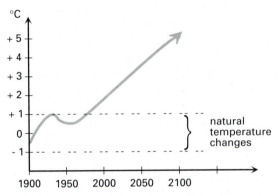

Chart 2: Development of energy consumption

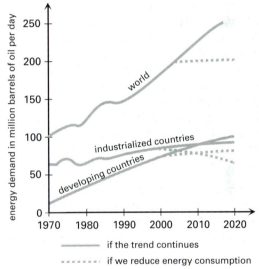

Graph 1 shows the development of world temperatures. Between 1900 and 1940 world temperatures rose significantly. From 1940 to 1980 they fell slightly. Since 1980 temperatures have increased constantly. If this trend continues, temperatures will be about 5 degrees higher in 2100 than in 1900.

trends	
increase	**decrease**
increase rise go up grow ⬆	decrease fall go down drop ⬇
remain	stable steady constant at the same level ➡

changes	
big changes	**small changes**
significant (ly) substantial (ly)	slight (ly) a little
fast changes	**slow changes**
sudden (ly) sharp (ly)	slow (ly) gradual (ly)

UNIT 7  PAGE 129 CONDITIONALS SEE PAGE 129 CONDITIONALS SEE PAGE 129 CONDITIONALS SEE P

1 How to save energy in your house

Darren and Kate Palmer have just bought a house in Seattle. The house is 25 years old and needs some repairs.
The Energy Council has sent them a brochure on ways they can save energy in their house.

Darren is showing Kate the brochure. He says "Look, it says here –

> **Example:** *"If we insulate our roof well, we will save a lot of energy."*

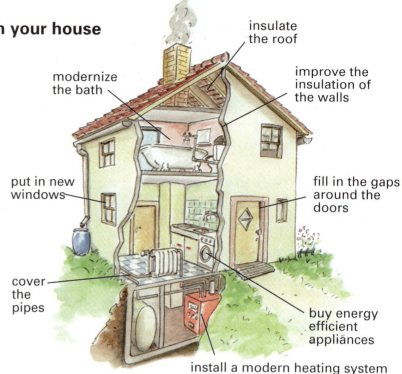

- Use the drawing and the phrases in the box to make at least eight sentences in the same way.

| lose less heat   save money   not use so much hot water   avoid a loss of heat   reduce our energy consumption   not pollute the environment so much   cut our water bill   not waste so much energy   save a lot of energy |

2 The advantages of alternative energy

Cathy Johnson, a politician and expert on energy questions, is giving a talk at a high school in Seattle. She is convinced that we depend too much on the use of fossil fuels (oil, gas and coal) as sources of energy. She believes that we should save energy and also look into the possibilities of the use of alternative energies more carefully. Here are some of her notes for her talk.

- Use the expressions in the box to express her opinions.

  1. First of all – must say
  2. Secondly – be of the opinion
  3. Thirdly – think
  4. At this point – must emphasize
  5. Moreover – must add
  6. In addition – believe
  7. Furthermore – must say
  8. Finally – be convinced

Example: 1. First of all I must say, if people used alternative forms of energy, they would contribute to a cleaner world.

1. people use alternative forms of energy – they contribute to a cleaner world
2. government spend more money on these alternatives – we all see the advantages in a few years
3. electricity companies replace old power stations in this area – they can produce electricity and not pollute the environment so much

CONDITIONALS SEE PAGE 129   CONDITIONALS   SEE PAGE 129   CONDITIONALS   SEE PAGE 129    UNIT 7

4. firms produce more energy efficient appliances for the home – we not need so many power stations
5. houseowners insulate their houses better – they can reduce their electricity bills
6. we use the sources of renewable energy in this part of the country – we save a lot of fossil fuels
7. people not travel by car so much – we not have such a big energy problem
8. we not waste energy as we do now – we have a cleaner and better world

3 Bob Flynn, the manager of a small company which develops solar systems, is thinking about his life

…didn't get good marks in the first year – because I didn't work hard.
…did well at college in the end – after I spent more time on my studies.

I …

- *Express his thoughts for him like this:*

> **Example:** If I had worked hard, I would have got good marks in the first year. If I hadn't spent more time on my studies, I wouldn't have done well at college in the end.

1. I got a job as an electrician – after I wrote a lot of letters of application.
2. I went to university – after I attended evening classes three times a week.
3. I studied electrical engineering – after I looked at the good job possibilities.
4. I passed my examinations at university – because I worked hard.
5. I didn't go straight into my own business – because I wasn't sure what to do after university.
6. I started up my own business – after a friend gave me some tips.
7. I bought a workshop – after the bank lent me $50,000.
8. I became interested in alternative forms of energy – after I joined an environmentalist group.
9. I started to develop solar systems – because I learnt all about solar energy at university.
10. I didn't invest more money in the business – because I didn't have enough money at that time.

4 Save energy now

Two students at a high school in Seattle have started a "Save Energy Now" group.
They are talking about the use of energy and how people have reacted to new developments.

- *Put the verbs in brackets into the correct form.*

Mary Jo: But we still aren't doing enough and if we **1.** (continue) to take so little care of our environment, soon we **2.** (not have) an environment at all.
Chuck: I know. But if people **3.** (know) years ago about the damage that power stations can do to the environment, I'm sure they **4.** (do) something about it a long time ago.
Mary Jo: Yes, but now we all know about it and we can all help. If a lot of people **5.** (not be) as lazy as they are, they **6.** (not waste) so much energy in their homes. It's the little things that help.
Chuck: Yes, you're right. I'm sure that if the school **7.** (not help) us with our project, then we **8.** (never be able to start) it, for example.
Mary Jo: That's true, and nowadays there are more people who are really interested in alternative forms of energy. If that **9.** (not be) so, we **10.** (not find) so many people at our meetings.

New U.S. energy alternatives

In the mid-1970s fewer than 1,000 U.S. homes generated their own power. Today however, 1993, that number has grown to 100,000 and this year 6,000 more will probably join those who are already off-the-grid. They are turning to wind, water and sunshine in order to generate power for their homes.

But why are more and more people doing this? Very often it is because these people live far away from the grid and cannot afford the cost of a power line to their home.

As a result of this strong interest, it has become big business to supply homes with renewable energy. The yearly sales for the solar-energy industry alone will soon be $1 billion, and wind and hydro systems for domestic users will add millions more. Last October, more than 150 off-the-grid homes in the USA opened their doors to show how they keep the beer cold, the shower warm and the reading lamp lit with no help from the local power station.

The most popular off-the-grid technology is the use of solar energy. Although photovoltaic (PV) systems are nearly twice as expensive as wind power and three times as expensive as a small hydro project, the sun provides energy for more than two thirds of America's off-the-grid homes. Wind power is generally too unreliable and hydro projects often take years to get approval from the state. Because solar energy is easy to install and doesn't need a lot of maintenance, the US Energy Department uses PV systems for energy programs in the country.

In the past, makers of PV systems sold 60% of their equipment to the government. However, their main customers now are private companies who have realized that PV systems are often cheaper. For example they can install a PV cell on phones or on highway signs which are far away from the grid and so it's not necessary to dig up roads and lay cables. Even the building industry is now showing an interest. It plans to market solar-equipped homes next year at no extra cost.

One of the most important developments recently is that now some electricity companies are even using solar power to avoid the need to build more traditional power plants. Last summer a Californian gas and electricity company supplied 150 homes in California with electricity from a number of PV panels. In this way it saved the $1 million it would have spent on a traditional system.

"All this is going in the right direction," says Tom Kelly, a solar research scientist, "but we must still make a number of engineering improvements before we are ready for the mass market." In fact research is going on all the time in order to find cheaper and better materials and to increase efficiency in solar energy installations. However, off-the-grid energy may get some help from politicians, who may introduce an extra tax on fossil fuels in order to limit global warming. If they do this, fossil fuel prices will increase and solar energy will therefore become more attractive. Such a measure could increase the number of off-the-grid homes from a minority to a majority.

518 words

a *Write a summary of this text.*

Follow these steps	Example for first section:
1. Read the text carefully and write the main idea in an introductory sentence.	*In his text "New U.S. energy alternatives" the author discusses the increase in the use of alternative energy sources, such as wind, sun and water.*
2. Divide the text into five main sections and find headlines for each.	*Section I (lines 1 – 10) Off-the-grid energy increasing in U.S.*
3. For each section write key points (not complete sentences). These must contain the main ideas in each section. Be careful not to include any unnecessary information or details.	*since 1970s – more U.S. country homes – off-the-grid power. alternative sources of energy – cheaper for them*
4. Decide what function each section has, e.g. introduction to subject matter, presentation of arguments for and against, examples, further information, results, contrast and conclusion.	*Section I – introduction to subject matter.*
5. Choose expressions from the list below which help you to present the ideas in the five sections. Firstly/On the one hand/On the other hand/Furthermore/Consequently/As a result/For example/For instance/The reason for/Although/In conclusion/All in all | the author points out, claims, states, maintains, mentions, argues, adds, goes on to say, concludes that …	*Firstly, the author points out that …*
6. Now write a summary of the text using your key words and notes. It should be about half the length of the original text and you should use your own words.	*In his text "New U.S. energy alternatives" the author discusses the increase in the use of alternative energy sources, such as wind, sun and water. Firstly, the author points out that it is mainly since the 1970s that U.S. country homes have turned to off-the-grid power. Alternative sources, says the author, are cheaper for them.*

b *Translate lines 49 to 62 (New U.S. energy alternatives).*

INFO-BOX: HOW TO WRITE A SUMMARY

1. Write the main idea of the text in an introductory sentence.
2. Divide the text into sections and find headlines for each one.
3. For each section write key points, giving the main ideas.
4. Decide what function each section has.
5. Choose expressions to present the ideas in each section.
6. Complete the summary in about half the length of the original text in your own words.

UNIT 7 **D**

1 The Idaho alternative power station

John James, an engineer from Britain, is on a business trip to Idaho in the U.S.A. He is talking to Chat Brown, production manager of an alternative power station which runs on manure. The pictures below show some things which are necessary for the production process.

furnace

fertilizer

storage pit

turbine and generator

 a *Listen to their conversation and put the pictures in the right order.*

b *Now describe the production process.*

2 Writing a report

Here are the notes which John James made during his visit to the Idaho alternative power station.

1) generator produces 12.5 megawatts
2) fuel cheap & environmentally-friendly
3) government money still necessary to keep station competitive
4) lorries deliver 25 tons manure to storage hall daily
5) low man-power costs: 2 employees only
6) furnace burns manure at 800 C
7) ash from furnace is quality fertilizer
8) turbine drives generator
9) greenhouse gas production 25% lower than from traditional power station
10) steam drives turbine
11) computer-controlled cranes take manure from storage hall to furnace
12) burning process produces steam

a *From the notes on the right make three lists to show:*
  1. the energy production process.
  2. the arguments for the process
  3. the arguments against the process

b *Use John James' notes to write a report.*
  1. Explain the process in the correct order.
  2. Write down points for and against the process in full sentences.

UNIT 8

Automation

- *Answer the following questions.*
    1. What differences can you see between the two production methods?
    2. When do you think the photos were taken?
    3. Where would you prefer to work and why?
    4. What changes in production methods will there be in the future? What do you think?

1 New production technologies

Modern life in the so-called civilized world needs all kinds of goods in increasing quantity and quality: computers, TV sets, toys, cars etc. There are many ways of producing goods, but for products that are sold in large quantities, the best way to make them is by mass production. Manufacturers are constantly trying to improve their productivity. That is why automation has been introduced to work faster, more accurately and more economically. As a result factories and shop floors look very different from the way they did in the past.

a The following three paragraphs describe three important developments in new technologies which are used in modern factories.
Read the three paragraphs and find out from the list on the right which terms go with each paragraph.

> robots, shop floors, Computer Aided Design (CAD), workers, research department, Computer Aided Manufacture (CAM).

1 The latest development in this area is that the "workers" are equipped with electronic sensors such as video cameras, microphones and touch sensors. Such a "worker" needs this equipment to do his work and also to send back information to the controlling computer. The computer is programmed to use this feedback to change its instructions to the "worker" if necessary.
2 With special programs designers can simulate on the computer what will happen if a particular design is chosen. In the past often unsuitable plans were drawn, just to find out later that they did not work. Now the computer helps to predict what will happen under different conditions – for example to a bridge in different winds. Moreover, these programs can also work out the most economical way of making something out of the materials available.
3 Machines that have to do the same job again and again can be operated automatically by this computer system. The computer programs in this system control the automated machines or tools. This software can be changed and so the machines can be programmed in different ways to make different products. The system is also used to monitor the production process and correct any faults.

b *Answer the following questions.*
1. What is the method of producing goods in large quantities called?
2. Why have most companies introduced automation in their factories?
3. How are technical drawings made nowadays?
4. What advantages does the CAD system have?
5. What does a CAM system control?
6. In what way is the CAM system flexible?
7. What electronic equipment do modern robots have?
8. Why are they equipped with these things?

c The most advanced systems link together CAD, CAM, robots and other automated machinery. One such system is called Computer Integrated Manufacture (CIM). It is shown on the right.
Describe in your own words how it works.

CPU — Central Processor Unit controls all operations

CAD (Design and Construction) → CAM (Manufacturing) → Storage → Delivery

2 Describing a production system

a *Match the words in the box with the parts of the car.*

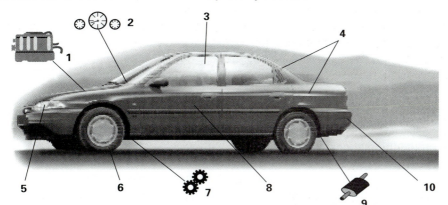

a) engine
b) doors
c) headlights
d) wheels
e) dashboard
f) windows
g) bumper
h) gearbox
i) exhaust pipe
j) car body

b In the diagram below you can see how a car is made in a modern car factory. *Describe the production system. Use the vocabulary in the box.*

Example: First lorries deliver the different parts of the car to the factory.

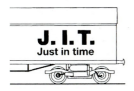
1

2

3

lorries, workers, machines, robots

spray, assemble, add, test, dip weld, dry, fit, deliver, drive away, put on

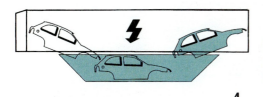
4

5

6

7

8

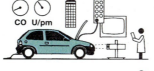
9

10

1 How is a car produced?

- *Describe the production process on page 67 in the passive voice. Add "by" if necessary.*

Example: The parts are delivered by lorries. The body is...

2 How should production be improved?

- In order to succeed on the international market a modern car has to be produced in only a few hours today. How can this be done?
  Here are some suggestions the workers have made. *Complete the sentences in the passive voice. "Must", "have to", "should", "can" or "could" should be used at least once.*

Example: 1. The workers should be trained more carefully.

1. workers / train more carefully
2. production process / organize better
3. cars / assemble / by groups of workers
4. important parts / make / by the workers
5. other parts / deliver "just-in-time"
6. better working conditions / introduce
7. a new kind of fast-drying paint / use
8. workers / give more responsibility
9. workers' suggestions / follow / by the management

3 Production in the past and today

Many years ago motor companies used only a few machines. So the workers did most of the hard and dirty work. After Henry Ford had invented the production line, motor companies started mass production. In the last few years companies especially in Japan have improved the production process. Nowadays European companies are also developing new production methods. If they did not do this, they would sell fewer cars, because motor companies in Japan or the US produce cars more cheaply. So companies have bought a lot of expensive machines. Today production lines transport the car bodies and robots do most of the work. More and more companies are introducing a system of computer integrated manufacture (CIM). Maybe in twenty years' time they will need no workers at all.

- *Describe the development of production in the passive voice.*

Example: Many years ago only a few machines were used by motor companies. So most of ...

4 A new job

Wesley Harding has applied for a job at a big motor company. This is what happened to him:

1. Before his interview/Wesley/a letter/send/the personnel manager
2. On the day of his interview/Mr Harding/questions/ask/about his qualifications
3. While he was waiting/the applicant/a cup of tea/serve/the tea-lady
4. Then/he/the new machines/show/the head technician
5. Afterwards/Wesley/lunch ticket/give/a secretary
6. In the afternoon/he/result/tell/the personnel manager
7. Wesley/job/give/the personnel manager
8. Before he left/Mr Harding/£20 travel expenses/pay

- *Make sentences both in the active and passive voice.*

> **Example:** 1. Before his interview the personnel manager sent a letter to Wesley.
> ...Wesley was sent a letter by the personnel manager.

5 Translation

- *Translate the following text. Watch out for the tenses.*

Die meisten Automobilfirmen wurden vor vielen Jahren gegründet. Zu jener Zeit wurden viele Arbeiter benötigt, um Autos zu produzieren. Es konnten pro Tag natürlich weniger Fahrzeuge als heute hergestellt werden. Aber nachdem neue Technologien eingeführt worden waren, wurden mehr und mehr Arbeiter entlassen (dismiss). Seit dem Beginn der Massenproduktion ist die Produktivität erhöht worden. Heute wird die Produktion von Robotern ausgeführt und von Computern kontrolliert. Der Prozess der Automatisierung kann nicht angehalten werden. In der Fabrik der Zukunft werden wahrscheinlich viele Produkte ohne Arbeitskräfte hergestellt werden. Allerdings werden auch dann qualifizierte (skilled) Arbeiter benötigt werden, weil nicht alle Tätigkeiten von Maschinen ausgeführt werden können. Zur Zeit werden Arbeitnehmer von verschiedenen Autoherstellern zu ihren Ideen befragt, wie die Produktion verbessert werden kann. Neue Technologien können auch zusammen mit den Gewerkschaften entwickelt und eingeführt werden. Aber natürlich weiß heute niemand genau, welche Autos in fünfzig Jahren produziert werden und wie der Produktionsprozess dann aussehen wird.

1 The new industrial revolution

Automation, computer-controlled robots, in recent years we have all seen pictures of modern production lines which are dominated by machines and where no humans can be seen.

However, in one German electronics firm in Cardiff, Wales, humans are making a comeback. Personnel manager Martin Wibberly told me "Nowadays we think of our workers not only as a cost factor, but as capital and so we invest in them." And the company invests in them because their flexibility is needed in today's market. Martin added "Flexibility means a faster and more customer-orientated service. Of course, we still use robots but the production lines of the past were too inflexible and complex and therefore too expensive to serve today's market. And so these methods have been replaced by much smaller and individual production units."

It's an arrangement which suits the workers equally well. Peter Brown, who was one of the 500 chosen from 25,000 applicants for jobs at the firm, explained the advantages of the new system for the workers. "As you know, past production methods were all based on mass production where each worker on the production line performed one small monotonous task. Now however, the work is done in groups which are completely responsible for one individual step in the production process. This arrangement is also more flexible for us because now we can arrange our own working schedules."

Today there are also opportunities for workers to train and get further qualifications so that they can do different jobs when this becomes necessary. This too, means that the work is much less repetitive and boring than in the past. The groups also meet regularly to discuss problems in the production process, to suggest solutions and to help to put them into practice. Peter Brown points out that when the workers have a say in the organization of their work, communication between workers and management is improved. He also enjoys the feeling of responsibility not only for his own work, but also for the success of the whole process.

These changes have been supported by the unions. They too, recognize the opportunities for personal development which workers will be given under this system. Lean management and productivity in the Japanese style can only be effective, they say, when all the employees have more say in the decision-making process.

387 words

a *Name two methods of production mentioned in the text.*

b *Find three groups of people who support the new method.*

c *List the disadvantages of the old system.*

d *List the advantages of the new system.*

e *Give the meaning of the following expressions from the text.*
   1. customer-orientated service (line 14)
   2. mass production (line 26/27)
   3. working schedules (line 33/34)
   4. further qualifications (line 36)
   5. lean management (line 52)
   6. decision-making process (line 55)

f *Write a summary of the text.*

g *Translate lines 35 to 48 (The new industrial revolution).*

2 Describing a process.

a A large German electronics firm has developed a new digital cassette recorder. They need the recording instructions in English. The production manager has given you this drawing.
Write the instructions in English for the export model.

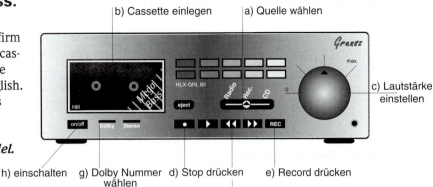

b) Cassette einlegen
a) Quelle wählen
c) Lautstärke einstellen
h) einschalten
g) Dolby Nummer wählen
d) Stop drücken
e) Record drücken
f) zurückspulen

Follow these steps	Example:
1. Put the instructions in the right order.	einschalten – Kassette einlegen …
2. Translate the instructions using the words in the box below. If you need more help, use your dictionary. einschalten: to switch on drücken: to press einstellen: to adjust zurückspulen: to rewind	einschalten = to switch on
3. Use infinitives, modals or passive forms.	*First, the recorder must be switched on. Then…*
4. Ask your partner to test the instructions at home.	

b Here is a new video recorder which has been produced by the same firm.
Write the operating instructions for this recorder.

> **INFO BOX: HOW TO DESCRIBE A PROCESS**
> 1. Put your information in the right order.
> 2. Use your dictionary to find exact meanings.
> 3. Write precise instructions. You can use infinitives, modals or passive forms.
> 4. Test out the instructions on the equipment.

1 Sales talk

a *Listen to the cassette and find out the following things:*
   1. Who is talking?
   2. Where are they talking?
   3. What are they talking about?

b *Listen to the cassette again and find out about the following:*
   1. speed 2. paper 3. print quality (resolution) 4. installation 5. service 6. price

2 Installing equipment

You have just bought the new Pineapple ink jet printer.
Unfortunately the instructions in the handbook are only in English. You also discover that these instructions are completely mixed up.

a *First find the correct headlines for the instructions.*

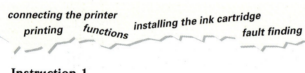

connecting the printer   installing the ink cartridge
printing   functions   fault finding

Instruction 1.
– tighten the screw of the interface connector.
– connect the other end of the interface cable to your printer.
– make sure that both the computer and the printer are turned off.
– connect one end of the interface cable to the computer

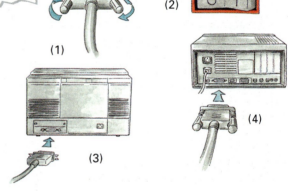

Instruction 2.
– put the printer cover back on.
– press the cartridge down until it snaps into position.
– take off the safety tape on the ink cartridge.
– remove the printer cover.

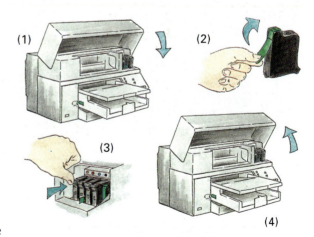

b *Now put the instructions into the correct order. The drawings will help you.*

c *Translate the instructions into German.*

d *You still need help to install the ink jet printer. The supplier of the printer comes to your house and shows you how to do this.*
   Work out the conversation you might have with this computer expert. Play these roles.

UNIT 9

Changes in the British industry

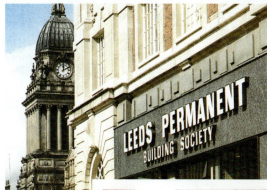

We've got everything you need

a   What do the photos tell us about Leeds?

b   Who do you think wrote the brochure and why?

c   Compare your town / region with Leeds.

d   Imagine you have to write a brochure in English for your town / region. Think of a slogan. What photos would you use? Give reasons for your choice.

1 Changes in the North of England

- *Look at the industrial map of Great Britain in the 1960s and the newspaper headlines below. Now answer the following questions.*

1. What kind of industries could you find in the Leeds/Newcastle area in the sixties?

2. What has happened to them?

3. What has happened to the workers?

4. Why do you think has there been such a development?

⚒ coal industry
⚙ steel industry
🏭 textile industry
🚢 shipbuilding industry

4,000 jobs lost in coal industry!

Newcastle shipyard closed!

Steel production reduced by 30%!

Textile Industry Goes East!

2 Newcastle takes off

Before ...

Newcastle Business Park, the £100 million development of a former industrial area, was officially opened yesterday.

The success of the Newcastle scheme is that 95 per cent of the 67,000 square metres of office buildings have already been let, mostly to computer companies and light industries.

The management of the new business park is giving financial help to new companies and is trying to provide the latest communications technology. The area also has the advantage of excellent road, rail and air links.

More than 3,500 people work on the 1.5 km site and this number is expected to reach 4,000 when all the available office buildings have been let. Decades ago the site was occupied by a large factory which produced machinery and arms. When the factory closed down, nobody was interested in taking over the site. However, unemployment figures were so high in Newcastle some years ago that the Newcastle Development Corporation decided to invest £100 million in this site. John Scally, the managing director, proudly says today: "Newcastle Business Park is an outstanding example of what cities can achieve."

181 words

and after ...

The European, London (adapted)

a *Compare the photos.*
   What has been done in the Newcastle area in the last few years?

b *Answer the following questions.*
   Some answers cannot just be taken directly from the text.
   1. What does a business park look like?
   2. What was produced on the site of the new business park years ago?
   3. Who (do you think) has given the money for the project to the Newcastle Development Corporation?
   4. Why (do you think) has so much money been invested?
   5. Why (do you think) are so many companies interested in the new office buildings?
   6. Why (do you think) were they not interested in the old site?

c *Now think of the town/area where you live. Describe a similar project that you have seen or heard of.*

UNIT 9 **B** INFINITIVE – GERUND SEE PAGES 130/131 INFINITIVE – GERUND SEE PAGES 130/131 INFINITI

A Canadian student at Newcastle college

1 Planning the visit

Craig Russell, a Canadian student from Vancouver, is planning to go on a year's exchange visit to Newcastle College in the north of England. He has never been to Europe before. So yesterday he asked Calvin, another student who had been on last year's exchange, for some help. Here are some of Craig's questions and the answers he received.

a *Match the answers to the questions.*

1. Who should I contact first at the college?
2. When should I write to my host family?
3. How should I travel from London Airport to Newcastle?
4. Where can I reserve a seat for that journey?
5. What should I give my host family as a present?
6. How much luggage should I take?
7. What should I wear at college?
8. Where can I find a good bank in Newcastle?

a) at a travel agent's
b) a month before you arrive
c) opposite the college
d) Ms Keegan, the head of department
e) not too much
f) by coach
g) casual clothes
h) something typically Canadian

b *Now report Calvin's answers like this :*

> **Example:** Calvin told him / advised him to contact Ms Keegan at the college.

c Craig has been at Newcastle College for one month now. This is part of Craig's letter home. As you can read the teachers **expect him to work** hard during his stay in Newcastle and sometimes they **make him do** some extra work. *Complete the letter with the verbs in the box.*

    let   expect   make   want   ask

Life at college is great. I am the second Canadian student to study here for a whole year. I get on well with the teachers here but they ..**1**.. me work quite hard. They ..**2**.. me to talk to the English students more about the Canadian college system. I didn't realize it was so complicated. In fact, the teachers ..**3**.. me to know a lot more than I actually do. Last week, for example, they ..**4**.. to show my photos of our college in Vancouver in order to give the English students a better idea of our work at Canadian colleges. But it is not all hard work. And if I want to do some sight-seeing at the weekend, the teachers ..**5**.. me go early on Fridays. By the way I have met …

2 Finding out useful information

a On the next page you can see a part of the students' notice board at Newcastle College. *Match the following sentences with the notices on the board.*

> **Example:** sentence 1 goes with notice F.

1. I'm interested in… more about France.
2. I'm tired of… with my parents and I need somewhere to live.
3. Students who are afraid of… their final tests should ring 347168.

4. ... is dangerous for your health.
5. Craig is going to the club because he is good at ... basketball.
6. We'll leave the car at home. ... and ... is stupid.
7. I'm looking forward to ... you on Friday evening.
8. If Gary takes me in his car, I won't have any more problems in ... to college on time.

b *Complete the sentences. Use the -ing form.*

Example: I'm interested in knowing more about France so I'll go to the French Club.

3 Talking about friends

Craig has met a lot of new friends at Newcastle College. Here are some remarks they have made about themselves.

Sharon:	"I play more hockey than volleyball at the Sports Club."
Kevin:	"I go to the cinema every week."
Emma:	"I don't smoke any more."
Bill and Ben:	"We don't eat in the college canteen. The food's not very good there."
Sam:	"That's one thing I hate – my alarm clock."
Mary Ann:	"I'm very interested in foreign languages."
Gary and Sue:	"We did the same test last year."
Lisa:	"I try not to be late for college. I take the early bus."
Mike:	"I spend all my free time at the Sports Club."
Tina:	"This book is very useful. I think you should read it."

• *Make statements about Craig's friends.*

The verbs in the box will help you.

like	hate	prefer	remember	stop
enjoy	avoid	suggest	dislike	love

Example: Sharon prefers playing hockey to volleyball at the Sports Club.

4 Translation

Imagine you were at Newcastle College on an exchange visit and that you had to write a report in English about your experiences there.

• *Translate these notes into English.*

1. Meine Gastfamilie ist sehr nett. Ich wohne gern bei ihr.
2. Aber zuerst hatte ich Schwierigkeiten, ihr Englisch zu verstehen.
3. Am Anfang hatte ich Angst, Fehler zu machen.
4. Die englischen Schüler im College sind sehr interessiert, mehr über Deutschland zu hören.
5. Im College lassen die Lehrer mich ziemlich hart arbeiten.
6. Sie erwarten, dass ich viel über das deutsche Schulsystem weiß.

Jobs – from France to Scotland

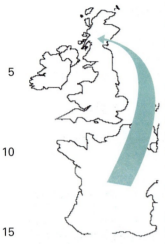

It was nothing unusual in the business world when MENOC, a big producer of household appliances, announced last month that it was closing down its vacuum-cleaner factory in France – with a loss of 600 jobs – in order to concentrate production in a single plant in Scotland. It all seemed logical: The company's production capacity in Europe was too high. In order to get 400 new jobs to Glasgow the workers at MENOC's Scottish plant were willing to accept wage cuts, flexible working hours and a longer working week. The company felt that in this way it would remain competitive in a more and more global business and that it could cut its costs by 25 per cent.

But French workers reacted quickly. MENOC employees in Dijon went on strike immediately. There was even talk of a nationwide boycott of MENOC products. "This is a disaster," said one striker. "It's impossible to find another job within hundreds of kilometres."

The French minister for industry and foreign trade accused the British workers of accepting bad conditions. He also said that Britain was lowering social standards and was stealing jobs from the rest of Europe.

The British Prime Minister, however, was proud of attracting MENOC to Britain. "It's not surprising that companies are coming to the U.K.," he said. "Our productivity is rising fast and relations between employers and unions have improved. It's now more economic to invest in Britain than it is in any other country in the European Union."

Unemployment in both countries is high. That fact explains the protest in France over the loss of just 600 jobs. It is a reminder that in hard economic times, nations, not to mention workers and unions, put their own interests before the needs of the European Union. Nowhere is this more true than in Glasgow, where unemployment is extremely high. Like other cities Glasgow has suffered as a result of the decline of its heavy industry. Europe's Single Market will do little to cut unemployment figures, at least not in the near future.

Today many European companies are trying to concentrate their production in order to save costs. In recent weeks several firms have also announced similar steps. For example a big German electronics firm which makes television sets in France wants to concentrate its production in Vienna, Austria, which will cost 890 jobs in France. The management says that the move will cut their costs by 8 per cent.

Of course, as Europe continues on its way to a true single market there will be more winners and losers. Few know this better than Glasgow officials these days. Just one day after the MENOC announcement they heard that a big Swiss food company would end its chocolate production in Glasgow, transferring the work to two other factories – one of them in France. The result: 500 jobs lost.

483 words

a Each of the following sentences represents a paragraph of the text.
Put the sentences in the order of the paragraphs.

1. At the moment many big companies are trying to save costs and so are closing down factories .
2. The French government and workers accuse the British workers and the British government of taking their jobs.
3. Not only France, but also Britain is losing jobs to other countries.
4. Britain is proud of its rising productivity and investment.
5. MENOC is giving up its vacuum-cleaner production in France.
6. As the unemployment rate is high in most countries, workers and their unions put their personal interests first.

b *Answer the following questions in complete sentences.*

1. Why is MENOC closing down its plant in France?
2. Why is the company carrying on its production of vacuum-cleaners in Scotland?
3. What effect does this decision have on the workers in Dijon?
4. What did the workers at MENOC do immediately?
5. Why are companies moving to Britain according to the British Prime Minister?
6. Why do European governments see the closing down of factories in their countries as a major political problem?
7. Why do many European companies concentrate their production in just one or two plants?

c "Workers should accept worse conditions (wage, working hours, working conditions, no strikes) in order to save their jobs or to create new jobs." Do you agree?
Write a comment:

Follow these steps	Example:
1. Write a general introduction to the topic, e.g. give reasons why the topic is of special importance today.	*Today the unemployment rate in many countries is high. So a lot of workers fear for their jobs, and the jobless are desperately looking for new jobs. Many of them are willing to accept lower pay and worse working conditions than before.*
2. Collect ideas for arguments for and against the statement above and put them in a suitable order.	*Arguments for:* *– lower costs for companies* *– more competitive on international markets* *Arguments against:* *– lower standard of living*
3. Then make complete sentences and decide which phrases may be suitable, e.g.: Firstly/In addition/On the one hand/On the other hand/In contrast, …	*On the one hand this brings many advantages to the companies. Firstly…*
4. Draw conclusions from the arguments above and state your point of view. Use these phrases: In conclusion/As a result/In my opinion/In my view/It is for this reason that …	*In conclusion I would say that workers should/should not…*

d *Translate lines 34 to 40 (Jobs – from France to Scotland).*

INFO-BOX : HOW TO WRITE A COMMENT
1. Write a general introduction to the topic.
2. Collect ideas for arguments for and against the statement and put them in a suitable order.
3. Choose expressions to present your arguments and write complete sentences.
4. Draw your conclusions from the arguments given and state your personal point of view.

Looking for a new location

Imagine you work for Samsons Ltd, an international manufacturer of high class racing bicycles. They are very interested in finding a new site for a new factory and offices in England. Your company has looked at a lot of promotion literature for development areas in Britain.

a *Read the two extracts below and do the following tasks.*

1. Find out where exactly the two areas are.
2. Make a list of the key points in both of the extracts.
3. Find out from your key points
   – which points are mentioned in both texts.
   – which are only in one of the texts.
4. Give a short report about the two areas.
5. Discuss your results in class. Which area do you think is better for your company? Give reasons.
6. Write a letter to both areas stating your situation, and ask for more information.

Extract 1:   England's Largest County is Getting Bigger!

Large investments by private developers in the North's most prosperous county allow us a wonderful opportunity to invite you to join our economic success. Fifteen new office and business parks are being developed both in town centres and out of town. Offices with up to 25,000 square feet will soon be available, while offices up to 35,000 square feet can be built to your own requirements.

North Yorkshire has a growing population, top schools, colleges and universities, good housing and shopping facilities, excellent road and rail links (only 2 hours from London) and highly developed business contacts.

Write or phone today for details of current opportunities.

The Economic Development Centre, North Yorkshire County Council, County Hall, Northallerton, North Yorkshire DL7 8AD, England. Telephone 0609 780780.

Extract 2:   WHERE ON EARTH SHOULD WE RELOCATE ?
The answer is easy: to the Black Country.

We're right in the centre of England which means there is direct access to London and the Channel Tunnel via the national motorway network. What else does the location offer? Plenty of skilled labour (after all we have represented the heart of Britain's manufacturing base for more than 200 years). Thousands of square metres of land for offices and factories. The buildings which have already been built are of the highest standard and we have not forgotten to build large car parks! In addition, we can provide all the back-up you need; from planning permission to expert help even financial assistance. The Black Country – your future in Europe has never looked brighter.

For more information, contact Linda Clement on **44 21 511 2000, or write to her – Black Country Development Corporation, Black Country House, Rounds Green Road, Olbury, West Midlands B69 2DG, England.

---

b *You are interested in finding out more about the two regions. Two colleagues have visited the areas.* **Listen to their reports and find out from their phone calls:**

1. which towns they have visited.
2. where these towns are.

c *Listen to the cassette again and find out more about the following:*

1. transport links
2. industry
3. price of land
4. housing
5. job situation
6. general impression

d *Which town would you now choose for a new site for your company? Work in groups and then write a report and give reasons for your decision.*

Immigration in the United States

Two hundred years ago the U.S. had a population of about 4 million people. Today the population has risen to about 260 million.

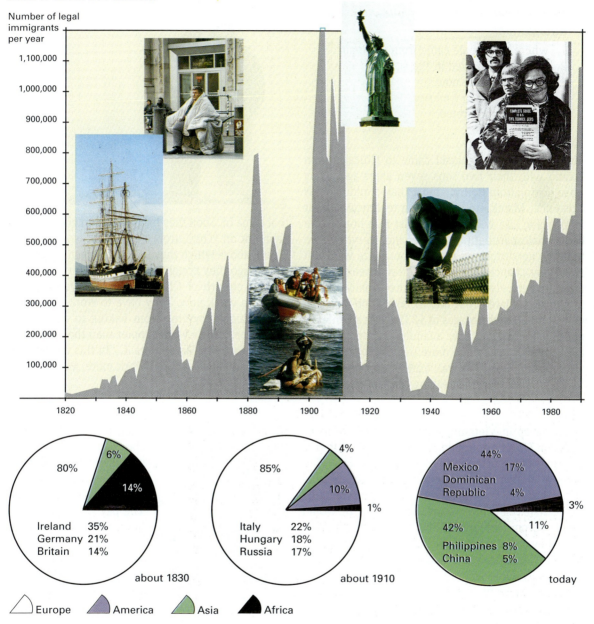

a Describe the development of immigration in the United States.

b Where have the different groups of immigrants come from over the years?

c What means of transport have immigrants used to get to the U.S.?

d What reasons have they had for coming?

1 Two faces of America

a *What do you think the title "Two faces of America" means?*

b *Find out from the texts the following information:*
1. where the people came from originally.
2. when they arrived in the U.S.
3. where they live now.
4. what they do in America.
5. why they emigrated.

Text 1

Marek and Lisa Leschinski came to Chicago from Poland with their two sons seven years ago. They were fleeing from nothing more than a middle-class existence. Marek, now 32, was a technical drawer
5 in Warsaw. Lisa was a receptionist in a hotel. "We had a small apartment, jobs, a car and everything we basically needed," says Marek, "but there were not really any chances for more." After three years of trying to get a visa to the States, they finally arrived
10 in Chicago. Marek first had to take a job as a machine operator with wages of $235 a week, which is not much when you have a family to support. However, a year later he had more than doubled his salary at another job. Lisa was working in a cookie fac-
15 tory, and they were just saving most of the money

that came in. Soon they had saved enough for a down payment on 'The European Cafe' on North Lincoln Street, above which they live in a 5-room apartment. A year ago they bought the 'Town Bakery' in a fashionable suburb of Chicago. Marek says they earn 20 $1200 a week now. They have to work 16 hours a day, doing everything from baking to making the deliveries, but they are happier than they have ever been before. As Marek puts it, "In this country you have the chance – if you work more, you can earn 25 more."

236 words

Text 2

Growing up in Vietnam, June Yen learnt to be an outsider. She is a so-called Amerasian. Her father is an American soldier she has never met. Her Vietnamese mother spent years explaining to her why
5 she looked different from her friends. When she came to the States eleven years ago she thought she would finally become integrated. She was wrong. "In Vietnam they called me American," the 25-year-old explained, "here, they don't know who I am and I still
10 don't really know where I belong." After arriving in America she went to school in Atlanta. There she was put into a class with children half her age because her English was not good enough. This made her feel like an outsider from the beginning. To make
15 matters worse one teacher there who had fought in the Vietnam war even told her, "Why don't you go back to your country?" This made June very sceptical and even afraid of her American teachers. June still cannot speak or write English very well and she

often feels like a second- 20 class person. After leaving school without any real qualifications she got a job in a Chinese restaurant. The pay was bad and the 25 hours long. Four years ago she met her Vietnamese husband. A year later they moved to Memphis where her husband found a new 30 job. June has given up work and now looks after their two children at home. As June says "Emigration to a new country takes a lot of courage and determination. Arriving in a foreign country with practically no possessions and not being able to speak the lan- 35 guage can be a very frightening experience. I only hope my children will have a better start in life than I did."

293 words

c *Find out from the texts why the following statements are true.*

1. Marek and Lisa were not poor immigrants.
2. It took 3 years before they could emigrate to America.
3. They started their own business in America.
4. The Leschinskis have found their happiness in America.
5. June Yen had identity problems in Vietnam.
6. She had problems at the school in Atlanta.
7. She still feels like a second-class citizen.
8. Her children will hopefully have a happier childhood.

d *Discuss the following quotations from the texts.*

1. "In America you have the chance – if you work more, you can earn more."
2. "Emigration takes courage and determination."

2 American immigrants: who are they and where do they go?

a *Link the five statements below with the states.*

b *Find out from the graphs the differences between the eastern and the western states.*

c *What else do the figures tell us?*

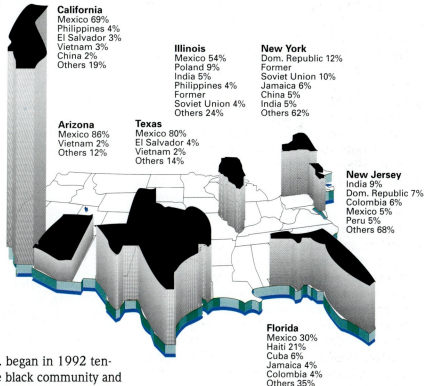

1. When the riots in L.A. began in 1992 tension grew between the black community and the new immigrants. 2000 Asian owned businesses were looted or damaged by fire.
2. More Poles live in Chicago than in any other city in the world except Warsaw. The city still attracts new Polish immigrants.
3. Ellis Island closed as a port of entry in 1954, but this city in the east still attracts more immigrants than any other city in America.
4. People from Latin America are still coming in great numbers to Miami.
5. Along its Mexican border, which is 1200 miles long, about 400,000 illegal immigrants are arrested every year.

1 California and the Chinese

The Californian population is a mixture of immigrants from many different nations **which includes** lots of Chinese. Most foreigners know the part of San Francisco **which is called** Chinatown. Today Chinatown has not only a lot of fine restaurants **which have been built** for the tourists, but it is also a place where some Chinese people do not have enough to eat. In some areas there are families with four or five children **who live** in a single room. And so you find many families **who use** the same kitchen and bathroom. Today Chinatown is not only a tourist attraction but also a place with a lot of poverty.

Meanwhile many young Chinese have left Chinatown for other places **which offer** better jobs. But most of the new immigrants **who come** from China cannot move because they do not know the language **which is spoken** outside the Chinese community.

The older Chinese people **who have been** there for decades do not want to move to another place. They hold on to their old ways, and they do not often ask for help from outside the community.

- *Replace the words in bold type by a present participle (ing-form) or past participle (third form of the verb).*

> **Example:** The Californian population is a mixture of immigrants from many different nations **including** lots of Chinese. Most foreigners know the part of San Francisco **called** Chinatown. Today Chinatown ...

2 Californian Indians

The American Indian was the first true Californian. The style of Indian art, music and clothing is part of the whole West, including California. But like other minorities, the Indians have had trouble in Californian society. In their case the problem is land. **As they believe** that they have been treated unfairly by the American politicians, many of them have become rather bitter. Others have started to make their voices heard in various protest actions. One group includes the Pitt River Indians. **Before they started** their protest action, they talked to several reporters.

The parts in bold type can be changed like this:

> **Example: Believing** that they have been treated unfairly ... **Before starting** their protest action ...

- *Now put the following statements about the Pitt River Indians into the same form as in the examples above.*

1. When they realized how much gold there was on our land, the whites decided to take it away from the Indians.
2. As they knew the Indians had been treated badly, later governments gave them money for their land.
3. Because the Indians want their land back and not the money, they have decided to start a protest action.
4. After they have made their protest here, they are going to fly to Washington.
5. As they know how difficult it is to get a meeting with the President, they are prepared to wait as long as necessary.
6. Before they leave Washington the Indians will give a press conference.

3 A Mexican immigrant

A Mexican immigrant talks about his life in the U.S. during a break in his work.

- *Infinite or ing-form? Fill in the correct form of the verb.*

> **Example:** 1. I'll never forget leaving my small Mexican hometown.
> 2. My mother told me: "Don't forget to write to us…

I'll never forget **1.** (leave) my small Mexican hometown. My mother told me: "Don't forget **2.** (write) to us when you're there. "I remember **3.** (cross) the border by night. I was very afraid of **4.** (be arrested), but I wanted **5.** (change) my life completely, so I decided **6.** (take) the chance. In the first town I stopped **7.** (get) some food. Inside the restaurant there was a sign **8.** (say) that they needed help in the kitchen. I remember **9.** (ask) the boss what he was prepared **10.** (pay). It wasn't much but **11.** (need) the money urgently I accepted it.

They made me **12.** (do) the dirty jobs. First I enjoyed **13.** (work) there because the other workers were friendly. But after **14.** (stay) there for six months I moved here to San Diego. I hope **15.** (find) my own apartment soon. I would like **16.** (stay) here forever. That's why I must remember **17.** (phone) the Housing Officer tomorrow. Most people don't care that I'm a so-called illegal. They let me **18.** (live) my own life. – Sorry, my break is over. I must stop **19.** (talk) now. I have **20.** (get) back to work again.

4 A German immigrant

Ursula Tischmann from Germany emigrated to America twenty years ago. Every year she writes a letter to some friends in Germany.

- *Translate the following part of one of her letters.*

Vor einigen Monaten zogen nebenan drei junge Leute ein. Nach einer Weile begannen sie, einige Arbeiten für die Nachbarn zu erledigen. Ich erinnere mich, dass ich Herrn Cheng, den Leiter des Supermarktes, gefragt hatte, wer sie waren. Er erzählte mir, dass sie deutsche Studenten waren, die eine Reise von Kalifornien nach New York planten. Deshalb hatten sie Herrn Cheng gebeten, ihnen eine Beschäftigung zu geben. Nachdem Herr Cheng mit ihnen gesprochen hatte, ließ er sie in seinem Geschäft arbeiten. Ich erinnere mich, dass ich sie eines Abends traf. Sie reparierten gerade ihren alten Lieferwagen. Ich hielt an, um ihnen meine Hilfe anzubieten. Es machte mir Spaß, wieder deutsch zu sprechen. Sie freuten sich darauf, die USA zu durchqueren und viele Sehenswürdigkeiten zu sehen. Mit dem Geld, das sie in Herrn Chengs Supermarkt verdient hatten, konnten sie letzte Woche aufhören zu arbeiten. Ich hoffe, dass sie es noch schaffen, New York zu sehen.

Immigration and welfare

Together with corn and cars, immigration has been one of the main factors of American economic growth. The traditional theory is simple: new workers increase the supply of goods and
5 *services with their labor and increase the demand for other goods and services by spending their wages. A circle of growth begins as a growing number of workers create a richer society for each other. Two hundred years of U.S. history seem to confirm this theory. But there is a feeling today that immigration is* 10
not so good for the economy any more.

The polls show that 62 per cent of U.S. citizens are worried that more immigrants will take jobs away from native-born workers. This can be true
15 in times of high unemployment. In California, for example, where the jobless rate is nine per cent, immigration is still rising and native-born Americans are actually leaving to find work in other states. So we must see both sides: "The short-
20 term costs of immigration are much higher today," says Michael Boston, one of the leading American economists, "but in the long run, immigrants are still great news for our economy. Normally, new jobs are created through the im-
25 migrants' own work. The immigrants' spending creates a demand for houses, food, etc. and their employers invest their growing profits in new machinery and jobs. That's how America got rich."

However, in the last two decades things have
30 changed. In the early days of immigration public education and some public health programs were the only services for those coming to New York or other Northeastern cities. One third of the new immigrants soon found out that America did not
35 offer the opportunities they were looking for and so they moved back home. Nowadays a lot of different welfare programs – from food stamps to unemployment benefit – help those who do not succeed in finding work and even attract immi-
40 grants who would otherwise stay in their home countries. Furthermore the level of skills of 90 per cent of the new immigrants is relatively low. And so are their earnings. 20 years ago the average immigrant earned 3 per cent more than a
45 native-born American, but today the new immigrants receive about 20 per cent less. Welfare costs for the new immigrants are steadily climbing and are now above those for native-born Americans.

Persecution and poverty in Europe made millions emigrate to the U.S. a century ago

The face of immigration has changed over the last few decades, adding non-European cultures, languages and religions

Of course, the welfare costs will decrease as the U.S. 50
economy recovers. The long-term benefits of immigrant labor will then be obvious. But the days of innocence for the U.S. as an immigration country are over.

422 words

a Which of the following topics are mentioned in the text?

> unemployment / transport / welfare costs / California / Texas / skills / wages / environment

b Answer the following questions in complete sentences.

1. How do immigrants help the economy
   – as workers?
   – as consumers?
2. What are many people afraid of in a bad economic situation?
3. How has the welfare state developed since 1900?
4. How has the level of immigrants' skills changed in the last few decades?
5. "The days of innocence are over." What do you think the author means by the last sentence of the text?

c List the costs and the benefits of immigration according to the text.

d Find more arguments and state your point of view.

e Write a comment: Immigration helps the economy. Do you agree?

f Translate the third paragraph.

Follow these steps	Example:
1. Read the whole text first, even if you only have to translate part of it. Make sure you understand the unknown words. Use your dictionary.	decade = Jahrzehnt, 10 Jahre
2. Translate the text into German in a way that you have a first draft. (word-by-word translation)	Jedoch in den letzten zwei Jahrzehnten haben sich die Dinge geändert.
3. Work through the text again. Compare the structure and the meaning of the English and the German sentence. Try to produce a suitable German final version.	In den letzten zwanzig Jahren hat sich jedoch die Situation geändert.

> **INFO-BOX : HOW TO WRITE A TRANSLATION**
>
> 1. Read and try to understand the complete text.
> 2. Look up unknown words in your dictionary.
> 3. Make a first draft in a word-by-word translation.
> 4. Go through the text again and produce a final version in good German.

1 The new majority

The Californian life style has grown out of many different cultures. People have been coming here from other American states and from foreign countries for a long time now. They have come to find better jobs, a better house, a better climate – in short a better way of life.

 a *Listen to the cassette.*

1. Put the photos into the correct order.
2. Find out where these people came from.
3. Find out where they live now in California.

Santiago Rodriguez

Lev Pischnik

Mom Chay Suth

b *Listen to the cassette again and find out the following information about the people:*

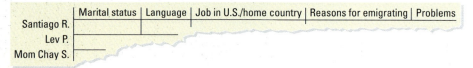

	Marital status	Language	Job in U.S./home country	Reasons for emigrating	Problems
Santiago R.					
Lev P.					
Mom Chay S.					

2 Minority groups

In many countries minority groups often face problems. Therefore some people are against immigration. On the other hand, immigration brings a lot of benefits to a country.

a *Make a list of all the benefits you can think of in the following areas.*

1. economy
2. employment
3. welfare
4. education
5. culture
6. language

b *A local newspaper has just published a letter from someone wanting to stop immigration. Write a letter to the editor of the newspaper, giving your arguments for immigration.*

FURTHER READING   FURTHER READING   FURTHER READING   FURTHER READING   FURTHER   READ

Free time

Computer games defended

In Britain alone there are now an estimated quarter of a million electronic games in amusement arcades, clubs, pubs and shops. For teenagers they appear to hold an almost hypnotic attraction, and many parents fear the possibly undesirable effects on their children's health and welfare. Parents are critical of games wondering whether they encourage aggressive behaviour. The games have also been blamed as being potentially dangerous, and there have been reported cases of epilepsy, and even heart attacks. The industry and their defenders claim the games have many positive benefits but that these have been neglected by the media. It claimed that acquiring the skills necessary to succeed at the games gives young people a new enthusiasm for learning. And learning to play well can speed reaction, increase assertiveness, teach patience and control, as well as helping a teenager use his or her memory to learn and apply the rules of the game. According to one American expert, computer games could even improve reading ability, because the required concentration and attention to detail is transferred to the reading process. Terry Pratt, who is editor of "Computer and Video Games" magazine for real fanatics, believes it's important to stress the positive benefits. "A lot of young people program their own games on their home computers and develop an interest in learning programming skills," he says. "And this is bound to help them in a few years' time when computers will play an even larger part in our everyday lives than they do at the moment." The fact that the games are enjoyable does make learning more fun, though many parents worry about the addictive nature of the electronic gadgets. How real is the danger? John Newson, Professor of Child Development at Nottingham University, explains the fascination. "Young people love button-pushing exercises and they like to see their own actions producing a result. The feedback is novel and not too predictable, so there's a strong urge to see whether it will happen again. Teenagers tend to be very speedy learners and quickly improve their skills with the machines. Though some American cardiologists claim computer games can induce heart stress and send blood pressure soaring, Professor Newson argues that a certain amount of stress is vital to our functioning. "I think young people have the capacity to switch off from excitement when they have had enough." The argument sounds logical, but anyone who has ever been gripped by the excitement of a small screen galactic invasion knows that to stop playing these games may not be easy. Terry Pratt of "Computer and Video Games", himself an enthusiast, agrees that there are problems. "Many young people play to the point of physical damage and pain. You often see young people play until their eyes ache from staring at a bright screen for too long."

471 words

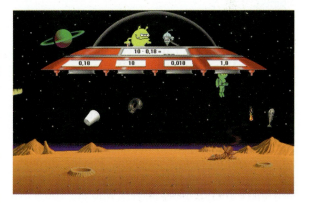

- *Answer the following questions on the text.*
  1. Why do many parents fear computer games?
  2. What are the main arguments against playing games?
  3. What arguments can be given in favour of computer games?

Sports

The crying game

A career in sport is very often short lived : start young, peak early, fade away as the next generation rises to steal your glory. But the punishing regime to which sportsmen and women subject their bodies leaves them exposed to the constant threat of injury – or even permanent injury – as in the case of Norman Whiteside.

His story reads like a fairytale, minus the happy ending. He became the youngest player to appear in the World Cup finals. At 17, he was putting on the jersey of one of the top football clubs in the world. And one day, he would score the winning goal in an English Cup Final at Wembley.

Now, at 29, Norman Whiteside is a student, getting the education he was warned would be necessary to fall back on. Whiteside took the short cut to fitness and found himself on the road to nowhere. Many had gone down the same road before, many more will follow. Even the elite in sport have, at best, only a decade at the top. Sudden death, broken bones, severed ligaments and over-training syndromes combine to make a dumping ground for sportsmen and women.

For Whiteside, it all started to go wrong before it went right. The knee injury which eventually finished his career began at the age of 15. Throughout his days at Manchester United, Whiteside played although he was not 100% fit.

"I think both me and the club were guilty. Each time, I thought it was just a minor injury that I could shake off. In fact, I had something like ten operations during my career, not just on the knee but on Achilles tendons and other foot problems. Playing through pain is part of a footballers life. In the English league now there are not many players who are 100% fit. You have always got an injury somewhere. But important clubs need you on the pitch because players are the most important assets."

Whiteside was only 26 when he was forced to quit. Now he is in his third year at University College Salford in the north west of England, studying podiatry (disorders of the feet) with the ambition to return to professional football in a related capacity. His injury is the most common type because the kneecap has two joints, allowing for rotation as well as extension. Knee straps are part of the kit in most

sports. The problems, coming from over-use, are unavoidable. Long term complications are not. "If only people would come to us when the injury occurs, " says Rose MacDonald, director of the Sports Injury Clinic at the Crystal Palace National Sports Centre in South London. "Most injuries have stages: you start by getting pain after activity; then comes pain during activity; then pain before, during and after activity. And in extreme cases, you get pain just walking around. We can treat them at the first stage because we can tell them what not to do. We can trace the cause of the injury. But for many sportsmen and women who do eventually come to us it is too late."

520 words

BBC WORLDWIDE (adapted)

- *Answer the following questions on the text.*
  1. Who is the story about and what is he famous for?
  2. Who does he blame for his long-term injury and why?
  3. Why are sports activities not always healthy?
  4. What is Norman doing nowadays?
  5. What is the main task of the Sports Injury Clinic?

Tourism

Tourists resort to all the comforts of home

In the resort of Cala Ratjada, it is easy to forget you are in Spain. The newspaper racks are loaded with copies of Frankfurter Allgemeine and Bild, while cafés and bierkellers advertise Dortmunder Pils. When you walk into a restaurant, you are much more likely to be greeted with a friendly "guten Abend" and handed a menu written in German than you are to hear "Buenas tardes".

A few kilometres along the Mallorcan coast at Malaguf it is a completely different story. The streets are lined with British pubs in which you can eat sausage and chips and buy "tea like mother made it" or drink all night at bars with names such as The Benny Hill and Lineker's.

Mallorca is the ultimate example of holiday colonialism. But as Europeans return to the beaches this year in their biggest numbers for years, the migratory habits of tourism from a particular country are becoming more and more pronounced.

A report by the French tourist board, for example, shows that visiting Germans are more inclined to avoid the cultural attractions of Paris in preference to heading off with a tent to the coast or the mountains. A spokesman for the German embassy explained: "The German character has always had a strong affinity with nature and a desire to be close to the earth. This is reflected in our literature and the romantic tradition. Camping gives the German an opportunity to fulfil this urge." The British, on the other hand, seem to prefer to stay in rented accommodation, though their hotels are less expensive than those booked by other European nationalities. France remains the most popular holiday destination in Europe, but signs are that other parts of the continent are doing better out of the tourist revival.

Much of the recovery in holidaymaking is due to the expansion in all-inclusive and cheaper package tours. And certainly the southern countries are prepared to go to the greatest lengths to make the package holidaymakers at home so that they do not suffer any form of cultural shock.

The sunshine islands of both Greece and Spain, in particular, have made every effort to create a home from home for their tourists. In Crete, Rhodes and Corfu, for instance, there is a proliferation of fish and chip shops and English pubs. But they cannot outdo the Balearic island of Menorca, which has the first ever purpose-built cricket pitch in Spain.

Just across the water from Menorca, the Mallorcan resort of Paguera has a street known as the "Bierstraße" where holidaymakers are much more likely to find Wiener Schnitzel and sauerkraut on the menu than tortilla espanol. The nearby beach of Playa del Palma was recently described as "Germany's 17th state" – a reference to the 2.4 million Germans who are expected to squeeze on to this 3,640 square kilometre island this year.

If the French are feeling left out in the scramble for a sunshine resort, they should not worry – the Greek island of Mykonos is all but theirs. Mykonos is top of their bookings by far because the boutiques there are affordable, it has plenty of bistros and cafes and the locals try to speak French.

529 words

The European, London (adapted)

- *Answer the following questions on the text.*
  1. Give examples from the text which underline the statement "As Europeans return to the beaches… the migratory habits from a particular country are becoming more pronounced."
  2. Why, according to the text, do Germans often go on camping holidays?
  3. Explain what an "all-inclusive package holiday" means.
  4. Which countries cater mostly to package holiday-makers and in what way?

Car technology

Back to the drawing board

Imagine you are an engineer at a major carmaker in charge of creating a new family car. What aspects would you have to think about? Clearly cars should not pollute the environment so much, but they should
5 also be cheap, comfortable, safe and above all fun to drive. These seemingly contradictory demands have sent the vehicle designers back to their drawing boards and computers.

Let us imagine you have been given a design envel-
10 ope that includes a number of typical guidelines to follow : the car must have space for four people, 0–100 kph acceleration in 9 seconds and 4 litres per 100 kilometres fuel consumption. You must build in safety devices such as dual air bags and crush zones
15 and side impact beams. And do not forget the vehicle must be built – and sold – at a reasonable price. Another significant guideline that you have to follow is based on the new tough environmental regulations.

20 Green has become the new colour of the automobile market. As a production manager of a leading car company says, "Today 10% of our investments are directly put into environmental protection. What must evolve is a new generation of vehicles which
25 reduce carbon dioxide emissions and at the same time increase fuel efficiency. Around the world car makers are experimenting with a range of new vehicles. At the moment models which carry both an internal combustion engine and an electric
30 motor, the so-called hybrid vehicles, seem to be very popular with most designers. However, other com-
35 panies are looking into the possibilities of producing vehicles which run on alternative fuels such as hy-
40 drogen, methane or even rape seed. The company which discovers a car which is practical, affordable
45 and runs on a non-polluting power source will be as successful as Henry Ford was when he standardized the production of the Model T.

Some of these "future" cars are already coming off the assembly lines, but most of the car makers pre-
50 fer to design first so-called "concept cars". These are forerunners of intended production vehicles. After the vehicles have been carefully designed to all the guidelines, they are shown at automobile shows around the world to test the public's reaction. These
55 concept cars give drivers a taste of the future. Moreover, they demonstrate that industrial design need not just follow the demands of the present market, but these cars also prepare the ground for future vehicles and to produce a sort of suggestion box on
60 wheels. If the public's reaction is positive, the manufacturers then start to use the concept car to test the limits of the technology available.

Over the years many significant developments have been made, especially in the field of electronics.
65 Anti-lock brakes and digital motor electronics are just two examples. Nevertheless, the main challenge the car makers and their designers will face in the future will be in the area of emissions, fuel efficiency and safety without losing the flair and spirit
70 of individual mobility that we have all got so used to. So back to your drawing boards you dream-machine designers!

509 words

Comprehension questions

- After you have read the text carefully, answer the following questions in your own words as far as possible.

    1. Which aspects do car designers have to consider nowadays?
    2. Why have car companies become environmentally conscious?
    3. Which new developments, according to the text, are being made in the field of emission reduction?
    4. What important role do concept cars play in the automobile industry?

Summary

- Using your own words, give a summary of the text. It should be about 250 words long.

Vocabulary

1. Explain the following:

    a) guidelines (line 10) *rules*
    b) internal combustion engine (line 29/30) *machine to move your car*
    c) fuel efficiency (line 26) *quantity of fuel per 100km*
    d) a suggestion box on wheels (line 60/61)
    e) individual mobility (line 71)

2. Look in the text to find antonyms for the following words:

    a) expensive *cheap*
    b) danger *safety*
    c) destruction *construction*
    d) increase *decrease*
    e) unimportant *important*

Translation

- Translate lines 64 to 73.

Comment

- Comment on the following statement, using your own knowledge and ideas.

    "Further technical developments in the car industry will solve all our future transport problems."

Grammar revision

1 Mixed tenses

- *Put the verbs in brackets into the correct tense.*

Dear Jim,

I write to you while on my journey to Scotland. Yes, I am on the train! I finally (**1.** sell) my car last year because of the damage cars do to the environment. Until then I (**2.** use) my car to visit my parents in Edinburgh, but last time I (**3.** go), the journey (**4.** take) 15 hours and we (**5.** not arrive) until midnight. The next day I (**6.** fall) asleep while we (**7.** watch) the Scotland v. England rugby game, which was the reason I (**8.** go) there in the first place. Travelling by train is definitely quicker and more environmentally-friendly and now at least I (**9.** know) that I (**10.** arrive) fresh and cheerful.
At the moment Graham is with me and we (**11.** enjoy) every minute. Perhaps there (**12.** be) time to go out for a meal in a restaurant with my parents this evening. We (**13.** not manage) to do that for many years now. My father (**14.** get) old and he (**15.** not go) out very often. Tomorrow, we (**16.** visit) an old friend of ours in Glasgow. We are near York now. The countryside (**17.** look) beautiful round here. I (**18.** not have) such a pleasant journey since I (**19.** be) at university. That was while I (**20.** study) in Bristol. At that time my parents (**21.** live) in London and I (**22.** use) the train to get home in the holidays.

Best wishes

2 Passive

- *Rewrite the parts in bold type in the passive form.*

Green cars
At an International Automobile show last autumn, **people ignored the usual talk of acceleration rates.** Instead, **car makers promoted environmentally-friendly cars.** Finally, **the car industry is reducing the amount of time and money spent on fast cars,** in order to protect the environment.
As governments increase efforts to reduce air pollution, more and more car makers have produced 'green' cars. And in the future, **they will introduce more cars with zero emissions and recyclable parts.**
Electric cars which run on batteries and do not pollute the environment are particularly popular. With some of these cars, **you can recharge the batteries** in only five minutes. In future too, **you won't need car scrap heaps** anymore, as **car companies take back and recycle certain models.** Big changes indeed in a big industry!

The internal combustion engine

a   *Look at the following drawing of an internal combustion engine and read the accompanying text.*

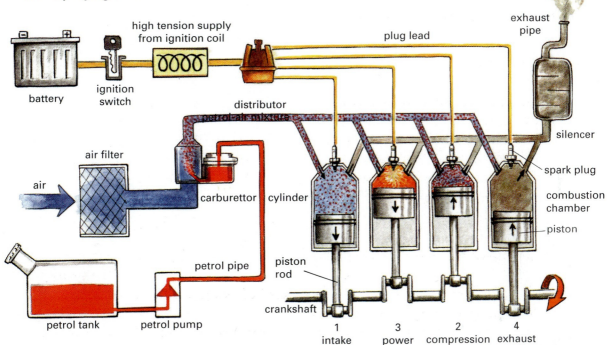

The function of the ignition system is to provide a spark in the combustion chamber to ignite the air/fuel mixture at the correct time. The system consists of an ignition switch, a battery, a coil, a distributor, spark plugs and leads.

The coil produces the high tension (high voltage) that is required to make the spark at the spark plugs. The distributor has the function of distributing the high tension supply to each spark at the correct moment. The spark plugs are screwed into the cylinder head at the top of the combustion chamber.

b   *Translate this information into German.*

c   *In the same way as above explain how the fuel system works.*

d   *Describe the four stages in a four-stroke engine with the help of the words in the box.*

move up/move down/push out/ compress/suck into/mix/create/ turn/ignite/repeat

Example: In the intake stroke the piston moves down and the petrol/air mixture is sucked into the cylinder. In the compression stroke...

e   *What would you suggest?*

It is a cold damp day and your car won't start. The engine turns over quite well but it sounds lifeless. There is a smell of petrol, too.

Energy production

Energy from the wind

When a small wind power company decided to build a wind farm near his home in Wales, Terry Williams was one of the first to welcome the decision.

However, that was several years ago. Now that the 103 wind turbines have been working for more than a year, his opinion has changed. "It's like being near a large air-conditioning unit," he says, "the noise comes from all directions. In some rooms you can hear it even with the double-glazed windows shut. And if it gets windy in the night, the turbines start and wake us up."

Other people living in the area have also noticed the noise, which is caused partly by the turbine blades and partly by the sound of the gear mechanisms. But for houses 600 metres or more from a turbine, this is not such a big problem as noise levels there are little above the natural background level of 19 decibels.

But noise is not the only problem connected with wind farms. The appearance is also a problem as some people consider that they are destroying the beauty of the Welsh countryside. Because of this, a group of experts have been examining the effects of existing wind farms. What they have found is that smaller wind farms needn't be an ugly addition to the landscape. The larger installations, however, can be seen more than nine miles away. This, the experts agree, spoils the view of the countryside.

Yet many of the people who live and work near the turbines are not disturbed by them. In one survey, 70% of the people in villages near wind farms said they would be happy to see more of them. Some even said, "Put them anywhere – they are pretty, they look like daffodils- they should be painted yellow."

At present, wind energy generates a very small amount of energy. The 103 turbines in Wales produce 300 kilowatts each when they are turning. Altogether their output is 30 times less than an average gas- or coal-fired power station. However, the potential is there. Countries, such as Denmark have realised that wind energy saves resources and produces neither dangerous emissions nor the toxic waste that nuclear power plants produce. So they

have gone ahead with the development of wind farms and are already successfully producing larger quantities of energy from wind power.

Nevertheless, the British government seems unwilling to support the growth of renewable forms of energy in general. Although its goal is to produce 4,500 megawatts of the nation's energy from renewables, wind, wave, geo-thermal or hydro-electric power by the year 2010, only 2% of its electricity tax money is spent on renewables, the other 98% supports nuclear power. There could be a quick and easy solution to the problems which wind energy, like every new technology, faces at the beginning. If the government spent more money on wind turbines, their effect on the landscape – both from the visual and the noise point of view would quickly be reduced and Terry Williams could enjoy the benefits of environmentally-friendly energy and sleep well again at night.

514 words

The Independent on Sunday (adapted)

Comprehension questions

- After you have read the text carefully, answer the following questions in your own words as far as possible.

  1. Why has Terry Williams' attitude to environmentally-friendly technology changed?
  2. What advantages do wind farms have compared with conventional power stations?
  3. What, according to the text, are the negative aspects of wind farms?
  4. What action is needed to eliminate the early problems in wind power technology?

Summary

- Using your own words, give a summary of the text. It should be about 250 words long.

Vocabulary

1. Explain the following:
   a) wind farm (line 24)
   b) natural background level (line 17)
   c) double-glazed windows (line 9)
   d) turbine (line 5)
   e) hydro-electric power (line 52)

2. Look in the text to find the opposites of these words:
   a) beautiful
   b) positive
   c) willing
   d) increase
   e) far away
   f) end
   g) badly
   h) disagree

Translation

- Translate lines 36 to 47.

Comment

- Comment on the following statement, using your own knowledge and ideas.

  "Alternative energy? – No, thank you."

97

Grammar revision

1 Mixed tenses

- Put the verbs in brackets into the correct tense.

Dear Patrick,

Recently I (**1.** join) the organization called 'Friends of the Earth'. I (**2.** not know) if I (**3.** tell) you this while I (**4.** stay) with you a couple of weeks ago. It's a group which (**5.** aim) to protect the environment.

I (**6.** expect) you (**7.** hear) of them already. Anyway, I have decided that I (**8.** attend) one of their meetings next week. Would you like to come with me? The subject which they (**9.** discuss) at this meeting is the energy supply in the Third World. It (**10.** seem) that they (**11.** find) it very expensive to supply remote villages with energy from a grid supply and so in future they probably (**12.** use) renewable energy sources.

I (**13.** send) you a copy of their leaflet if you like, so that you can read about it yourself. Until I (**14.** read) it last week, I hadn't known much about the problem. I certainly (**15.** not realise) before that how many people in the Third World live without an energy supply.

Apparently 70% of the population of the developing world (**16.** not have) any electricity at all. But in the last few years some Third World governments (**17.** start) to build solar, water and wind power installations. The main problem is that these installations also (**18.** cost) a lot of money. To help pay these costs, at present some renewable energy companies in the industrialised world (**19.** organize) special funds. The World Bank believes that developing countries (**20.** invest) $1 trillion in power systems of one sort or another in the next ten years. You can learn more about it next week.

See you at the meeting? Sally

2 Conditionals

- Put the verbs in brackets into the correct tense.

Two engineers are talking about wind energy.

If the government (**1.** not support) nuclear energy in the way they do, there (**2.** be) much more money left to develop environmentally-friendly methods of energy production, like wind energy. I know, if the government (**3.** continue) to spend so little money on renewables, the technology (**4.** not develop) fast enough and that means critics (**5.** have) even more time to find arguments against it.

Yes, it makes me furious. If they (**6.** start) to build wind farms years ago, by now the problems (**7.** solve). A colleague of mine who lives in Wales says that if they (**8.** have) a coal-fired power station near them instead of a wind farm, he (**9.** find) it much uglier. The wind farms look pretty, he thinks.

Electricity supply

Here is a diagram of an energy supply system from power station to consumer.

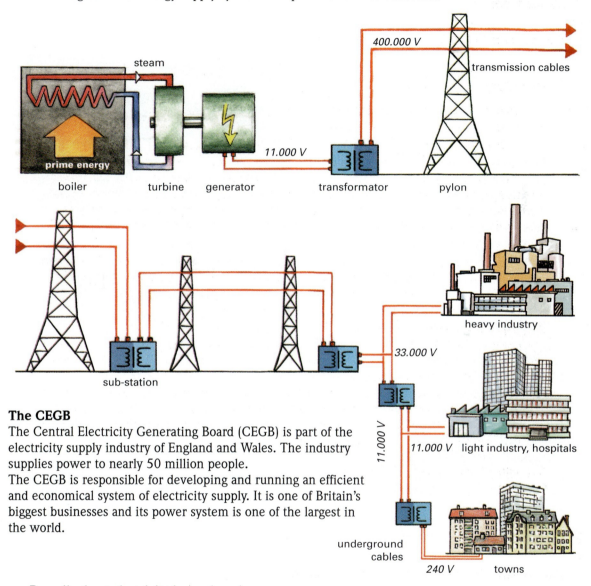

The CEGB
The Central Electricity Generating Board (CEGB) is part of the electricity supply industry of England and Wales. The industry supplies power to nearly 50 million people.
The CEGB is responsible for developing and running an efficient and economical system of electricity supply. It is one of Britain's biggest businesses and its power system is one of the largest in the world.

a *Describe how electricity is produced.*

b *Describe how electricity is supplied to the consumer (households/factories).*

c When electricity is supplied, the voltage is changed at various points.
   Give examples of such changes.
   Why are these changes necessary?

d *Translate the text.*

99

Technology and pollution

A future for the earth?

"One generation passes away, and another generation comes: but the earth lives on forever."
(Holy Bible)

No, not forever. For man has now reached a point in his evolution where he has the power to influence the present and the future state of the planet, for better or for worse.

Since the beginning of the Industrial Revolution, smokestacks have released harmful gases into the atmosphere, factories have dumped toxic wastes into rivers and streams, cars have consumed irreplaceable fossil fuels and polluted the air with their exhaust gases. In the name of progress, forests have been cut down and lakes and oceans poisoned with pesticides and chemicals.

The continuing destruction of the atmosphere's ozone layer is partly caused by the use of atmosphere-destroying chlorofluorcarbons (CFCs) in different types of foam, insulation and air-conditioners. Perhaps most threatening of all, the destruction of the tropical forests, home to at least half the earth's plant and animal species, continues at a rate equal to one football field a second. The resulting worldwide extinction of species promises to be at least as great as the mass extinction that happened at the end of the age of dinosaurs.

For a long time scientists have pointed to the damage and its possible consequences. But no one has paid much attention. Now things have become so bad that people are beginning to listen. Surely everyone must now notice that the Earth is in danger. In the U.S. heat waves every summer now drive temperatures above 40 degrees Centigrade across much of the country, raising fears that the "greenhouse effect" – global warming – is already under way. Because of the lack of rain, the western forests, including the Yellowstone National Park, have already gone up in flames several times. And on many beaches, garbage, raw sewage and medical waste spoil the fun of bathers and confront them personally with the growing pollution of the oceans. Similar pollution in Europe has closed beaches on the Mediterranean, the North Sea and the English Channel. Thousands of seals have died because their immune systems have been weakened by pollution.

What will happen, if nothing is done? The increase of CO_2 in the atmosphere could raise the planet's average temperature by 2 to 6 degrees Centigrade within the next fifty years. That could cause the oceans to rise by several metres, flooding coastal areas and ruining huge parts of farmland. Changing weather conditions can make large areas infertile and uninhabitable, resulting in migration on a scale which we have not experienced up till now.

Let there be no illusion. Taking effective action to halt the massive damage to the earth's environment will require a mobilization of political will, international cooperation and sacrifice unknown except in wartime. But humanity is at war right now, and it is no exaggeration to call it a war for survival. It is a war in which all nations must be allies. Both the causes and effects of the problems that threaten the earth are global, and they must be attacked globally.

Every individual on the planet must be made aware of the serious situation and of the need to do something. No attempt to protect the environment will be successful in the long run unless ordinary people – the American housewife, the Chinese factory worker, the African farmer and the European office worker – are willing to change their life-styles.

544 words

Comprehension questions

- After you have read the text carefully, answer the following questions in your own words as far as possible.

  1. How has man, in the name of progress, changed the earth's environment?
  2. How has nature reacted to such treatment?
  3. What will happen if nothing is done about this serious situation?
  4. Why does the author say that humanity is at war right now?

Summary

- Using your own words, give a summary of the text. It should be about 250 words long.

Vocabulary

1. Find antonyms for the following words taken from the text:

   a) forever (line 1) *for a short time*
   b) better (line 4) *worse*
   c) much (line 26) *little*
   d) harmful (line 6) *harmless*
   e) irreplaceable (line 8/9) *replacable*
   f) destruction (line 13) *construction*
   g) danger (line 28) *safety*
   h) weaken (line 42) *strengthen*

2. Look in the text to find the corresponding verbs for these nouns:

   a) life *live*
   b) poison *poison*
   c) threat *threaten*
   d) confrontation *oppose*
   e) requirement *demand*
   f) protection *protect*

Translation

- Translate lines 52 to 60.

Comment

- Using your own knowledge and ideas, describe the measures that governments, industry and ordinary people can take in order to improve the environment.
  Do you believe that these measures will be successful in the near future? Give reasons.

101

Grammar revision

1 Mixed tenses

- *Put the verbs in brackets into the correct tense.*

Feeling the Heat

For more than twenty years now, scientists (**1.** warn) about the gases from cars and factories. This (**2.** produce) massive climate changes in the next few years. The temperature of the earth (**3.** already/rise) by some degrees. Years ago nobody (**4.** pay) much attention. But then NASA's Institute for Space Studies (**5.** turn) global warming into front-page news. James Hansen, head of the institute, (**6.** say) that global warming (**7.** change) from theory into fact. Since then the amount of CO_2 in the atmosphere (**8.** increase) everywhere. So if we (**9.** not/change) our energy consumption habits, our planet (**10.** become) uninhabitable. For that reason many countries (**11.** already/introduce) higher petrol taxes, and others (**12.** plan) a CO_2 tax on all fossil-fuel energy sources.

2 Infinitive or "ing"-form?

- *Fill in the infinitive with or without "to" or a suitable "ing"-form.*

A hundred-year plan for the future

Japan has made impressive steps on its way to become a First World leader in (**1.** control) air pollution, in (**2.** reduce) energy consumption and in (**3.** provide) its citizens with clean water. By (**4.** pass) the Basic Environmental Law (**5.** include) a national environmental plan and (**6.** establish) a Central Environmental Council, Japan has opened a new round of "green" laws. This will not only make companies (**7.** reduce) emissions, but it will also help them (**8.** develop) clean energy sources.

Most Japanese companies are now interested in (**9.** become) environmentally correct. For example Chiyoda Corp. has developed a method of (**10.** clean) power plant exhaust. After (**11.** work) on it for several years Nippon Steel Corp. has announced a new waste-melting system. This process will reduce the volume of toxic waste by (**12.** convert) most of it into recyclable material.

On the other hand critics still point out that, for example, the country's industry has caused a lot of damage by (**13.** use) wood (**14.** come) from the tropical forests in Southeast Asia. When we asked him (**15.** give) a statement, Saburo Kato, president of an environmental research institute, said: "There are still some difficulties in (**16.** cooperate) on an international level, but we aren't afraid of (**17.** face) competition in the environmental field."

Waste management

About 800 000 tonnes of electric and electronic appliances are thrown away per year. Except for some fridges and washing machines most of these products end up on the scrap heap. The amount of electronic scrap is steadily increasing: TV-sets are often thrown away after seven or eight years, personal computers are technically out-of-date after only three or four years. So what to do with the rubbish? Today more and more firms are trying to avoid or substitute harmful materials and to reduce the amount of scrap.

a **Describe the decisions you should make at the different checks in the diagram below. Use the words in the box.**

> clean, recharge, maintain, burn, avoid, substitute, reduce, treat, repair, melt, re-use, recycle, dump

Example: At check 1 you must decide if you can substitute materials or...
At check 2 you...

b **What would you do with the following parts of electronic appliances? Think of reducing, substituting, recycling and incinerating.**

1. plastic parts
2. paint
3. cardboard packaging
4. oil
5. batteries
6. mixture of plastic, metal, glass

c **Give reasons and possible disadvantages of your suggestions.**

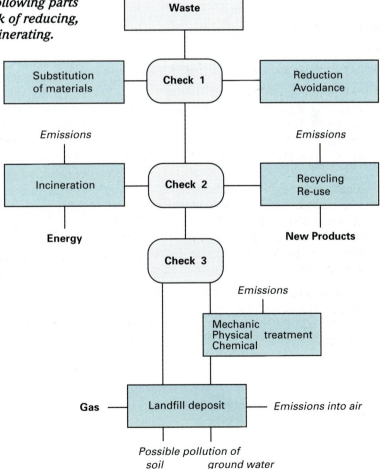

UNIT 14

CAD/CAM/CIM

Automating design

In the biggest factory in the world, the new Boeing is being put together. Next month, it will be rolled out of the doors and will then take off into the skies over Seattle. Boeing and its customers hope that this twin-engined airliner will be a special machine in many ways. In some ways, it already is. Normally the company builds models of a new aeroplane to make sure that its millions of parts fit together. However, in this case no such prototypes have been built. The first plane, which is now being produced, will be a fully functioning aeroplane.

Of course, a model of the plane does exist, namely in trillions of bytes of information stored in the company's computers. The development of the new model has been the biggest single test of computer-aided design (CAD) so far. By using the computer's designs of the parts, engineers with the help of their computer programs checked that the whole thing would fit together before any pieces were made. So far, their checking seems to have been extremely successful, all the parts fit to within a thousandth of an inch.

CAD programs are not spectacular, but they give the designer new tools and allow companies to change the ways they organise design. Good design is the key to sucessful manufacturing.

The advantages of automation have always been time and accuracy. CAD has both of these. Technical drawing of designs takes a long time and research shows that CAD programs can cut the time it takes to draw a design by as much as 90%. Perfect copies can be made by simply pressing a button and changes to the design can be made quickly and easily. A CAD design can be transmitted perfectly and passed relatively easily into CNC (computer numerically controlled) tool systems. This system is known as CIM – computer integrated manufacture. And if the CNC tools are as accurate as they should be, the parts will fit perfectly. This integrated system has the further advantage of cutting costs.

CAD has also led to the breaking down of the wall between design and production in a process known as 'concurrent design'. The idea of concurrent design is that the designers work closely with all those who play important parts in the production process. In this way, manufacturers can follow the design process and can influence it. In the past, there was no need for concurrent design as everything happened in one man's head. The designer built the product or at least oversaw its building. The aim of a good concurrent design team is to function together as one man's mind and to consider all the sides of a process at the same time. However, to get several heads within one company working together as one is not always easy. They all have to communicate with each other very clearly. They also have to know when a change has been made and what its effects might be. This is what integrated CAD systems can provide. They allow designers to see the effects of changes in ways that were not possible in the past. So, as well as a design tool, CAD is also a communications technology which ties all the knowledge in the team together, allowing them to plan ahead and make the right decisions before it's too late.

557 words

© The Economist, London (5 March, 1994) (adapted)

(handwritten at top: who did the introduction of CAD CAM CIM Technologies change the way airplanes are made)

Comprehension questions

- After you have read the text carefully, answer the following questions in your own words as far as possible.

    1. What difference is there between the new Boeing and any aeroplane built before that?
    2. What influence does CAD have on the manufacturing process? *(handwritten: time is reduced, much more accurate)*
    3. Describe briefly how the CIM system functions?
    4. What improvements does the use of integrated technology have both for the product and the company? *(handwritten: less time, costs reduced, changes in design can be implemented very quickly)*

Summary

- Using your own words, give a summary of the text. It should be about 250 words long.

Vocabulary

1. Explain the following:
    a) twin-engined airliner (line 5) *(handwritten: aircraft operating two engines)*
    b) prototype (line 9)
    c) CNC tool systems (line 39/40)
    d) manufacturers (line 52) *(handwritten: company who produces something)*
    e) computer integrated manufacture (CIM) (line 41/42)

2. Look in the text to find synonyms for these words:
    a) biggest
    b) to assemble
    c) to make sure
    d) to shorten
    e) fast
    f) goal *(handwritten: aim)*
    g) brain *(handwritten: mind)*
    h) to talk to each other

Translation

- Translate lines 27 to 46.

Comment

- Comment on the following statement, using your own knowledge and ideas.

    "Computers are steadily improving the quality of our working and living conditions."

Grammar revision

1 Mixed tenses

- Put the verbs in brackets into the correct tense.

Dear Sam,

I'm sorry that I (**1.** not write) to you for such a long time. Last birthday my parents (**2.** give) me a computer and I (**3.** spend) most of my time with it since then. However, last week, my father (**4.** buy) a modem for our system, so we regularly (**5.** link) up with a lot of other computer users. When (**6.** get) you your system? You (**7.** tell) me last summer while I (**8.** stay) at your house that you wanted one, so I expect that you (**9.** buy) it by now. Before we (**10.** install) the computer, my father and I (**11.** not get on) too well together, but now we have a common interest and lots of new friends. We (**12.** have) a lot of fun together at the moment. I hope that you (**13.** visit) us soon and then you (**14.** be able) to join us.

Sometimes we (**15.** take) part in very interesting debates on-line. Last week we (**16.** talk) to a man who (**17.** work) on a pipeline in Alaska. He (**18.** not get out) much there in those cold conditions. Just imagine, soon we (**19.** have) friends all over the world.

Best wishes

David

2 Modal auxiliaries

- Put the correct modal or its auxiliary form into these sentences.

Visual engineering

Car makers have recently introduced a new system of manufacturing engineering, called visual engineering. It means that designers (**1**) draw their designs by hand anymore. In future, sophisticated computers (**2**) build solid models on the screen for them instead. Up to now, designers (**3**) use old-fashioned design and development techniques with drawings and real models. But now already they (**4**) assemble parts on the screen to see if they work. In this way car makers (**5**) cut the time needed to develop the product considerably. In order to keep up with these developments in the manufacturing process, firms (**6**) make other changes too. The office work (**7**) slow down the process or the manufacturing advantages will be lost. There are still some problems to be solved, but soon car makers (**8**) design cars electronically from start to finish.

T 14 UNIT 14 UNIT 14 UNIT 14 UNIT 14 EXAM PREPARATION UNIT 14 UNIT 14 UNIT 14 UNIT 14  UNIT 14

Industrial processes

a *Describe the function of these hardware parts.*

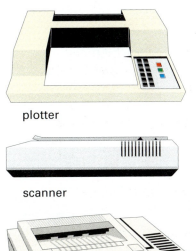

plotter

scanner

laser printer

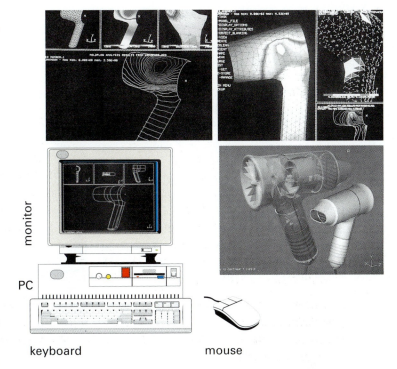

monitor

PC

keyboard

mouse

b *Translate the following text.*

Implementing a CAD program is an enormously complicated task for a computer, which is why CAD use was limited until recently to large computers.
Work with a large computer is as a rule, organized in such a way that one central computer supplies several terminals with the required data. As a result of the large quantities of data which are often produced by CAD programs, the time it takes to produce an answer is relatively long and can have a negative effect on a continuous work process. On the basis of the current level of technological progress, an average answer time which is one second or more is not acceptable.

c *Describe the stages in the process from design to production. (CIM-Configuration)*

CIM-Configuration

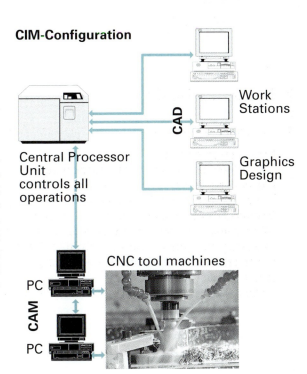

Central Processor Unit controls all operations

CAD

Work Stations

Graphics Design

CAM

PC

PC

CNC tool machines

107

Civil engineering

The Golden Gate Bridge

The Golden Gate suspension bridge is an example of the challenge which bridge builders face. To build a suspension bridge you need two or four big steel cables between two support towers. Between these towers there is a span of unsupported distance. In the case of the Golden Gate Bridge this span is 1280 metres.

Moreover, you require many smaller cables, hanging down from the main cables, to hold the road or railway. Suspension bridges are the most technically difficult bridges to build, but in this case it was the only way. Two factors made any other kind of bridge impossible. The first was that some of the largest ships in the world used the Bay of San Francisco to enter the main harbour of the city and they needed to use the deepest part of the channel for this purpose. The second factor which influenced the engineers' decision to design a long suspension bridge was that the channel is not only deep but is also affected by strong tides and big waves in bad weather. Therefore supports in the middle of the channel could not be erected.

Work on the bridge began in 1933 after an engineer named Joseph Strauss had finished his plans for the suspension bridge. Obviously the work during construction was going to be very dangerous, so Strauss designed a big net to go under the bridge to catch workers who fell. It was also the first time that construction workers had to wear protection helmets and safety belts with ropes on a building site. The first part of the work was to build the two support towers. Both of these towers had to be built on the ground which was under the water level. Consequently, a cofferdam was constructed. When the water had been pumped out of the cofferdam, both men and machines went into the dry area and dug down ten metres below the sea level. While they were digging, the sharp edges on the bottom of the heavy cofferdam pressed down further into the ground. Then concrete was pumped in to make the foundations for the tall towers. Strauss designed the tower foundations to move under the towers in case of an earthquake. So he did not connect the towers to the concrete. In that way, the bridge was safe. Next it was time for teams of workers to put the steel beams of the towers into place. Then the towers were raised up to 227 metres above the water.

After both towers had been completed, the main cables had to be put into position. These cables needed to be both strong and flexible because they had to bend over the tops of the towers and down to the ground behind them on the land. Here they were connected to heavy concrete anchorages in the ground. Having spanned these main suspension cables across the water, smaller cables, so-called suspenders were attached to them. The suspenders hung down in tension with the main cables. Then the road support and the road itself were connected to the suspenders. The road was wide enough for six lanes of traffic. Finally workers painted the bridge to protect it from the salt water and the misty air. In 1937 the bridge was opened.

545 words

Comprehension questions

- After you have read the text carefully, answer the following questions in your own words as far as possible.

  1. Why did engineers decide to build a suspension bridge over the Bay of San Francisco?
  2. Which changes in workers' safety came with the building of the Golden Gate Bridge?
  3. Why was a cofferdam used?
  4. Why were the towers not connected to the concrete below them?
  5. What function do suspenders have?

Summary

Using your own words, give a summary of the text. It should be about 250 words long.

Vocabulary

1. Explain the following:

   a) unsupported distance (line 5)
   b) strong tides (line 20)
   c) protection helmets (line 29)
   d) foundation (line 40/41)
   e) in tension (line 57)

2. Look in the text to find nouns for the following verbs.

   a) require
   b) construct
   c) build
   d) enter
   e) move

Translation

- Translate lines 48 to 62.

Comment

- Comment on the following statement, using your own knowledge and ideas.

"The construction of new roads, houses and bridges often destroys both the landscape and the quality of peoples' lives. Governments should stop new planning and concentrate on conserving the environment."

Grammar revision

1 Mixed forms

- Put the verbs in brackets into the correct form.

(**1.** think) you ever about the work which (**2.** go on) before a house (**3.** build)? Putting up new houses on new sites (**4.** require) much careful preparation. For example it (**5.** be) always very important to find out the kind of soil you (**6.** plan) to build on. If you (**7.** not do) soil tests, building on the wrong type of soil (**8.** cause) the houses (**9.** sink) slowly. Besides (**10.** test) the soil, it is necessary (**11.** measure) the level of the ground water. Let us imagine this for one moment. If a house (**12.** construct), (**13.** use) wooden supports which (**14.** remain) partly below and partly above the ground water level, these supports or piles (**15.** rot away) in a short time. The result (**16.** be) that the house (**17.** collapse) soon. Once the site (**18.** test) thoroughly, roads can (**19.** build) and site toilets for the builders can (**20.** put up) on or near the site. Now work may (**21.** start) with the plotting of the area on which the houses (**22.** build).

2 Reported speech

- Write a report on this speech by John Charlton to some visitors to Newcastle-upon-Tyne. Use as many different reporting verbs as you can.

The new shopping centre
"I would first like to welcome you to Newcastle. My name is John Charlton and I am Newcastle-upon Tyne's planning officer. This evening I am going to give a short talk on the development of Newcastle's inner city. After lots of careful planning and public discussion we now have completed our new shopping centre right here in the city centre. We are very proud of it. It has been developed as a system of pedestrian malls. Most of these malls are at a higher level than the streets. Our city buses and service vehicles operate below the pedestrian shopping zones. Of course we didn't forget the cars which many people use to travel to the city centre. Multi-storey car parks have been built at the edge of the central area. We, as planners, had two main objectives while we were designing this project. On the one hand, we didn't want to destroy the existing historical buildings and on the other hand we wanted to concentrate the shopping facilities in a more convenient and compact area. As you can see from this drawing shoppers can do all their shopping in the dry and are not bothered by the noise and fumes of the traffic. If you have any questions, don't hesitate to ask. Yes. The lady over there in the red dress. Madam, what's your question, please?" ...

A new highway

When civil engineers planned the U.S. Interstate Highway System, they had to make some difficult decisions. In planning a highway between Adamsville and River City, engineers thought of three plans.

- Look at the drawing of the three plans and consider the advantages and the disadvantages of each plan. The notes below will help you.
- Then write a report describing the three plans and decide which of the plans you prefer. Give reasons.

Plan A:
- lower hills and raise valleys
- build bridge over South Road
- build bridge over the West Branch River
- destroy homes in the Lower River City
- use 16 kilometres of pavement
- spend $15 million

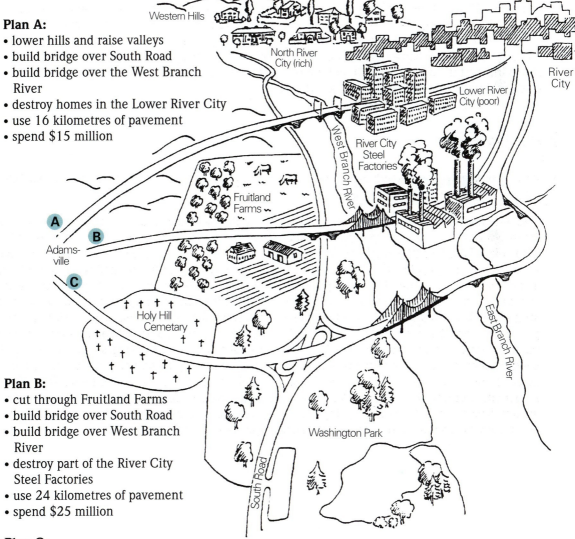

Plan B:
- cut through Fruitland Farms
- build bridge over South Road
- build bridge over West Branch River
- destroy part of the River City Steel Factories
- use 24 kilometres of pavement
- spend $25 million

Plan C:
- build around Fruitland Farms
- cut through Holy Hill Cemetary
- cut through Washington Park
- build a flyover over South Road
- build bridge across the West Branch River
- build two bridges across the East Branch River
- build around the River City Steel Factories
- use 35 kilometres of pavement
- spend $34 million

Indefinite article ➡ UNIT 1 (Workbook)
(Unbestimmter Artikel)

Form

a	college student university	vor **gesprochenen** Konsonanten
an	interview address hour	vor **gesprochenen** Vokalen

Verwendung

I have bought **a** book for you.	für zählbare Begriffe in der Einzahl
He is **a** teacher.	vor Berufsbezeichnungen

Definite article ➡ UNIT 1 (Workbook)
(Bestimmter Artikel)

the	course language European	vor **gesprochenen** Konsonanten Aussprache [ðə]
the	engineer office hour	vor **gesprochenen** Vokalen Aussprache [ðiː]

Verwendung

the people of London **the** life of Lucy Jordan **the** University of Manchester	bei Substantiven (Personen, Dingen, Abstrakta), wenn sie näher bestimmt sind oder werden
the Americans	für die Gesamtheit von Personen
the United States	für Ländernamen im Plural
the Thames, **the** North Sea	für Flüsse und Meere
the Browns	für Eigennamen im Plural
On their tour they visited **the** church.	für die konkrete Bedeutung als Gebäude

Verwendung ohne Artikel

	Der Artikel wird abweichend vom Deutschen **nicht** verwendet:
nature, life, time, people	für abstrakte Begriffe und Sammelbezeichnungen, wenn sie nicht näher bestimmt sind oder werden
Trafalgar Square, Buckingham Palace	für Ortsbezeichnungen
Switzerland, Normandy, Lake Windermere	für Länder, Berge und Seen im Singular
church, school, college When does church begin?	für Gebäudebezeichnungen, wenn die normale Nutzung gemeint ist
Americans	für einzelne Angehörige einer Personengruppe

Plural ➡ UNIT 1 (Workbook)
(Mehrzahl)

Form

student college	student**s** college**s**	Die meisten Nomen bilden den Plural durch Anhängen von -s.
universit**y** cit**y**	universit**ies** cit**ies**	Konsonant + y wird zu -ies.
addre**ss** mat**ch**	address**es** match**es**	Nach Zischlauten (z.B. s,ss,ch,sh) wird -es angehängt.
man woman child life	**men women children lives**	Einige Nomen haben unregelmäßige Pluralformen.

Verwendung

information, weather, nature, knowledge, work, furniture	Einige Nomen treten nur im Singular auf.
trousers, jeans, glasses, clothes, thanks	Einige Nomen treten nur im Plural auf.
news, the United States, the United Nations, economics, mathematics, electronics No news **is** good news.	Einige Nomen treten nur in der Pluralform auf, das Verb steht jedoch im Singular.

Some important prepositions ➡ UNIT 2 (Workbook)

Zeitliche Präpositionen

on 20th September **on** Saturday **on** weekdays	**at** six o'clock **at** the age of 16 **at** night **at** noon **at** midnight	**by** day
in 1992 **in** the morning **in** the evening		twelve minutes **to** five
		a quarter **past** six

Präpositionen der Art und Weise

go **by** bus, car, bike
go **on** foot

Räumliche Präpositionen

go **to** the cinema go **to** college I've been **to** Scotland
at home **at** school **at** the supermarket

Possessive case ➡ UNIT 2 (Workbook)
(Genitiv)

s'-Genitiv

Verwendung bei Personen, Tieren, Zeiten	
Henry**'s** exam the baker**'s** (shop)	Nomen im Singular + **'s**
his parents**'** computer shop the Greens**'** house	Nomen im Plural + **'**
people**'s** faces children**'s** books	bei Nomen im Plural **ohne** "s" Anhängung von **'s**
today**'s** newspaper two weeks**'** pay	Bei Zeiten gelten die gleichen Regeln.

of-Genitiv

Verwendung bei Sachen	
the title **of** the book the price **of** the computers	Der *of*-Genitiv wird im Singular und im Plural verwendet.

Comparison of adjectives ⇒ UNIT 3 (Workbook)
(Steigerung von Adjektiven)

Form

cheap small	cheap**er** small**er**	cheap**est** small**est**	Steigerung der kurzen Adjektive mit -er und -est
nice	nic**er**	nic**est**	stummes -e entfällt
heavy	heav**ier**	heav**iest**	-y wird zu -ier und -iest
big	bi**gg**er	bi**gg**est	Nach kurzen Vokalen wird der Endkonsonant verdoppelt.
good bad little	**better** **worse** **less**	**best** **worst** **least**	Einige Adjektive haben unregelmäßige Steigerungsformen.
careful difficult	**more** careful **more** difficult	**most** careful **most** difficult	Alle dreisilbigen und mehrsilbigen Adjektive und alle zweisilbigen Adjektive, die nicht auf -er, -le, -y, -ow enden, werden mit *more* und *most* gesteigert.
careful difficult	**less** careful **less** difficult	**least** careful **least** difficult	Eine Verminderung der Adjektive ist mit *less* und *least* möglich.

Verwendung

In town centres walking is often **as fast as** going by car.	Gleichheiten werden mit *as ... as* ausgedrückt
Travelling by plane is **faster than** travelling by train. Travelling by car is **more expensive than** walking.	Komparative werden mit *... than* gebildet.
A bicycle is **not so expensive as** (isn't as expensive as) a car. A bicycle is **less expensive than** a car.	Eine andere Form, Ungleichheit auszudrücken, ist *not so ... as* oder umgangssprachlich *not as ... as*. Wie im Deutschen kann man auch "weniger als" verwenden.
The Concorde is **the fastest** airliner from Paris to New York.	Der Superlativ wird nur benutzt, wenn mehr als zwei Dinge miteinander verglichen werden.

Adjective and adverb ➡ UNIT 4
(Adjektiv und Adverb)

Form

Adjective	Adverb	
cheap	cheap**ly**	Das Adverb wird gebildet aus Adjektiv + -ly.
lazy	laz**ily**	-y wird zu -ily
horrible	horri**bly**	-le wird zu -ly
economic	econom**ically**	-ic wird zu -ically
fast	**fast**	Einige Adverbien bilden unregelmäßige Formen.
good	**well**	

Adjective	Adverb	Adverb	
late	**late** (spät)	**lately** (in letzter Zeit)	Einige Adverbien bilden mehrere Formen.
hard	**hard** (hart)	**hardly** (kaum)	
near	**near** (nah)	**nearly** (beinahe)	

Verwendung

There are many **new devices** on the market. **They** are still **expensive**.	Adjektive beziehen sich auf Nomen oder Pronomen.
We can't **control** the technology **exactly**. Comics are **really popular** with children. Modern computers work **extremely quickly**. **Fortunately**, she faxed the information to me in time.	Adverbien beziehen sich auf – Verben – Adjektive – Adverbien – ganze Sätze.
He **felt nervous** about his new job.	Nach Verben, die einen Zustand darstellen, (z.B. *feel, be, become, get, seem, appear, keep*) folgt ein Adjektiv.

Word order with adverbs and adverbials → UNIT 5 (Workbook)

(Wortstellung bei Adverbien und adverbialen Bestimmungen)

Die Stellung der Adverbien und adverbialen Bestimmungen (a. B.) ist im Englischen sehr flexibel. Folgende Stellungen sind allerdings üblich:	
At nine o'clock he caught the bus **to work**.	Adverbien/a. B. der Zeit stehen am Anfang oder Ende des Satzes. Adverbien/a. B. des Ortes stehen in der Regel am Ende des Satzes.
Mr Woods **always** travels to work by train. It arrives **punctually**.	Adverbien/a. B. der Häufigkeit stehen vor dem (Haupt)verb. Adverbien/a. B. der Art und Weise stehen in der Regel nach dem Verb (den Verben).
The bus drove **slowly** through **London during the rush hour**.	Treten mehrere Adverbien/a. B. zur gleichen Zeit auf, gilt die Regel: Art und Weise vor Ort und Zeit.

Some or any? → UNIT 4 (Workbook)

Verwendung

I need **some** help with this program. **Some** newspapers in Britain only appear on Sundays.	in Aussagesätzen vor unbestimmten Mengen (etwas) oder Anzahlen (einige)
They didn't make **any** money with the new campaign. Some TV stations do not show **any** adverts.	in verneinten Sätzen vor unbestimmten Mengen oder Anzahlen (kein oder keine usw.)
Have they done **any** research on the new product? Have you got **any** ideas for a new logo?	in Fragesätzen vor unbestimmten Mengen (etwas) oder Anzahlen (welche?)
Would you like me to show you **some** examples?	in Fragesätzen, wenn sie eine Aufforderung, Bitte oder Angebot enthalten
We never needed **any** electronic devices in the past.	nach Wörtern mit negativer Bedeutung

Some/Any + -one/-body/-thing/-where

Somebody wants to see you. We haven't been **anywhere** this weekend. Have you got **anything** to say?	Die Regeln zum Gebrauch von *some* and *any* gelten auch für diese Formen.

Much – many – a lot of ⇒ UNIT 4 (Workbook)

Form

much a lot of	viel	nicht zählbar
many a lot of	viele	zählbar

Verwendung

He spends **a lot of** time practising his communication skills. **A lot of** (many) people have computers in their homes.	In Aussagesätzen wird in der Regel *a lot of* bevorzugt.
I don't have **a lot of / much** money to spend on computers. There aren't **a lot of / many** experts on the staff.	In verneinten Sätzen kann man beide Formen gebrauchen.
How **much** money do you earn? How **many** adverts did they show?	Nach *how* müssen *much* oder *many* stehen.

Little/a little – Few/a few ⇒ UNIT 4 (Workbook)

Form

We had **little** help during our training. John had only **a little** time to explain.	wenig ein bisschen	unzählbar
Few computers never break down. There are **a few** good adverts on TV.	wenige ein paar	zählbar

Modal auxiliaries → UNIT 5
(Modale Hilfsverben)

Form

Modale Form	Ersatzform	Bedeutung
must	have to	müssen
can	be able to	können
can	be allowed to	dürfen
mustn't / can't	not be allowed to	nicht dürfen
can't	not be able to	nicht können
needn't	not have to	nicht brauchen / nicht müssen

Verwendung

Cars **must/have to** stop at red lights. You **needn't/don't have to** pay in that car park. John **can't/isn't able to** find a parking space.	In der Gegenwart kann entweder die modale oder die Ersatzform benutzt werden.
We **had to** turn right at the traffic lights. He **didn't have to** wait as the lights were green. Jane **couldn't/wasn't allowed to** leave her car outside the house, as there was a "No Parking" sign.	Mit Ausnahme von *could* oder *couldn't* können die modalen Hilfsverben keine anderen Zeiten bilden. Für die anderen Zeiten werden die Ersatzformen verwendet.

Defining relative clauses ➡ UNIT 5
(Notwendige Relativsätze)

Verwendung

Ein Relativsatz ist notwendig, wenn die darin enthaltene Information nötig ist, um zu erkennen, welche Person oder Sache gemeint ist.	
The man **who/that** is getting on the bus is on his way to the office.	Bei Personen werden die Relativpronomen *who* oder *that* verwendet.
The bus **which/that** is waiting at the traffic lights is going to London.	Bei Sachen wird *which* oder *that* verwendet.
He greeted the man **(who)** he saw on the platform. He read the paper **(which)** he had bought that morning.	Wenn das Relativpronomen Objekt des Satzes ist, kann es weggelassen werden.

Non-defining relative clauses
(Nicht notwendige Relativsätze)

Verwendung

Ein Relativsatz ist nicht notwendig, wenn die darin enthaltene Information nicht nötig ist um zu erkennen, welche Person oder Sache gemeint ist.	
Henry's wife, **who is 58**, was waiting for him at the station.	Ein Relativsatz wird durch Kommas vom Hauptsatz getrennt.
The train, **which was an Intercity**, left punctually.	*that* darf hier nicht verwendet werden.
Henry, **who I met at the station**, is retiring next week.	Wenn das Relativpronomen Objekt eines Relativsatzes ist, darf es nicht weggelassen werden.

The Tenses *(Die Zeiten)*
Present simple ➡ UNIT 1

Form

I/you/we/they He/she/it	**live** **lives**	in Leeds.	Aussage
I/you/we/they He/she/it	**do not (don't) live** **does not (doesn't) live**	in Birmingham.	Verneinung

Do **Does**	I/you/we/they he/she/it	**(not)**	**live**	in Liverpool?	(verneinte) Frage
Where Why	**do** you **does** she			**live?** **smoke?**	

Who **How many students**	**likes** **live**	basketball? at home?	Ist das Fragewort Subjekt oder Teil des Subjekts, wird *do/does* nicht verwendet.

Besonderheiten bei der Schreibung der s-Endung:

go, do	go**es**, do**es**
watch, kiss	watch**es**, kiss**es**
carry, try	carr**ies**, tr**ies**

Verwendung

She **has** a brother.	bei einem Dauerzustand
She **(usually) goes** to college by bus. He **(often) helps** at home.	bei regelmäßigen oder wiederholten Handlungen (oft mit Häufigkeitsadverbien wie *usually, normally, often, sometimes, never, always*)
She **doesn't smoke**.	bei Gewohnheiten
He **has** a flat in Mayfield. I **think** that this **is** a good idea.	bei bestimmten Verben, wenn sie einen Zustand beschreiben, z.B. *be, have, look, think, see, know, like, want*
The train **arrives** at 8 o'clock tomorrow morning.	bei Fahrplänen und Veranstaltungsprogrammen (mit Zukunftsbezug)

Present continuous ➡ UNIT 1

Form

| I
You/We/They
He/She/It | **am**
are
is | (**not**) | **reading** a book. | Aussage und Verneinung |

Kurzform der Verneinung: aren't, isn't

| **Am**
Are
Is | I
you/we/they
he/she/it | (**not**) | **reading** a magazine? | Frage und
verneinte Frage |

Besonderheiten bei der Schreibung

| come, take | co**m**ing, ta**k**ing |
| sit, run | si**tt**ing, ru**nn**ing |

Verwendung

They **are talking** about their courses.	bei Handlungen, die im Moment des Sprechens stattfinden
She **is studying** for her exam this year.	bei Handlungen, die vorübergehend stattfinden, nicht aber unbedingt im Augenblick
She **is having** a good time. A lot of people **are thinking** about their future.	bei bestimmten Verben (siehe *present simple*), wenn sie eine vorübergehende Handlung und keinen Zustand beschreiben
I **am meeting** him tomorrow.	bei zukünftigen Handlungen (mit Zeitbestimmung)
Some students **are always complaining**.	zur gefühlsbetonten Darstellung von Handlungen in Verbindung mit *always*

Past simple ➡ UNIT 2/3

Form

| She
You | work**ed**
need**ed** | in Glasgow
a new car. | last year. | Aussagen
Grundform + -ed
(Infinitiv) |

Besonderheiten

move	moved	stummes -e entfällt
try	tried	Konsonant + y wird zu ie
stop	stopped	Lautverdopplung
go meet	went met	unregelmäßige Verben haben besondere Formen für das *simple past*- dabei wird die 2. Form verwendet

| He
We | did not
(didn't) | need
lose | special software.
the money. | Verneinung |

| Did | you
they
it | (not) | move
live
take | to Glasgow?
in Birmingham?
more than 6 months? | (verneinte)
Frage |
| Why did | he | (not) | stop | in Liverpool? | |

Verwendung

| Jane **moved** to Glasgow 7 years ago.
First she **worked** for a computer company. | bei Handlungen zu einem bestimmten Zeitpunkt oder in einem abgeschlossenen Zeitraum in der Vergangenheit (oft mit einer Zeitbestimmung wie z.B. *yesterday, last year, in 1988, ...ago, from... until*) |

Past continuous ➡ UNIT 3

Form

| I/He/She/It | was | (not)
(wasn't) | standing | on the platform. | (verneinte)
Aussage |
| We/You/They | were | (not)
(weren't) | | | |

Verwendung

As/while he **was driving** to the airport, it started to rain. A lot of passengers **were waiting** at the counter when Jason went into the bank.	für eine Handlung, die schon im Gange war, als eine neue Handlung eintrat
While I **was reading** a book, my friend **was writing** a letter.	Bei gleichzeitigem Verlauf zweier Handlungen steht die Verlaufsform in beiden Fällen.
What **did** you **do** when Susan **came** in? When she **came** in I **put** down my newspaper and talked to her.	Für Handlungen, die nacheinander stattfanden, wird in beiden Fällen *past simple* benutzt.

Present perfect simple ➡ UNIT 2

Form

I/you/we/they	**have**	(not) (haven't)	**had** a car for three years. **sold** 120 million cassettes. **been** to Scotland.	(verneinte) Aussage have/has + 3. Form
He/she/it	**has**	(not) (hasn't)		

Have	I/you/we/they	(not)	**made** a loss? **taken** a photo? **been** here?	(verneinte) Frage
Has	he/she/it			

Verwendung

I **have repaired** the car.	bei Handlungen in der Vergangenheit ohne Zeitangabe – das Ergebnis ist oft wichtiger als die Zeitangabe
They **have sold** 50,000 cars **up till now**.	mit Zeitbestimmungen, die einen Zeitraum beschreiben, der noch andauert: z.B. *today, this week, so far, in the last ten years*
He has **already paid** the bill.	mit bestimmten Adverbien: z.B. *ever, never, always, yet, just, already*
How long have you **known** about this book? The Browns **have lived** there **for** 3 years. We **have lived** here **since** 1986.	bei nicht abgeschlossenen Zuständen mit *how long, since* und *for* – *since* bezieht sich dabei auf einen Zeitpunkt, *for* auf einen Zeitraum

Present perfect continuous ➡ UNIT 2

Form

I/you/we/they	**have**	**been standing**.	Present simple von *have* + *been* + -ing-Form

Verwendung

How long have you been waiting? I've been waiting – for half an hour. – since ten o'clock.	bei Handlungen, die in der Vergangenheit begannen und noch andauern – meist in Verbindung mit *how long, since, for*

Past perfect simple ➡ UNIT 3

Form

I/You/He/She/ It/We/They	**had**	**(not)** (**hadn't**)	**travelled** to Paris.	(verneinte) Aussage

Verwendung

After he **had arrived** at the hotel, he went to his room. When I arrived at the station, the ticket office **had** already **closed**.	für Handlungen oder Zustände, die vor einem Zeitpunkt in der Vergangenheit abgeschlossen waren

Future with 'going to' → UNIT 4

Form

I/You He/She/It We/They	am ('m) is ('s) are ('re)	(not)	going to watch TV.	(verneinte) Aussage
Am **Is** **Are**	I he/she/it we/they	**going to have**	a cup of coffee?	Frage

Verwendung

She **is going to answer** the phone	bei Absichten und Vorhaben
That fax machine **is going to** break down.	bei Vorhersagen, die aufgrund bereits bekannter Fakten oder bisheriger Erfahrungen sicher oder logischerweise in Erfüllung gehen müssen

Future with 'will' → UNIT 4

Form

I/You He/She/It We/They	**will** **will not (won't)**	**use** alternative energy **waste** water.	Aussage Verneinung
Will	I/you, he/she/it we/they	**use** talking computers?	Frage

Verwendung

Computers **will probably do** most of the work.	bei Vorhersagen mit *I suppose/expect* und *probably*
Just a minute, **I'll help** you with your shopping.	bei Entscheidungen, die im Moment des Sprechens getroffen werden
I'll phone you tomorrow, I promise.	bei Versprechen
Will you **make** some coffee, please.	um eine Bitte auszudrücken

Question tags → UNIT 5 (Workbook)
(*Frageanhängsel*)

Form

Aussagesatz	Frageanhängsel	
You can drive,	**can't you?**	Das Hilfverb wird in dem Frageanhängsel wiederholt.
Pollution is increasing,	**isn't it?**	Ist der Aussagesatz bejaht, so wird das Frageanhängsel verneint.
Trams will improve our public transport service,	**won't they?**	
Statistics aren't always correct,	**are they?**	Ist der Aussagesatz verneint, so wird das Frageanhängsel bejaht.
You mustn't drive over 70 mph on motorways,	**must you?**	
We enjoyed the journey,	**didn't we?**	Wenn der Aussagesatz kein Hilfsverb enthält, wird das Frageanhängsel mit 'to do' in der Zeit des Aussagesatzes gebildet.
She usually goes to Britain,	**doesn't she?**	

Verwendung

	Frageanhängsel werden verwendet:
Air travel is really comfortable, **isn't it?**	beim Wunsch nach Bestätigung
You didn't walk here, **did you?**	bei Überraschung
Oh, it's not another traffic jam, **is it?**	bei Verärgerung
Well, that's a really new idea, **isn't it?**	bei ironischen Aussagen

Reported speech ⇒ UNIT 6
(Indirekte Rede)

Form

Aussagen	Die Zeitformen ändern sich:
"We are protesting about pollution." Harry said they **were protesting** about pollution. "He doesn't buy cans." June told me he **didn't buy** cans.	*Present tenses* werden zu *past tenses*.
"Watsons opened four supermarkets in 1995." Fred pointed out that Watsons **had opened** four supermakets in 1995. "They have started a bus service." He added that they **had started** a bus service.	*Simple past* und *present perfect* werden zu *past perfect*.
"There will be more 'green' products." Sue went on to say that there **would be** more 'green' products.	*will* wird zu *would*.
"I can save more energy." Harry told me that **he** could save more energy.	Die Pronomen werden angepasst.
"We are meeting the town planner tomorrow." Sue added that they were meeting the town planner **the next day**. "I bought the car three days ago." He said that he had bought the car **three days before**.	Orts- (z.B. *here* wird zu *there*) und Zeitbestimmungen werden angepasst.

Fragen

"What are you doing about waste?" **They asked what we were doing** about waste. "When did you introduce bicycle routes?" **We wanted to know when they had introduced** bicycle routes.	Bei Fragen wird die Wortstellung geändert.

Verwendung

Indirekte Rede wird benutzt, wenn berichtet werden soll, was jemand gesagt oder gefragt hat.

Conditionals ➡ UNIT 7
(Bedingungssätze)

Form

Type 1		
If-Satz	Hauptsatz	
If **we fit** a shower,	**we will** save water.	*Present simple* wird für das Verb in dem If-Satz, Futur mit *will* für das Verb in dem Hauptsatz verwendet.

Type 2		
If-Satz	Hauptsatz	
If the government **developed** solar energy,	there **would be** less pollution.	*Past simple* wird für das Verb in dem If-Satz, *Conditional I* für das Verb in dem Hauptsatz verwendet.
If I **were** Environment Minister,	I **could** put my ideas about energy into practice.	*could* oder *might* sind Alternativen zu *would* in dem Hauptsatz.

Type 3		
If-Satz	Hauptsatz	
If Tom and Kate **had insulated** their roof years ago,	they **would have saved** a lot of money.	*Past perfect* wird für das Verb in dem If-Satz, *Conditional II* für das Verb in dem Hauptsatz verwendet.

Verwendung

Type 1 wird gebraucht, wenn die Voraussetzungen für die Erfüllung der Bedingung schon existieren und es deswegen wahrscheinlich ist, dass die Handlung in dem If-Satz in Erfüllung gehen wird (wir planen, eine Dusche einzubauen).
Type 2 wird gebraucht, wenn a) wir nicht erwarten, dass die Handlung in dem If-Satz eintreten wird. Wir stellen uns die Situation rein theoretisch vor. b) die Handlung in dem If-Satz gar nicht eintreten kann, weil sie in Gegensatz zu den Tatsachen steht (ich bin nicht der Umweltminister).
Type 3 wird gebraucht, wenn die Handlung in dem If-Satz nicht eintreten kann, weil sie in der Vergangenheit liegt. Es kann an der Situation nichts mehr geändert werden.

Passive voice ➡ UNIT 8
(Das Passiv)

Form

The robots **are equipped** with sensors. This motor **was not made** in Great Britain. **Will** the new car **be sold** in Japan?	Form von *be* in der jeweiligen Zeit + Partizip Perfekt (3. Form) des Verbes
Now the wheels **can be fitted**. The car **must be tested** first.	auch mit Hilfsverben

Verwendung

These cars **were made** in Germany. The handbook **is written** in English.	hauptsächlich in der Schriftsprache, wenn der Ausführende unbekannt, unwichtig oder selbstverständlich ist
This information **is checked by** the central computer.	Wenn der Ausführende allerdings genannt werden soll, dann benutzt man die Präposition *by (by-agent)*.
It is said **It is reported** that computers will become **It is believed** even more important in the **It is supposed** future. **He is said** to be rich.	bei Verben des Meinens und Berichtens
English **is spoken** here. = Man spricht Englisch. We **will be told** the result later. = Man wird uns später das Ergebnis sagen.	im Deutschen wird ein Aktivsatz mit ‚man' bevorzugt

Infinitive ➡ UNIT 9
(Infinitiv)

Verwendung

ohne *to*	
We **must write** a report about our trip to England.	nach den meisten Hilfsverben
Our new teachers **make us work** very hard, but on Friday they **let us go** home early.	nach *make* und *let* + direktem Objekt

	mit *to*
The teacher **asked me to show** my photos of Newcastle. She **told them to wait** outside for a moment.	nach bestimmten Verben *(ask/tell/advise/expect etc.)*
This is not **easy to understand.** I am **surprised to hear** that.	nach Adjektiven
I do not know **what to do.** I soon found out **where to go.**	nach Fragewörtern

Gerund ⇒ UNIT 9
(Gerundium)

Verwendung

Drinking and **driving** is dangerous.	als Subjekt
I **enjoy swimming.**	als Objekt nach Verben ohne Präpositionen, wenn eine allgemeingültige Situation beschrieben wird: z.B *enjoy/like/dislike/ hate/stop/ start/ avoid/suggest/mind/love/recommend/ prefer*
I **look forward to seeing** you again. He is **tired of waiting** here. They saw the **danger of destroying** the environment.	nach Verben/Adjektiven/Substantiven mit Präpositionen
He has helped me a lot **by giving** me that map of Newcastle. The child crossed the road **without looking.**	nach Präpositionen mit adverbialer Bedeutung, z.B. *by/without/instead of*
Normally I enjoy swimming but today I **would prefer to play** tennis.	aber kein Gerundium, wenn es sich um eine Ausnahmesituation handelt (oft mit *would*)
I remember learning those rules. = Ich erinnere mich daran, daß ich die Regeln gelernt habe. I must remember to learn these rules. = Ich muß daran denken, diese Regeln zu lernen.	oder wenn die Bedeutung es nicht zulässt, z.B. bei *stop/start/remember*

131

Participle ➡ UNIT 10
(Partizip)

Form

Das Partizip besteht aus zwei Formen

waiting/going/watching	Partizip Präsens
waited/gone/watched	Partizip Perfekt

Verwendung

The weather forecast for the **coming** week… The weather in New York last week was rather **mixed.**	als Adjektiv
You can find several families **living** in one flat. There are a lot of restaurants there especially **built** for the tourists.	anstelle von Relativsätzen
After talking to the press they started their demonstration. **Having discussed** the problem with the President personally, they flew home to California.	als Verkürzung von Adverbialsätzen *(after/before/ because/while etc.)*

VOCABULARY

(unitbegleitend)

Unit 1

Starter

Bachelor of Arts (B.A.) ['bætʃələr_əv ɑːts]	niedrigster akad. Grad
BTEC National Diploma [,biː,tiː,i:'siː 'næʃənl dɪ'pləʊmə]	etwa: Fachhochschulreifeprüfung
certificate [sə'tɪfɪkət]	Zeugnis
comprehensive school [,kɒmprɪ'hensɪv skuːl]	Gesamtschule
degree [dɪ'griː]	akad. Grad (z. B. B.A., M.A.), Diplom
GCSE = General Certificate of Secondary Education [,dʒiː,siː,es'iː] ['dʒenərəl sə'tɪfɪkət əv 'sekəndrɪ ,edʒʊ'keɪʃn]	etwa: Fachoberschulreife

A1

accountancy [ə'kaʊntənsɪ]	Rechnungswesen
advanced [əd'vɑːnst]	fortgeschritten
application [,æplɪ'keɪʃn]	Anwendung
basic ['beɪsɪk]	Grund-; grundlegend
bus pass [bʌs pɑːs]	Busausweis
CAD (Computer Aided Design) [,siː,eɪ'diː] [kəm'pjuːtər_eɪdɪd_dɪ'zaɪn]	Computerunterstützte Zeichnung
CAM (Computer Aided Manufacture) [,siː,eɪ'em] [kəm'pjuːtər_eɪdɪd ,mænjʊ'fæktʃə]	Computerunterstützte Fertigung
civil engineering ['sɪvl ,endʒɪ'nɪərɪŋ]	Bauwesen
control [kən'trəʊl]	Kontrolle, hier: Regeltechnik
electrical engineering [ɪ'lektrɪkl ,endʒɪ'nɪərɪŋ]	Elektrotechnik
finance ['faɪnæns]	Finanzwesen
full-time [fʊl taɪm]	Vollzeit
general science ['dʒenərəl 'saɪəns]	allgemeine Naturwissenschaften
grant [grɑːnt]	Zuschuss, Bafög
industrial [ɪn'dʌstrɪəl]	industriell
instrumentation [,ɪnstrʊmen'teɪʃn]	Messtechnik
level ['levl]	Stufe, Niveau
Local Education Authority (L.E.A.) ['ləʊkl_,edʒʊ'keɪʃn ɔː'θɒrətɪ] [,el,iː'eɪ]	örtliche Schulbehörde
mechanical engineering [mə'kænɪkl ,endʒɪ'nɪərɪŋ]	Maschinenbau
office skills ['ɒfɪs_skɪlz]	Bürofertigkeiten
paragraph ['pærəgrɑːf]	Absatz
part-time [pɑːt_taɪm]	Teilzeit
principle ['prɪnsəpl]	Grundsatz, Prinzip
qualification [,kwɒlɪfɪ'keɪʃn]	Qualifikation, Befähigung
statistics [stə'tɪstɪks]	Statistik
studies ['stʌdɪz]	Kurs, Studium

A2

bedsitter [,bed'sɪtə]	Einzimmerwohnung
beginner [bɪ'gɪnə]	Anfänger(in)
canteen [kæn'tiːn]	Kantine
coach [kəʊtʃ]	Trainer
dialogue ['daɪəlɒg]	Dialog
female ['fiːmeɪl]	weiblich
formula ['fɔːmjʊlə]	Formel
information sheet [,ɪnfə'meɪʃn ʃiːt]	Informationsblatt
male [meɪl]	männlich
packing ['pækɪŋ]	Verpackung
to rush [rʌʃ]	eilen
social studies ['səʊʃl 'stʌdɪz]	Sozialwissenschaften

C1

a couple of [ə 'kʌpl_əv]	ein paar
to be about [biː_ə'baʊt]	sich um etwas handeln
adventure [əd'ventʃə]	Abenteuer
as well as [əz_'wel_əz]	sowie
biscuit ['bɪskɪt]	Keks
bold type [bəʊld taɪp]	Fettdruck
to broaden the mind ['brɔːdn ðə maɪnd]	den Horizont erweitern
comment ['kɒment]	Bemerkung, Kommentar
to cope [kəʊp]	mit etwas klarkommen
district ['dɪstrɪkt]	Gegend
exchange [ɪks'tʃeɪndʒ]	Austausch
to get on like a house on fire [get_ɒn laɪk_ə haʊs_ɒn 'faɪə]	sich sehr gut verstehen
to get to know [get_tʊ 'nəʊ]	kennenlernen
head of department [hed_əv dɪ'pɑːtmənt]	hier: Fachbereichsleiter(in)
heavy metal [,hevɪ 'metl]	Heavy Metal (harte Rockmusik)
host [həʊst]	Gastgeber
to be into (sth.) [biː_'ɪntuː]	Fan von (etwas) sein
joint [dʒɔɪnt]	gemeinsam
metal ['metl]	Metall
moor [mɔː]	Moor
organizer ['ɔːgənaɪzə]	Veranstalter(in)
project ['prɒdʒekt]	Projekt
to put to the test [pʊt_tʊ ðə 'test]	jmdn./etwas auf die Probe stellen
remark [rɪ'mɑːk]	Bemerkung
smoker ['sməʊkə]	Raucher(in)
staffroom ['stɑːfruːm]	Lehrerzimmer
workshop ['wɜːkʃɒp]	Werkstatt

C2

can't stand [kɑːnt ˈstænd]	nicht ausstehen können
informal [ɪnˈfɔːml]	informell
to look like [lʊk laɪk]	aussehen wie
personality [ˌpɜːsəˈnæləti]	Persönlichkeit
scheme [skiːm]	Projekt, Plan, Programm
Yours [jɔːz]	dein(e)

D1

a bit [ə bɪt]	ein bisschen
enthusiastic [ɪnˌθjuːziˈæstɪk]	begeistert
for instance [fər ˈɪnstəns]	beispielsweise
hard-working [ˌhɑːdˈwɜːkɪŋ]	fleißig
in my view [ɪn ˈmaɪ vjuː]	meiner Ansicht nach
phrase [freɪz]	Ausdruck

Unit 2

Starter

active [ˈæktɪv]	aktiv
advertising manager [ˈædvətaɪzɪŋ ˈmænɪdʒə]	Werbeleiter(in)
creative [kriːˈeɪtɪv]	kreativ
dancer [ˈdɑːnsə]	Tänzer(in)
to discover [dɪˈskʌvə]	entdecken
hairdresser [ˈheəˌdresə]	Friseur, Friseurin
independent [ˌɪndɪˈpendənt]	unabhängig
logical [ˈlɒdʒɪkl]	logisch
mark [mɑːk]	Zensur, Note
novel [ˈnɒvl]	Roman
officer [ˈɒfɪsə]	Beamter, Beamtin, Offizier
office worker [ˈɒfɪs ˈwɜːkə]	Büroangestellte(r)
on your own [ɒn jər ˈəʊn]	allein
per [pə]	pro
practical [ˈpræktɪkl]	praktisch
puzzle [ˈpʌzl]	Rätsel
saleswoman [ˈseɪlzˌwʊmən]	Verkäuferin
singer [ˈsɪŋə]	Sänger(in)
specialist [ˈspeʃlɪst]	Spezialist(in)
sportsman [ˈspɔːtsmən]	Sportler
sportswoman [ˈspɔːtsˌwʊmən]	Sportlerin
suggestion [səˈdʒestʃən]	Vorschlag
suitable [ˈsjuːtəbl]	geeignet
tourist guide [ˈtʊərɪst gaɪd]	Fremdenführer(in)
well-paid [wel peɪd]	gut bezahlt
to work out [wɜːk aʊt]	herausfinden, ausarbeiten, lösen

A1

to adapt [əˈdæpt]	bearbeiten
adjective [ˈædʒɪktɪv]	Adjektiv
alive [əˈlaɪv]	lebend, lebendig, aktiv
enormous [ɪˈnɔːməs]	gewaltig, enorm
to expand [ɪkˈspænd]	ausdehnen
fortune [ˈfɔːtʃuːn]	Glück, Reichtum
to graduate [ˈgrædʒʊeɪt]	das Studium beenden
in the meantime [ɪn ðə ˈmiːntaɪm]	in der Zwischenzeit
moreover [mɔːˈrəʊvə]	überdies, außerdem
natural [ˈnætʃərəl]	natürlich
noun [naʊn]	Substantiv
risk [rɪsk]	Risiko
sales [seɪlz]	Verkaufszahlen
self-employed [ˌselfɪmˈplɔɪd]	selbständig
to service [ˈsɜːvɪs]	(Auto, Maschine etc.) warten
to sum up [sʌm ʌp]	zusammenfassen
to a great extent [tʊ ə greɪt ɪkˈstent]	in großem Umfang
turnover [ˈtɜːnəʊvə]	Umsatz
unlimited (company) [ˌʌnˈlɪmɪtɪd / ˈkʌmpəni]	Gesellschaft mit unbeschränkter Haftung
wage [weɪdʒ]	Lohn

A2

to afford [əˈfɔːd]	sich leisten
to close down [kləʊz daʊn]	schließen
equipment [ɪˈkwɪpmənt]	Ausrüstung
income [ˈɪŋkʌm]	Einkommen
to link [lɪŋk]	verbinden
listener [ˈlɪsnə]	Zuhörer(in)
main [meɪn]	Haupt-
to make up one's mind [meɪk ʌp wʌnz ˈmaɪnd]	sich entschließen
market development [ˈmɑːkɪt dɪˈveləpmənt]	Marktentwicklung
namely [neɪmli]	nämlich
nevertheless [ˌnevəðəˈles]	dennoch
photographer [fəˈtɒgrəfə]	Fotograf(in)
to point out [pɔɪnt aʊt]	hinweisen auf
to react [riˈækt]	reagieren
to record [rɪˈkɔːd]	aufnehmen (Ton, Video etc.)
to start up (business) [stɑːt ʌp / ˈbɪznɪs]	(Geschäft) anfangen
tense [tens]	Zeitform
thought [θɔːt]	Gedanke
video production [ˈvɪdiəʊ prəˈdʌkʃn]	Videoproduktion
wedding [ˈwedɪŋ]	Hochzeit

C1

amount [əˈmaʊnt]	Betrag, Menge
attitude [ˈætɪtjuːd]	Haltung, Einstellung
average [ˈævərɪdʒ]	Durchschnitt
bank holiday [bæŋk ˈhɒlɪdeɪ]	öffentl. Feiertag (Brit.)
benefit [ˈbenɪfɪt]	Zuwendung, soziale Leistung
to carry out [ˈkæri aʊt]	ausführen
condition [kənˈdɪʃn]	Bedingung
Dutch [dʌtʃ]	Niederländer(in); niederländisch
employee [ˌemplɔɪˈiː]	Arbeitnehmer(in), Angestellte(r)
except [ɪkˈsept]	außer
to get on with [get ɒn wɪð]	auskommen mit
Greek [griːk]	Grieche, Griechin; griechisch
to have in common [hæv ɪn ˈkɒmən]	gemeinsam haben
to identify [aɪˈdentɪfaɪ]	identifizieren
in general [ɪn ˈdʒenərəl]	im Allgemeinen
on the other hand [ɒn ði ˈʌðə hænd]	auf der anderen Seite
satisfaction [ˌsætɪsˈfækʃn]	Zufriedenheit
satisfied [ˈsætɪsfaɪd]	zufrieden
sick leave [sɪk liːv]	krankheitsbedingte Abwesenheit
survey [ˈsɜːveɪ]	Untersuchung, Umfrage
underpaid [ˌʌndəˈpeɪd]	unterbezahlt
to vary [ˈveəri]	sich ändern, unterschiedlich sein
working class [ˈwɜːkɪŋ klɑːs]	Arbeiterklasse
working hours [ˈwɜːkɪŋ aʊəz]	Arbeitszeit
workmate [ˈwɜːkmeɪt]	Kollege, Kollegin

C2

in order to [ɪn ˈɔːdə tuː]	um zu
secure [sɪˈkjʊə]	sicher
would like [wʊd laɪk]	würde(n) gerne

D

aged ... [eɪdʒd]	... Jahre alt
applicant [ˈæplɪkənt]	Bewerber(in)
to apply [əˈplaɪ]	sich bewerben
assistant [əˈsɪstənt]	Assistent(in)
attendance [əˈtendəns]	Besuch
candidate [ˈkændɪdət]	Kandidat(in), Bewerber(in)
commercial [kəˈmɜːʃl]	kaufmännisch
company car [ˈkʌmpəni kɑː]	Firmenwagen
contract [ˈkɒntrækt]	Vertrag
CV= curriculum vitae [ˌsiːˈviː] [kəˌrɪkjələm ˈviːtaɪ]	Lebenslauf
data [ˈdeɪtə]	Daten
Dear Sir [dɪə sɜː]	Sehr geehrter Herr
Dear Madam [dɪə ˈmædəm]	Sehr geehrte Dame
to enclose [ɪnˈkləʊz]	beilegen
essential [ɪˈsenʃl]	wesentlich
export assistant [ˈekspɔːt əˈsɪstənt]	etwa: Außenhandelskaufmann, -frau
foreign [ˈfɒrən]	ausländisch
to look forward to (-ing) [lʊk ˈfɔːwəd tuː]	sich freuen auf (Schlussformel im Geschäftsbrief)
marital status [ˈmærɪtl ˈsteɪtəs]	Familienstand
nationality [ˌnæʃəˈnæləti]	Nationalität
overseas [ˌəʊvəˈsiːz]	in Übersee
professional [prəˈfeʃənl]	beruflich
reference [ˈrefrəns]	Referenz
renewable [rɪˈnjuːəbl]	erneuerbar
to require [rɪˈkwaɪə]	benötigen, erfordern
responsible [rɪˈspɒnsəbl]	verantwortlich
salary [ˈsæləri]	Gehalt
sales department [seɪls dɪˈpɑːtmənt]	Verkaufsabteilung
similar [ˈsɪmələ]	ähnlich
sports [spɔːts]	Sport
step [step]	Schritt, Stufe
task [tɑːsk]	Aufgabe
vacancy [ˈveɪkənsi]	freie Stelle
willing [ˈwɪlɪŋ]	bereit
with reference to [wɪð ˈrefrəns tuː]	mit Bezug auf
Yours faithfully [jɔːz ˈfeɪθfʊli]	Hochachtungsvoll
Yours sincerely [jɔːz sɪnˈsɪəli]	Mit freundlichen Grüßen

Unit 3

Starter

adult [ˈædʌlt]	Erwachsene(r)
capital city [ˈkæpɪtl ˈsɪti]	Hauptstadt
European Union [ˌjʊərəˈpɪən ˈjuːnjən]	Europäische Union (die EC wurde im November 1993 in die EU umbenannt)

A1

anger [ˈæŋgə]	Zorn, Wut
to apologize [əˈpɒlədʒaɪz]	sich entschuldigen
Belgian [ˈbeldʒən]	Belgier(in); belgisch
bookshop [ˈbʊkʃɒp]	Buchhandlung
chain [tʃeɪn]	Kette
currency [ˈkʌrənsi]	Währung

to demand [dɪˈmɑːnd]	verlangen	to slow down [sləʊ daʊn]	verlangsamen
ECU (European Currency Unit) [ˈekjuː] [ˌjʊərəpɪən ˈkʌrənsɪ ˈjuːnɪt]	Europäische Währungseinheit (Dezember 1995: in EURO umbenannt)	Spain [speɪn]	Spanien
		state [steɪt]	Staat
		treaty [ˈtriːtɪ]	Vertrag
edition [ɪˈdɪʃn]	Ausgabe	wealthy [ˈwelθɪ]	wohlhabend
to examine [ɪgˈzæmɪn]	untersuchen, überprüfen		
exchange rate [ɪksˈtʃeɪndʒ reɪt]	Wechselkurs	**C1**	
		according to (him)/(her) [əˈkɔːdɪŋ tʊ / hɪm/hɜː]	(seiner)/(ihrer) Meinung nach, laut
France [frɑːns]	Frankreich		
French [frentʃ]	französisch; Franzose, Französin	to act [ækt]	handeln
		to argue [ˈɑːgjuː]	argumentieren
handful [ˈhændfʊl]	Handvoll	continent [ˈkɒntɪnənt]	Kontinent, Erdteil
to impress [ɪmˈpres]	beeindrucken	to defend [dɪˈfend]	verteidigen
impression [ɪmˈpreʃn]	Eindruck	democracy [dɪˈmɒkrəsɪ]	Demokratie
in the end [ɪn ðɪ ˈend]	schließlich	eastern [ˈiːstən]	Ost-; östlich
on the road [ɒn ðə ˈrəʊd]	auf dem Weg	efficiency [ɪˈfɪʃənsɪ]	Leistungsfähigkeit
payment [ˈpeɪmənt]	Zahlung	efficient [ɪˈfɪʃənt]	leistungsfähig
pound note [paʊnd nəʊt]	Pfundnote	financial [faɪˈnænʃl]	finanziell
to realize [ˈrɪəlaɪz] *	erkennen, bemerken	to found [faʊnd]	gründen
to refuse [rɪˈfjuːz]	ablehnen, verweigern	freedom [ˈfriːdəm]	Freiheit
Scottish [ˈskɒtɪʃ]	schottisch	institute [ˈɪnstɪtjuːt]	Institut
shop assistant [ˈʃɒp əˈsɪstənt]	Verkäufer(in)	otherwise [ˈʌðəwaɪz]	sonst, anderenfalls
		pleasant [ˈplezənt]	angenehm
single [ˈsɪŋgl]	einzig, hier: einheitlich	powerful [ˈpaʊəfʊl]	stark, mächtig
suspicious of [səsˈpɪʃəs əv]	misstrauisch gegenüber	prefix [ˈpriːfɪks]	Vorsilbe
to turn over [tɜːn əʊvə]	umdrehen	relation [rɪˈleɪʃn]	Beziehung
united [juːˈnaɪtɪd]	vereinigt	southern [ˈsʌðən]	Süd-; südlich
unity [ˈjuːnətɪ]	Einheit	stable [ˈsteɪbl]	stabil
up until now [ʌp ənˌtɪl ˈnaʊ]	bis jetzt	such as [sʌtʃ əz]	wie (zum Beispiel)
		to suffer from [ˈsʌfə frəm]	leiden unter
A2		undemocratic [ˌʌndeməˈkrætɪk]	undemokratisch
Belgium [ˈbeldʒəm]	Belgien		
British [ˈbrɪtɪʃ]	britisch	wealth [welθ]	Wohlstand, Reichtum
to come into operation [kʌm ˌɪntʊ ˌɒpəˈreɪʃn]	in Kraft treten	western [ˈwestən]	West-, westlich
		D	
democratic [ˌdeməˈkrætɪk]	demokratisch	to appoint [əˈpɔɪnt]	ernennen, bestimmen
Denmark [ˈdenmɑːk]	Dänemark	archbishop [ˌɑːtʃˈbɪʃəp]	Erzbischof
economic [ˌiːkəˈnɒmɪk]	Wirtschafts-; wirtschaftlich	cabinet [ˈkæbɪnət]	Kabinett
election [ɪˈlekʃn]	Wahl	cassette [kəˈset]	Kassette
factor [ˈfæktə]	Faktor	conservative [kənˈsɜːvətɪv]	konservativ
flag [flæg]	Fahne	constituency [kənˈstɪtjʊənsɪ]	Wahlbezirk
Germany [ˈdʒɜːmənɪ]	Deutschland		
Great Britain [ˌgreɪt ˈbrɪtn]	Großbritannien	to consult [kənˈsʌlt]	sich beraten, zu Rate ziehen
Greece [griːs]	Griechenland	delay [dɪˈleɪ]	Verzögerung, Verspätung
Ireland [ˈaɪələnd]	Irland	democrat [ˈdeməkræt]	Demokrat(in)
Italy [ˈɪtəlɪ]	Italien	diagram [ˈdaɪəgræm]	Diagramm
Luxembourg [ˈlʌksəmbɜːg]	Luxemburg	economics [ˌiːkəˈnɒmɪks]	Wirtschaft(swissenschaft)
membership [ˈmembəʃɪp]	Mitgliedschaft	to elect [ɪˈlekt]	wählen
Netherlands [ˈneðələndz]	Niederlande	electrician [ˌɪlekˈtrɪʃn]	Elektriker(in)
parliament [ˈpɑːləmənt]	Parlament	former [ˈfɔːmə]	ehemalig
past tense [pɑːst tens]	Vergangenheitsform	House of Commons [haʊs əv ˈkɒmənz]	Unterhaus
peaceful [ˈpiːsfʊl]	friedlich		
political [pəˈlɪtɪkl]	politisch	House of Lords [haʊs əv ˈlɔːdz]	Oberhaus
process [ˈprəʊses]	Vorgang, Prozess		
to resign [rɪˈzaɪn]	zurücktreten		

* *Bei vielen Verben sind die Endungen "-ize" oder "-ise" möglich.*

labour ['leɪbə]	Arbeit	object ['ɒbdʒɪkt]	Gegenstand
legislation [ˌledʒɪs'leɪʃn]	Gesetzgebung	paradise ['pærədaɪs]	Paradies
life peers [laɪf pɪəz]	Peer auf Lebenszeit	private ['praɪvət]	privat
on recommendation [ɒn ˌrekəmen'deɪʃn]	auf Empfehlung	poverty ['pɒvətɪ]	Armut
parliamentary [ˌpɑːlə'mentərɪ]	parlamentarisch	recognition [ˌrekəg'nɪʃn]	(Wieder-)Erkennung
		remote control [rɪ'məʊt kən'trəʊl]	Fernbedienung
previous ['priːvɪəs]	vorhergehend, früher	screen [skriːn]	Bildschirm, Leinwand
prime minister [praɪm 'mɪnɪstə]	Premierminister(in)	sound wave [saʊnd weɪv]	Schallwelle
proportion [prə'pɔːʃn]	Verhältnis, Teil, Anteil	transmission [træns'mɪʃn]	Übertragung
proportional representation [prə'pɔːʃənl ˌreprɪzen'teɪʃn]	Verhältniswahl	TV set [ˌtiː'viː set]	Fernsehgerät
		user ['juːzə]	Benutzer(in)
to register ['redʒɪstə]	registrieren, anmelden,		
simple majority voting system ['sɪmpl mə'dʒɒrətɪ 'vəʊtɪŋ 'sɪstəm]	Mehrheitswahlsystem	**A2**	
		bar graph ['bɑːgrɑːf]	Säulendiagramm
		cable TV ['keɪbl ˌtiː'viː]	Kabelfernsehen
sovereign ['sɒvrɪn]	Souverän, Herrscher(in)	figure ['fɪgə]	Zahl, Figur
to take notes [teɪk nəʊts]	Notizen machen	household ['haʊshəʊld]	Haushalt
to vote [vəʊt]	wählen	percentage [pə'sentɪdʒ]	prozentualer Anteil
voter ['vəʊtə]	Wähler(in)		
voting system ['vəʊtɪŋ 'sɪstəm]	Wahlsystem	**C**	
		advertiser ['ædvəˌtaɪzə]	Inserent(in), Auftraggeber(in) von Werbesendungen

Unit 4

Starter

medicine ['medsɪn]	Medizin, Medikament

A1

actual ['æktʃʊəl]	tatsächlich	airtime ['eətaɪm]	Sendezeit
apparatus [ˌæpə'reɪtəs]	Gerät	author ['ɔːθə]	Autor(in), Verfasser(in)
appliance [ə'plaɪəns]	Gerät	background ['bækgraʊnd]	Hintergrund
to blink [blɪŋk]	blinken	best-known ['best nəʊn]	bekanntester, -e, -es
bubble ['bʌbl]	Blase	campaign [kæm'peɪn]	Kampagne, Werbefeldzug
to call up [kɔːl ʌp]	anrufen	commercial [kə'mɜːʃl]	hier: Werbespot
to combine [kəm'baɪn]	verbinden, vereinigen	contrast ['kɒntrɑːst]	Gegensatz
complex ['kɒmpleks]	komplex, kompliziert	to decrease [dɪ'kriːs]	abnehmen, vermindern
complicated ['kɒmplɪkeɪtɪd]	kompliziert	to fail [feɪl]	scheitern
consumer [kən'sjuːmə]	Verbraucher(in)	habit ['hæbɪt]	Gewohnheit
device [dɪ'vaɪs]	Gerät	logo ['ləʊgəʊ]	Logo, (Firmen-)Emblem
diary [daɪərɪ]	Tagebuch, Terminkalender	on the one hand [ɒn ðə 'wʌn hænd]	auf der einen Seite
digital ['dɪdʒɪtl]	digital	outdoor [ˌaʊt'dɔː]	draußen, im Freien
document ['dɒkjʊmənt]	Dokument, Unterlage	to overestimate [ˌəʊvər'estɪmeɪt]	überschätzen
easy-to-use [ˌiːzɪ tʊ 'juːz]	einfach zu bedienen		
electronic [ˌɪlek'trɒnɪk]	elektronisch	pleased [pliːzd]	zufrieden, erfreut
to enable (so. to do sth.) [ɪ'neɪbl]	(es jmdm.) möglich machen, (etwas zu tun)	to recognize ['rekəgnaɪz]	(wieder-)erkennen
		share [ʃeə]	Anteil
in addition [ɪn ə'dɪʃn]	zusätzlich	to switch [swɪtʃ]	umschalten, schalten
in this way [ɪn ðɪs weɪ]	auf diese Weise	tennis serve ['tenɪs sɜːv]	Aufschlag (Tennis)
media ['miːdjə]	Medien	value ['væljuː]	Wert
microphone ['maɪkrəfəʊn]	Mikrofon	viewer ['vjʊə]	Zuschauer(in)
multi- ['mʌltɪ]	Mehr-, Viel-	viewpoint ['vjuːpɔɪnt]	Standpunkt
network ['netwɜːk]	Netz	whereas [weəræz]	während
		worldwide [ˌwɜːld'waɪd]	weltweit

D1

polite [pə'laɪt]	höflich
superb [sjuː'pɜːb]	erstklassig
superfast [ˌsjuːpə'fɑːst]	außerordentlich schnell

137

D2

advert ['ædvɜːt]	Kurzform von "advertisement" = Werbeanzeige
to aim (at) [eɪm]	zielen (auf)
to associate [əˈsəʊʃɪeɪt]	assoziieren, in Verbindung bringen
brand name [brænd ˌneɪm]	Markenname
life-style [ˈlaɪfstaɪl]	Lebensstil
slogan [ˈsləʊgən]	Slogan, Werbespruch
target group [ˈtɑːgɪt gruːp]	Zielgruppe

Unit 5

Starter

to reduce [rɪdjuːs]	verringern, senken
view [vjuː]	Sicht, Ansicht, Aussicht

A1

congested [kənˈdʒestɪd]	überfüllt, verstopft
congestion [kənˈdʒestʃən]	Stau
day by day [ˌdeɪ baɪ ˈdeɪ]	Tag für Tag
fumes [fjuːmz]	Rauch, Dämpfe, Abgase
to get used to [get ˈjuːst tuː]	sich gewöhnen an
innovation [ˌɪnəˈveɪʃn]	Neuerung
to look into [lʊk ˈɪntuː]	untersuchen, prüfen
major [ˈmeɪdʒə]	bedeutend
motorway [ˈməʊtəweɪ]	Autobahn
navigation system [ˌnævɪˈgeɪʃn ˈsɪstəm]	Navigationssystem
overcrowded [ˌəʊvəˈkraʊdɪd]	überfüllt
standstill [ˈstændstɪl]	Stillstand
technological [ˌteknəˈlɒdʒɪkl]	technologisch, technisch
to thicken [ˈθɪkən]	dicker werden, dicker machen
town centre thrombosis [taʊn ˈsentə θrɒmˈbəʊsɪs]	Verkehrsinfarkt
traffic jam [ˈtræfɪk dʒæm]	Verkehrsstau
tram [træm]	Straßenbahn

A2

a number of [ə ˈnʌmbər əv]	einige
ahead of someone [əˈhed əv ˈsʌmwʌn]	vor jemandem
aid [eɪd]	Hilfe, Hilfsmittel
to avoid [əˈvɔɪd]	vermeiden
battery [ˈbætərɪ]	Batterie
dashboard [ˈdæʃbɔːd]	Armaturenbrett
destination [ˌdestɪˈneɪʃn]	Reiseziel, Zielort
(to) display [dɪˈspleɪ]	Anzeige; anzeigen
diversion [daɪˈvɜːʃn]	Umleitung
due to [djuː tuː]	aufgrund
electrical supply [ɪˈlektrɪkl səˈplaɪ]	Stromversorgung
to equip [ɪˈkwɪp]	ausrüsten
fog [fɒg]	Nebel
fuel consumption [fjʊəl kənˈsʌmpʃn]	Kraftstoffverbrauch
function [ˈfʌŋkʃn]	Funktion, Aufgabe
infra-red [ˌɪnfrəˈred]	infrarot
to install [ɪnˈstɔːl]	einbauen
jam buster [ˈdʒæm ˌbʌstə]	"Stauknacker"
mileage [ˈmaɪlɪdʒ]	Meilen, Meilenstand
mph (miles per hour) [ˌemˌpiːˈeɪtʃ] [ˌmaɪlz pər ˈaʊə]	Meilen pro Stunde
to operate [ˈɒpəreɪt]	bedienen, verkehren
planner [ˈplænə]	Planer
to plug [plʌg]	stecken
portable [ˈpɔːtəbl]	tragbar
punctual [ˈpʌŋktʃʊəl]	pünktlich
re-route [ˌriːˈruːt]	Umleitung
recently [ˈriːsəntlɪ]	kürzlich
to rewrite [ˌriːˈraɪt]	neu schreiben, umschreiben
to run on [rʌn ɒn]	laufen mit
sensor [ˈsensə]	Sensor, Fühler
series [ˈsɪərɪːz]	Reihe, Folge
to suggest [səˈdʒest]	vorschlagen
to take care [teɪk ˌkeə]	aufpassen
traffic flow [ˈtræfɪk fləʊ]	Verkehrsfluss
to transmit [trænzˈmɪt]	übermitteln

C1

attractive [əˈtræktɪv]	reizvoll, anziehend, attraktiv
cost-efficient [kɒst ɪˈfɪʃənt]	kostengünstig
crazy [ˈkreɪzɪ]	verrückt
convenient [kənˈviːnɪənt]	günstig, praktisch
to double [ˈdʌbl]	(sich) verdoppeln
ecological [ˌiːkəˈlɒdʒɪkl]	ökologisch, umweltfreundlich
electrically-driven [ɪˈlektrɪklɪ ˌdrɪvən]	elektrisch angetrieben
environmentalist [ɪnˌvaɪrənˈmentəlɪst]	Umweltschützer(in)
to estimate [ˈestɪmeɪt]	schätzen
expert [ˈekspɜːt]	Experte, Expertin
fixed-route [ˌfɪkstˈruːt]	schienengebunden
flexible [ˈfleksɪbl]	flexibel
to get rid of [get ˈrɪd əv]	loswerden, abschaffen
heading [ˈhedɪŋ]	Überschrift
in favour of [ɪn ˈfeɪvər əv]	zugunsten von
individual [ˌɪndɪˈvɪdjʊəl]	individuell
inner [ˈɪnə]	Innen-; inner-
to make sense [meɪk sens]	einen Sinn ergeben

medium-sized [ˌmiːdjəm ˈsaɪzd]	mittelgroß
peak [piːk]	Spitze, Gipfel, Höhepunkt
progress [ˈprəʊgres]	Fortschritt
to provide [prəˈvaɪd]	sorgen für, liefern, bereitstellen
rail [reɪl]	Schiene
sort [sɔːt]	Art, Sorte
tramway [ˈtræmweɪ]	Straßenbahngleis
underground [ˈʌndəgraʊnd]	Untergrund, U-Bahn
unpopular [ˌʌnˈpɒpjʊlə]	unpopulär

C2
definite [ˈdefɪnɪt]	eindeutig, bestimmt

D1
gate [geɪt]	Flugsteig
motorist [ˈməʊtərɪst]	Autofahrer(in)

D2
base [beɪs]	Basis, Stützpunkt, Ausgangspunkt
by rail [baɪ ˈreɪl]	mit der Bahn
coaching days [ˈkəʊtʃɪŋ deɪz]	Postkutschenzeit
to concentrate on [ˈkɒnsəntreɪt ɒn]	konzentrieren auf
conference [ˈkɒnfərəns]	Konferenz, Tagung
continental [ˌkɒntɪˈnentl]	kontinental
crossroads [ˈkrɒsrəʊdz]	Kreuzung
hourly [ˈaʊəlɪ]	stündlich
intercontinental [ˌɪntəkɒntɪˈnentl]	interkontinental
link [lɪŋk]	Verbindung
on top of [ɒn ˈtɒp əv]	zusätzlich zu
promotion [prəˈməʊʃn]	Werbung, Beförderung
town hall [taʊn hɔːl]	Rathaus
via [ˈvaɪə]	über

Unit 6

Starter
chart [tʃɑːt]	Tabelle, Schaubild
household waste [ˌhaʊshəʊld ˈweɪst]	Hausmüll
per capita [pəˈkæpɪtə]	pro Kopf
plastic [ˈplæstɪk]	Kunststoff, Plastik
tonne [tʌn]	Tonne

A1
acid rain [ˈæsɪd reɪn]	saurer Regen
advertising campaign [ˈædvətaɪzɪŋ kæmˈpeɪn]	Werbekampagne
at all costs [ət ɔːl ˈkɒsts]	um jeden Preis
bulb [bʌlb]	(Glüh)birne
conscious [ˈkɒnʃəs]	bewusst
to contribute [kənˈtrɪbjuːt]	beitragen
contribution [ˌkɒntrɪˈbjuːʃn]	Beitrag
disposal [dɪsˈpəʊzl]	Beseitigung, Entsorgung
emission [ɪˈmɪʃn]	Emission, Ausstoß
emphasis [ˈemfəsɪs]	Betonung
to emphasize [ˈemfəsaɪz]	betonen
environmental [ɪnˌvaɪrənˈmentl]	Umwelt-
in conclusion [ɪn kənˈkluːʒn]	abschließend
to insulate [ˈɪnsjʊleɪt]	isolieren
insulation [ˌɪnsjʊˈleɪʃn]	Isolierung
lighting [ˈlaɪtɪŋ]	Beleuchtung
to manufacture [ˌmænjʊˈfæktʃə]	herstellen
manufacturer [ˌmænjʊˈfæktʃərə]	Hersteller
to meet the growing demand [miːt ðə ˈgrəʊɪŋ dɪˈmɑːnd]	der wachsenden Nachfrage gerecht werden
non-returnable [ˌnɒnrɪˈtɜːnəbl]	Einweg-
once again [wʌns əˈgen]	noch einmal
ozone hole [ˈəʊzəʊn həʊl]	Ozonloch
packaging [ˈpækɪdʒɪŋ]	Verpackung
power station [ˈpaʊə ˌsteɪʃn]	Kraftwerk, Elektrizitätswerk
range [reɪndʒ]	Sortiment, Umfang, Reichweite
reaction [rɪˈækʃn]	Reaktion
recyclable [ˌriːˈsaɪkləbl]	wiederverwertbar
reduction [rɪˈdʌkʃn]	Verminderung
responsibility [rɪˌspɒnsəˈbɪlɪtɪ]	Verantwortung
retailer [ˈriːteɪlə]	Einzelhändler(in)
rubbish [ˈrʌbɪʃ]	Abfall, Müll
so-called [ˌsəʊˈkɔːld]	sogenannt
to turn to [tɜːn tuː]	sich zuwenden
wasteful [ˈweɪstfʊl]	verschwenderisch

A2
additional [əˈdɪʃənl]	zusätzlich
all over the world [ɔːl ˈəʊvə ðə wɜːld]	in der ganzen Welt
CFC [ˌsiːˌefˈsiː]	FCKW (Fluorchlorkohlenwasserstoff)
chemist [ˈkemɪst]	Chemiker(in)
convinced [kənˈvɪnst]	überzeugt
direct speech [daɪˈrekt spiːtʃ]	direkte Rede

disagreement [ˌdɪsəˈɡriːmənt]	abweichende Meinung, Meinungsverschiedenheit	fear [fɪə]	Furcht
elsewhere [ˌelsˈweə]	woanders	mining [ˈmaɪnɪŋ]	Bergbau
furthermore [ˈfɜːðəmɔː]	außerdem	nature [ˈneɪtʃə]	Natur
improvement [ɪmˈpruːvmənt]	Verbesserung	ore [ɔː]	Erz
to maintain [meɪnˈteɪn]	behaupten	recording [rɪˈkɔːdɪŋ]	Aufnahme
ought to [ɔːt tuː]	sollte(n)	summary [ˈsʌməri]	Zusammenfassung
to take the view [teɪk ðə vjuː]	der Ansicht sein	technologist [tekˈnɒlədʒɪst]	Technologe, Technologin
		zinc [zɪŋk]	Zink

C

D2

(not) any more [nɒt / ˌeni ˈmɔː]	nicht länger	attraction [əˈtrækʃn]	Attraktion, Anziehungskraft
approach [əˈprəʊtʃ]	Ansatz, Annäherung	coastal [ˈkəʊstl]	Küsten-
to attack [əˈtæk]	in Angriff nehmen, angreifen	concerned [kənˈsɜːnd]	betroffen, interessiert
by-product [ˈbaɪˌprɒdʌkt]	Nebenprodukt	housing estate [ˈhaʊzɪŋ ɪˌsteɪt]	Siedlung
card [kɑːd]	Karte	issue [ˈɪʃuː]	Thema, Frage
to come true [kʌm truː]	wahr werden	MP (Member of Parliament) [ˌemˈpiː] [ˈmembər əv ˈpɑːləmənt]	Mitglied des Parlaments
to consist of [kənˈsɪst əv]	bestehen aus		
dealer [ˈdiːlə]	Händler(in)	primary school [ˈpraɪməri skuːl]	Grundschule
to dismantle [dɪsˈmæntl]	zerlegen, demontieren	reported speech [rɪˈpɔːtɪd spiːtʃ]	indirekte Rede
(to) dump [dʌmp]	Müllkippe, (Müll) abladen	role [rəʊl]	Rolle
foam [fəʊm]	Schaum	seaside resort [ˈsiːsaɪd rɪˈzɔːt]	Seebad
Friends of the Earth [ˌfrendz əv ðɪ ˈɜːθ]	Name einer Umweltschutzorganisation	surface [ˈsɜːfɪs]	Oberfläche
over and over again [ˈəʊvər ən ˈəʊvər əˈɡen]	immer wieder		

Unit 7

Starter

(to) paraphrase [ˈpærəfreɪz]	Umschreibung; umschreiben	machinery [məˈʃiːnəri]	Maschinen
precise [prɪˈsaɪs]	genau	peat bog [piːt bɒɡ]	Torfmoor
raw [rɔː]	Roh-; roh	resources [rɪˈsɔːsɪz] [rɪˈzɔːsɪz]	Boden-, Naturschätze, Mittel

A1

to re-use [ˌriːˈjuːz]	wiederverwenden	antonym [ˈæntəʊnɪm]	Antonym, Wort mit gegensätzlicher Bedeutung
to recycle [ˌriːˈsaɪkl]	wiederverwerten		
to refer to [rɪˈfɜː tuː]	(sich) beziehen auf	availability [əˌveɪləˈbɪlɪti]	Vorhandensein, Verfügbarkeit
scrap [skræp]	Schrott, Fetzen		
to separate [ˈsepərət]	getrennt	billion [ˈbɪljən]	Billion (Am.: Milliarde)
to shift [ʃɪft]	verlagern	citizen [ˈsɪtɪzn]	Bürger(in)
(to) substitute [ˈsʌbstɪtjuːt]	Ersatz -; ersetzen	developing country [dɪˌveləpɪŋ ˈkʌntri]	Entwicklungsland
supplier [səˈplaɪə]	Lieferant(in)	fossil fuels [ˌfɒsl ˈfjuːəlz]	fossile Brennstoffe
to take to pieces [teɪk tʊ ˈpiːsɪz]	zerlegen	geographical [ˌdʒɪəˈɡræfɪkl]	geographisch
textile [ˈtekstaɪl]	Stoff	global warming [ˌɡləʊbl ˈwɔːmɪŋ]	weltweiter Temperaturanstieg
unknown [ˌʌnˈnəʊn]	unbekannt		
unlikely [ʌnˈlaɪkli]	unwahrscheinlich	to harm [hɑːm]	schädigen
up to now [ʌp tʊ ˈnaʊ]	bis jetzt	industrialized [ɪnˈdʌstrɪəlaɪzd]	industrialisiert
waste management [weɪst ˈmænɪdʒmənt]	Abfallwirtschaft		
		mankind [mænˈkaɪnd]	Menschheit
		plentiful [ˈplentɪfʊl]	reichlich, häufig

D1

countryside [ˈkʌntrisaɪd]	Landschaft
to create [kriːˈeɪt]	schaffen, verursachen
deposit [dɪˈpɒzɪt]	Lagerstätte, Guthaben
ecology [ɪˈkɒlədʒi]	Ökologie

plenty ['plentɪ]	viel, eine Menge	off-the-grid [ˌɒf ðə 'grɪd]	nicht an das Versorgungsnetz angeschlossen
to predict [prɪ'dɪkt]	vorhersagen	panel ['pænl]	Schalttafel
significant [sɪg'nɪfɪkənt]	bedeutend, bedeutsam	photovoltaic (PV) [ˌfəʊtəʊvɒl'teɪɪk] [ˌpiː'viː]	fotoelektrisch
slight [slaɪt]	leicht, schwach, gering	power line ['paʊə laɪn]	(Stark-) Stromleitung
solar power [ˌsəʊlə 'paʊə]	Sonnenenergie	research ['riːsɜːtʃ]	Forschung
source [sɔːs]	Quelle	scientist ['saɪəntɪst]	Wissenschaftler(in)
standard of living ['stændəd əv 'lɪvɪŋ]	Lebensstandard	shower ['ʃaʊə]	Dusche
to take action [teɪk 'ækʃn]	etwas unternehmen	to state [steɪt]	darlegen, vortragen, nennen
total ['təʊtl]	gesamt	subject matter ['sʌbdʒɪkt ˌmætə]	Stoff, Inhalt
to transfer [træns'fɜː]	übertragen	traditional [trə'dɪʃənl]	traditionell, herkömmlich
trillion ['trɪljən]	Trillion (Am.: Billion)	unreliable [ˌʌnrɪ'laɪəbl]	unzuverlässig
what ... like? [wɒt ... laɪk]	wie...?	yearly ['jɪəlɪ]	jährlich

A2

constant ['kɒnstənt]	ständig, gleichbleibend
to drop [drɒp]	fallen, fallen lassen
gradual ['grædjʊəl]	allmählich, sanft (ansteigen, abfallen)
graph [grɑːf]	Schaubild, mathematische Kurve
sharp [ʃɑːp]	scharf, deutlich, steil
stable ['steɪbl]	stabil, dauerhaft
steady ['stedɪ]	stabil, gleichbleibend
substantial [səb'stænʃl]	beträchtlich, erheblich
temperature ['temprətʃə]	Temperatur

D1

boiler room ['bɔɪlə ruːm]	Kesselraum
conversation [ˌkɒnvə'seɪʃn]	Unterhaltung, Gespräch
crane [kreɪn]	Kran
delivery hall [dɪ'lɪvrɪ hɔːl]	Auslieferungshalle
fertilizer ['fɜːtəlaɪzə]	Dünger
to fix [fɪks]	vorhaben, organisieren
furnace ['fɜːnɪs]	Ofen
generator ['dʒenəreɪtə]	Generator, Lichtmaschine
manure [mə'njʊə]	Dung
megawatt ['megəwɒt]	Megawatt
neat [niːt]	ordentlich, gelungen, schlau
output ['aʊtpʊt]	(Produktions-)Leistung
pit [pɪt]	Grube
steam [stiːm]	Dampf
storage ['stɔːrɪdʒ]	Lagerung, Aufbewahrung
straight in [streɪt ɪn]	(gerade) direkt hinein
turbine ['tɜːbaɪn]	Turbine

C

approval [ə'pruːvl]	Zustimmung
to argue ['ɑːgjuː]	streiten, hier: behaupten
as a result [əz ə rɪ'zʌlt]	folglich
beer [bɪə]	Bier
cell [sel]	Zelle
consequently ['kɒnsɪkwəntlɪ]	folglich
to dig [dɪg]	graben
domestic [də'mestɪk]	häuslich
e.g. [ˌiː'dʒiː] [fər ɪg'zɑːmpl]	z. B. (zum Beispiel)
to generate ['dʒenəreɪt]	erzeugen
grid [grɪd]	Versorgungsnetz
highway ['haɪweɪ]	Landstraße
hydro ['haɪdrəʊ]	Wasser-
in the mid [ɪn ðə 'mɪd]	in der Mitte von, Mitte der ...
introductory [ˌɪntrə'dʌktərɪ]	einleitend
key point [kiː pɔɪnt]	springender Punkt
to light, lit, lit [laɪt lɪt lɪt]	anzünden, (be)leuchten
maintenance ['meɪntənəns]	Wartung, Instandhaltung
majority [mə'dʒɒrətɪ]	Mehrheit
maker ['meɪkə]	Hersteller(in)
measure ['meʒə]	Maßnahme
minority [maɪ'nɒrətɪ]	Minderheit

D2

ash [æʃ]	Asche
competitive [kəm'petətɪv]	wettbewerbsfähig
greenhouse ['griːnhaʊs]	Treibhaus, Gewächshaus
man-power ['mænˌpaʊə]	Arbeitskräfte
ton [tʌn]	Tonne

Unit 8

A1

again and again [ə'gen ən ə'gen]	immer wieder
all kind(s) of [ɔːl 'kaɪndz əv]	alle Arten von, alle möglichen
to automate ['ɔːtəmeɪt]	automatisieren
automatic [ˌɔːtə'mætɪk]	automatisch

available [əˈveɪləbl]	verfügbar, vorhanden	lean management [liːn ˈmænɪdʒmənt]	„schlankes" Management
civilized [ˈsɪvɪlaɪzd]	zivilisiert	monotonous [məˈnɒtənəs]	eintönig, monoton
CIM (Computer Integrated Manufacture) [ˌsiːˌaɪˈem] [kəmˈpjuːtər ˌɪntɪgreɪtɪd ˌmænjʊˈfæktʃə]	computerintegrierte Fertigung	opportunity [ɒpəˈtjuːnəti]	Gelegenheit, Möglichkeit
		to perform [pəˈfɔːm]	ausführen, vollbringen
		personnel [ˌpɜːsəˈnel]	Personal
designer [dɪˈzaɪnə]	Zeichner(in), Designer(in)	production line [prəˈdʌkʃn laɪn]	Fertigungsstraße, Fließband
economical [ˌiːkəˈnɒmɪkl]	sparsam, wirtschaftlich	repetitive [rɪˈpetətɪv]	(sich) wiederholend, eintönig
etc. (et cetera) [ˌiːˌtiːˈsiː] [ɪtˈsetərə]	und so weiter		
fault [fɔːlt]	Fehler, Schuld, Mangel	schedule [ˈʃedjuːl]	(Zeit-, Fahr-) Plan; Programm
feedback [ˈfiːdbæk]	Rückmeldung, Feedback		
latest [ˈleɪtɪst]	der, die, das Neueste	style [staɪl]	Stil, Art
to link together [lɪŋk təˈgeðə]	miteinander verbinden	union [ˈjuːnjən]	Gewerkschaft
		unit [ˈjuːnɪt]	Einheit, Gruppe
particular [pəˈtɪkjʊlə]	besonderer, -e, -es	**C2**	
productivity [ˌprɒdʌkˈtɪvəti]	Produktivität, Leistungsfähigkeit	to adjust [əˈdʒʌst]	einstellen
		to eject [ɪˈdʒekt]	auswerfen
research department [ˈriːsɜːtʃ dɪˈpɑːtmənt]	Forschungsabteilung	infinitive [ɪnˈfɪnətɪv]	Infinitiv, Grundform
		modal [ˈməʊdl]	(modales) Hilfsverb
robot [ˈrəʊbɒt]	Roboter, vollautomatische Vorrichtung	model [ˈmɒdl]	Modell
		passive [ˈpæsɪv]	Passiv
shop floor [ˈʃɒp flɔː]	Produktionsstätte, -halle	recording instruction [rɪˈkɔːdɪŋ ɪnˈstrʌkʃn]	Aufnahmeanleitung
to simulate [ˈsɪmjʊleɪt]	simulieren		
term [tɜːm]	Ausdruck, Wort	to reset [ˌriːˈset]	zurückstellen
(to) touch [tʌtʃ]	Berührung; berühren	to rewind [ˌriːˈwaɪnd]	zurückspulen
unsuitable [ˌʌnˈsjuːtəbl]	unpassend, ungeeignet	volume [ˈvɒljuːm]	Lautstärke
A2		**D 1**	
to assemble [əˈsembl]	zusammenbauen	to print [prɪnt]	drucken
bumper [ˈbʌmpə]	Stoßstange	printer [ˈprɪntə]	Drucker
car body [kɑː ˈbɒdi]	Karosserie	resolution [ˌrezəˈluːʃn]	Auflösung
exhaust pipe [ɪgˈzɔːst paɪp]	Auspuffrohr	**D 2**	
to fit [fɪt]	einbauen, anbringen	cartridge [ˈkɑːtrɪdʒ]	Kassette, Patrone
gearbox [ˈgɪəbɒks]	Getriebe	connector [kəˈnektə]	Verbinder, Stecker
headlight [ˈhedlaɪt]	Scheinwerfer	cover [ˈkʌvə]	Abdeckung
(to) spray [spreɪ]	Spray; sprühen, spritzen, lackieren	handbook [ˈhændbʊk]	Handbuch
		ink [ɪŋk]	Tinte
to weld [weld]	schweißen	ink jet printer [ˈɪŋkdʒet ˈprɪntə]	Tintenstrahldrucker
C1		installation [ˌɪnstəˈleɪʃn]	Installation, Anschluss
to arrange [əˈreɪndʒ]	aufstellen, planen, veranlassen	interface [ˈɪntəfeɪs]	Schnittstelle
		to make sure [meɪk ʃʊə]	sich überzeugen
arrangement [əˈreɪndʒmənt]	Vereinbarung, Arrangement	to mix up [mɪks ʌp]	vertauschen
		to remove [rɪˈmuːv]	entfernen
customer-orientated [ˈkʌstəmər ˈɔːrɪənteɪtɪd]	kundenorientiert	(to) screw [skruː]	Schraube; schrauben
		to snap [snæp]	einrasten
decision-making process [dɪˈsɪʒn ˌmeɪkɪŋ ˈprəʊses]	Entscheidungsprozess	to take off [teɪk ɒf]	abnehmen
		tape [teɪp]	Band, Klebestreifen
to dominate [ˈdɒmɪneɪt]	beherrschen, dominieren	to tighten [ˈtaɪtn]	(fest) anziehen, verschärfen
flexibility [ˌfleksəˈbɪləti]	Flexibilität		
inflexible [ɪnˈfleksəbl]	unflexibel		
Japanese [ˌdʒæpəˈniːz]	Japaner(in); japanisch		

Unit 9

A1

shipbuilding [ˈʃɪpˌbɪldɪŋ]		Schiffbau
shipyard [ˈʃɪpjɑːd]		Werft
steel [stiːl]		Stahl

A2

to achieve [əˈtʃiːv]	erreichen, erzielen
arms [ɑːmz]	Waffen
corporation [ˌkɔːpəˈreɪʃn]	Gesellschaft, Körperschaft
decade [ˈdekeɪd]	Jahrzehnt, Dekade
managing director [ˈmænɪdʒɪŋ daɪˈrektə]	Geschäftsführer(in)
to occupy [ˈɒkjupaɪ]	einnehmen, besetzen, beschäftigen
official [əˈfɪʃl]	offiziell; Beamter, Beamtin, Funktionär
outstanding [ˌaʊtˈstændɪŋ]	hervorragend, außergewöhnlich
site [saɪt]	Grundstück, Sitz, Standort
square [skweə]	Quadrat
to take over [teɪk ˈəʊvə]	übernehmen

C

to accuse [əˈkjuːz]	beschuldigen, anklagen
Austria [ˈɒstrɪə]	Österreich
(to) boycott [ˈbɔɪkɒt]	Boykott; boykottieren
capacity [kəˈpæsəti]	Kapazität, Leistungsfähigkeit
to correspond [ˌkɒrɪˈspɒnd]	entsprechen, übereinstimmen, korrespondieren
(to) decline [dɪˈklaɪn]	Niedergang, Verschlechterung; sich verschlechtern, sinken
desperate [ˈdespərət]	verzweifelt
disaster [dɪˈzɑːstə]	Katastrophe
extreme [ɪkˈstriːm]	extrem, äußerst, höchst
(to) gain [geɪn]	Gewinn; gewinnen
global [ˈgləʊbl]	global, weltweit
to go on strike [gəʊ ɒn straɪk]	in den Streik treten
household appliance [ˈhaʊshəʊld əˈplaɪəns]	Haushaltsgerät
in contrast [ɪn ˈkɒntrɑːst]	im Gegensatz
investment [ɪnˈvestmənt]	Investition, (Kapital-)Anlage
jobless [ˈdʒɒbləs]	arbeitslos
to lower [ˈləʊə]	senken, herabsetzen
nationwide [ˈneɪʃnwaɪd]	landesweit
point of view [pɔɪnt əv ˈvjuː]	Standpunkt
rate [reɪt]	Rate, (Prozent-)Satz
reminder [rɪˈmaɪndə]	Erinnerung, Mahnung
to steal [stiːl]	stehlen
striker [ˈstraɪkə]	Streikende(r)
suitable [ˈsjuːtəbl]	passend, geeignet
to take away [teɪk əˈweɪ]	wegnehmen
topic [ˈtɒpɪk]	Thema
unusual [ˌʌnˈjuːʒʊəl]	ungewöhnlich
vacuum-cleaner [ˈvækjəːmˌkliːnə]	Staubsauger
Vienna [vɪˈenə]	Wien
winner [ˈwɪnə]	Gewinner(in)
working week [ˈwɜːkɪŋ wiːk]	Arbeitswoche

D

access [ˈækses]	Zugang, Zutritt
assistance [əˈsɪstəns]	Hilfe
back-up [ˈbækʊp]	Unterstützung
bright [braɪt]	hell, strahlend
car park [ˈkɑːpɑːk]	Parkplatz
colleague [ˈkɒliːg]	Kollege, Kollegin
council [ˈkaʊnsl]	(Stadt-, Grafschafts-)Rat
county [ˈkaʊnti]	Grafschaft, Bezirk
current [ˈkʌrənt]	aktuell, gegenwärtig
developer [dɪˈveləpə]	Entwickler(in), Bauunternehmer(in)
extract [ˈekstrækt]	Auszug, Extrakt
facility [fəˈsɪləti]	Einrichtung, Möglichkeit
high class [ˌhaɪˈklɑːs]	hochwertig, erstklassig
housing [ˈhaʊzɪŋ]	Unterkunft, Wohnungen
literature [ˈlɪtrətʃə]	Literatur, Informationsmaterial
location [ləʊˈkeɪʃn]	Lage, Standort
out of town [aʊt əv ˈtaʊn]	außerhalb der Stadt
permission [pəˈmɪʃn]	Erlaubnis
phone call [ˈfəʊnkɔːl]	Anruf
prosperous [ˈprɒspərəs]	erfolgreich, florierend
racing bicycle [ˈreɪsɪŋ ˌbaɪsɪkl]	Rennrad
region [ˈriːdʒən]	Gebiet, Bezirk
to relocate [ˌriːləʊˈkeɪt]	(Geschäftssitz) verlegen
requirement [rɪˈkwaɪəmənt]	Bedarf, Erfordernis
shopping [ˈʃɒpɪŋ]	Einkauf(en)
skilled [skɪld]	qualifiziert, ausgebildet
standard [ˈstændəd]	Niveau, Standard, Maßstab
up to [ʊp tuː]	bis zu

Unit 10

Starter

China [ˈtʃaɪnə]	China
Dominican Republic [dəˈmɪnɪkən rɪˈpʌblɪk]	Dominikanische Republik
Hungary [ˈhʌŋgəri]	Ungarn
immigration [ˌɪmɪˈgreɪʃn]	Einwanderung

143

legal ['li:gl]	legal, gesetzlich zulässig	illegal [ɪ'li:gl]	illegal, gesetzlich unzulässig
means [mi:nz]	Mittel, Möglichkeiten	India ['ɪndɪə]	Indien
Mexico ['meksɪkəʊ]	Mexiko	Latin America [ˌlætɪn_ə'merɪkə]	Lateinamerika
Philippines ['fɪlɪpi:nz]	Philippinen	to loot [lu:t]	plündern
Russia ['rʌʃə]	Russland	Mexican ['meksɪkən]	Mexikaner(in); mexikanisch

A1

Amerasian [ˌæmər'eɪʒn]	amerikanisch-asiatisch	Poland ['pəʊlənd]	Polen
childhood ['tʃaɪldhʊd]	Kindheit	Pole ['pəʊl]	Pole, Polin
Chinese [tʃaɪ'ni:z]	Chinese(in); chinesisch	Polish ['pəʊlɪʃ]	polnisch
cookie ['kʊkɪ]	Keks, Plätzchen	riot ['raɪət]	Aufruhr, Krawall
courage ['kʌrɪdʒ]	Mut	tension ['tenʃn]	Spannung
determination [dɪˌtɜ:mɪ'neɪʃn]	Entschlossenheit, Bestimmung		
down payment [ˌdaʊn_'peɪmənt]	Anzahlung	**C**	
		circle ['sɜ:kl]	Kreis, Kreislauf
drawer ['drɔ:ə]	Zeichner(in)	confirm [kən'fɜ:m]	bestätigen
to emigrate ['emɪgreɪt]	auswandern	corn [kɔ:n]	Getreide, Mais, Korn
emigration [ˌemɪ'greɪʃn]	Auswanderung	culture ['kʌltʃə]	Kultur
existence [ɪg'zɪstəns]	Existenz, Dasein	(to) draft [drɑ:ft]	Entwurf, Konzept; entwerfen
fashionable ['fæʃnəbl]	modisch	earnings ['ɜ:nɪŋz]	Einkommen, Verdienst, Ertrag
to flee [fli:]	fliehen, flüchten		
to frighten ['fraɪtn]	erschrecken, Angst machen	economist [ɪ'kɒnəmɪst]	Wirtschaftswissenschaftler(in)
to grow up [grəʊ_ʌp]	aufwachsen		
happiness ['hæpɪnɪs]	Glück, Heiterkeit, Zufriedenheit	food stamp [fu:d_stæmp]	Essensmarke
		in the long run [ɪn_ðə_'lɒŋ_rʌn]	auf lange Sicht
hopeful ['həʊpfʊl]	zuversichtlich, vielversprechend		
		innocence ['ɪnəsəns]	Unschuld
identity [aɪ'dentətɪ]	Identität, Übereinstimmung	long-term ['lɒŋtɜ:m]	langfristig
		native-born [ˌneɪtɪv'bɔ:n]	gebürtig
to integrate ['ɪntɪgreɪt]	integrieren	non- [nɒn]	Nicht-
operator ['ɒpəreɪtə]	(Maschinen-)Bediener(in), Telefonvermittler(in)	obvious ['ɒbvɪəs]	offensichtlich
		persecution [ˌpɜ:sɪ'kju:ʃn]	Verfolgung
original [ə'rɪdʒənl]	ursprünglich, originell	poll [pəʊl]	Umfrage, Abstimmung, Wahl
outsider [ˌaʊt'saɪdə]	Außenseiter(in)		
possession [pə'zeʃn]	Besitz	to recover [rɪ'kʌvə]	sich erholen
quotation [kwəʊ'teɪʃn]	Zitat; Kostenvoranschlag	short-term ['ʃɔ:ttɜ:m]	kurzfristig
sceptical ['skeptɪkl]	skeptisch	society [sə'saɪətɪ]	Gesellschaft
soldier ['səʊldʒə]	Soldat	structure ['strʌktʃə]	Struktur
title ['taɪtl]	Titel	theory ['θɪərɪ]	Theorie
Vietnamese [ˌvjetnə'mi:z]	Vietnamese, Vietnamesin, vietnamesisch	unemployment benefit [ˌʌnɪm'plɔɪmənt_'benɪfɪt]	Arbeitslosenunterstützung
visa ['vi:zə]	Visum	version ['vɜ:ʃn]	Version, Fassung
Warsaw ['wɔ:sɔ:]	Warschau	welfare ['welfeə]	Wohl, Wohlfahrt, Sozialhilfe
		word-by-word [ˌwɜ:d_baɪ_'wɜ:d]	Wort für Wort
A2			
(to) arrest [ə'rest]	verhaften; Verhaftung	worried ['wʌrɪd]	besorgt
Asian ['eɪʒn]	Asiat(in); asiatisch		
Colombia [kə'lɒmbɪə]	Kolumbien	**D1**	
community [kə'mju:nətɪ]	Bevölkerungsgruppe, Gemeinde	climate ['klaɪmət]	Klima
		way of life [weɪ_əv_'laɪf]	Lebensweise
Cuba ['kju:bə]	Kuba		
entry ['entrɪ]	Einreise, Eingang, Eintritt		
former Soviet Union ['fɔ:mə ˌsəʊvɪət_'ju:njən]	ehemalige Sowjetunion		

D2

editor ['edɪtə]	Herausgeber(in), Redakteur(in)
to face (a problem) [feɪs / ə 'prɒbləm]	(einem Problem) gegenüberstehen
to publish ['pʌblɪʃ]	veröffentlichen

Further Reading 1
Free time
Computer games defended

ability [ə'bɪlətɪ]	Fähigkeit
(to) ache [eɪk]	Schmerz; schmerzen
to acquire [ə'kwaɪə]	sich aneignen
addictive [ə'dɪktɪv]	süchtig machend
aggressive [ə'ɡresɪv]	aggressiv
amusement arcade [ə'mjuːzmənt ɑː'keɪd]	Spielhalle
assertiveness [ə'sɜːtɪvnəs]	Selbstbewusstsein
behaviour [bɪ'heɪvjə]	Benehmen
to be bound (to do sth.) [baʊnd]	(etwas) bestimmt (tun); verpflichtet, unterwegs
cardiologist [ˌkɑːdɪ'ɒlədʒɪst]	Herzspezialist(in)
(to) claim [kleɪm]	Anspruch; behaupten, beanspruchen
concentration [ˌkɒnsən'treɪʃn]	Konzentration
critical ['krɪtɪkl]	kritisch
defender [dɪ'fendə]	Verteidiger(in)
enthusiasm [ɪn'θjuːzɪæzm]	Begeisterung, Enthusiasmus
enthusiast [ɪn'θjuːzɪæst]	Begeisterte(r), Enthusiast(in)
epilepsy ['epɪlepsɪ]	Epilepsie
especial [ɪ'speʃl]	besondere(r)
excitement [ɪk'saɪtmənt]	Aufregung, Begeisterung
fanatic [fə'nætɪk]	Fanatiker(in); fanatisch
fascination [ˌfæsɪ'neɪʃn]	Faszination
gadget ['ɡædʒɪt]	Gerät, Apparat
galactic [ɡə'læktɪk]	Weltraum-; galaktisch
(to) grip [ɡrɪp]	Griff, Halt; (er-)greifen, fesseln
heart attack [hɑːt ə'tæk]	Herzanfall
hypnotic [hɪp'nɒtɪk]	hypnotisch
to induce [ɪn'djuːs]	verursachen, herbeiführen
to involve [ɪn'vɒlv]	beteiligen, verwickeln
memory ['memərɪ]	Gedächtnis
to neglect [nɪ'ɡlekt]	vernachlässigen
pain [peɪn]	Schmerz
patience ['peɪʃəns]	Geduld
player ['pleɪə]	Spieler(in)
predictable [prɪ'dɪktəbl]	vorhersagbar, vorhersehbar
pressure ['preʃə]	Druck
(to) punch [pʌntʃ]	Schlag; schlagen
to soar [sɔː]	(stark) ansteigen
social ['səʊʃl]	gesellschaftlich, sozial
speedy ['spiːdɪ]	schnell
to stare [steə]	starren
to tend [tend]	tendieren
unable [ˌʌn'eɪbl]	nicht in der Lage (sein)
undesirable [ˌʌndɪ'zaɪərəbl]	unerwünscht
(to) urge [ɜːdʒ]	Drang; drängen
vital ['vaɪtl]	lebenswichtig, entscheidend
(to) wonder ['wʌndə]	Wunder; sich fragen, sich wundern
to worry ['wʌrɪ]	sich sorgen, beunruhigen

Further Reading 2
Sports
The crying game

Achilles tendon [ə'kɪliːz 'tendən]	Achillessehne
ambition [æm'bɪʃn]	Ehrgeiz, Ambition
asset ['æset]	Vermögen(-swert), Besitz
bone [bəʊn]	Knochen
common ['kɒmən]	gemeinsam, gewöhnlich, verbreitet
complication [ˌkɒmplɪ'keɪʃn]	Komplikation
director [daɪ'rektə]	Leiter(in), Direktor(in), Regisseur(in)
disorder [dɪs'ɔːdə]	Durcheinander, Funktionsstörung
dumping ground ['dʌmpɪŋ ɡraʊnd]	Müllabladeplatz
eventual(ly) [ɪ'ventʃʊəl / ɪ'ventʃʊəlɪ]	am Ende, schließlich
exposed [ɪk'spəʊzd]	ungeschützt, ausgesetzt
extension [ɪk'stenʃn]	(Aus-)Strecken, Verlängerung
to fade (away) [feɪd / feɪd ə'weɪ]	verblassen, nachlassen, verwelken
fairytale ['feərɪteɪl]	Märchen
footballer ['fʊtbɔːlə]	Fußballspieler(in)
glory ['ɡlɔːrɪ]	Ruhm
guilty ['ɡɪltɪ]	schuldig
injury ['ɪndʒərɪ]	Verletzung
jersey ['dʒɜːzɪ]	Trikot
kit [kɪt]	Ausrüstung, Bausatz, Set
knee-cap ['niːkæp]	Kniescheibe
league [liːɡ]	Liga
ligament ['lɪɡəmənt]	Band (z. B. am Knie)
minor ['maɪnə]	kleiner, weniger bedeutend, leicht
minus ['maɪnəs]	minus, ohne, abzüglich

to occur [əˈkɜː]	auftreten
over-training [ˌəʊvəˈtreɪnɪŋ]	zu häufiges Training
over-use [ˌəʊvəˈjuːs]	zu häufiger Gebrauch
to peak [piːk]	seine Spitzenform erreichen
permanent [ˈpɜːmənənt]	(be)ständig, bleibend
pitch [pɪtʃ]	Spielfeld
podiatry [ˈpəʊdɪətrɪ]	Lehre von den Fußkrankheiten
to punish [ˈpʌnɪʃ]	(be)strafen
punishing [ˈpʌnɪʃɪŋ]	mörderisch, hart
to quit [kwɪt]	verlassen, aufhören, aufgeben
related [rɪˈleɪtɪd]	verwandt
rotation [rəʊˈteɪʃn]	Drehung
(to) score [skɔː]	Spielstand; (Treffer) erzielen
to sever [ˈsevə]	durchtrennen, abbrechen
to shake (off) [ʃeɪk ɒf]	(ab)schütteln
short cut [ˈʃɔːtkʌt]	Abkürzung
somewhere [ˈsʌmweə]	irgendwo, ungefähr
strap [stræp]	Riemen, Träger, Bandage
syndrome [ˈsɪndrəʊm]	Syndrom
throughout [θruːˈaʊt]	die ganze Zeit, stets
(to) trace [treɪs]	Spur; nachgehen, nachspüren
unavoidable [ˌʌnəˈvɔɪdəbl]	unvermeidbar

Further Reading 3

Tourism

Tourists resort to all the comforts of home

accommodation [əˌkɒməˈdeɪʃn]	Unterkunft, Zimmer
affinity [əˈfɪnətɪ]	Verbundenheit, Verwandtschaft
affordable [əˈfɔːdəbl]	erschwinglich
all but [ɔːl bʌt]	fast
all-inclusive [ˌɔːlɪnˈkluːsɪv]	alles beinhaltend
booking [ˈbʊkɪŋ]	Buchung
by far [baɪ ˈfɑː]	bei weitem
to cater to [ˈkeɪtə tuː]	ausgerichtet sein auf
copy [ˈkɒpɪ]	(Zeitungs)Exemplar
Crete [kriːt]	Kreta
cricket pitch [ˈkrɪkɪt pɪtʃ]	Kricketfeld
cultural shock [ˈkʌltʃərəl ʃɒk]	Kulturschock
effort [ˈefət]	Anstrengung, Mühe, Versuch
embassy [ˈembəsɪ]	Botschaft
expansion [ɪkˈspænʃn]	Ausweitung
to fulfil [fʊlˈfɪl]	erfüllen, entsprechen
to go to the greatest lengths [gəʊ tʊ ðə ˈgreɪtɪst leŋkθs]	sich die größte Mühe geben
to head off [hed ɒf]	(hin-)fahren (nach), losfahren
holidaymaker [ˈhɒlɪdɪˌmeɪkə]	Urlauber(in)
home from home [həʊm frəm həʊm]	zweites Zuhause
(to be) inclined (to do sth.) [biː ɪnˈklaɪnd]	(dazu) neigen, (etwas zu tun)
(to feel) left out [fiːl left ˈaʊt]	(sich) ausgeschlossen (fühlen)
likely [ˈlaɪklɪ]	wahrscheinlich
lined with [laɪnd wɪð]	gesäumt von
loaded with [ˈləʊdɪd wɪð]	überladen mit
menu [ˈmenjuː]	Speisekarte
migratory habits [maɪˈgreɪtərɪ ˈhæbɪts]	Reisegewohnheiten
to outdo [ˌaʊtˈduː]	übertreffen, überbieten
package tour [ˈpækɪdʒ tʊə]	Pauschalreise
(in) preference (to) [ɪn ˈprefrəns tuː]	(unter) Bevorzugung (von)
proliferation [prəʊˌlɪfəˈreɪʃn]	Ausbreitung, Umsichgreifen
pronounced [prəˈnaʊnst]	ausgeprägt, deutlich
purpose-built [ˈpɜːpəs bɪlt]	eigens zu diesem Zweck angefertigt
rack [ræk]	Ständer, Regal
recovery [rɪˈkʌvərɪ]	Erholung
reference (to) [ˈrefrəns tuː]	hier: Anspielung (auf)
to reflect [rɪˈflekt]	widerspiegeln
resort [rɪˈzɔːt]	Urlaubsort
revival [rɪˈvaɪvl]	Wiederaufleben, (-aufblühen)
Rhodes [rəʊdz]	Rhodos
romantic [rəʊˈmæntɪk]	romantisch
sausage [ˈsɒsɪdʒ]	Wurst
scramble [ˈskræmbl]	Gerangel, Gedränge
spokesman [ˈspəʊksmən]	Sprecher
to squeeze [skwiːz]	sich drängen, quetschen
tent [tent]	Zelt
tourism [ˈtʊərɪzəm]	Tourismus
tourist board [ˈtʊərɪst bɔːd]	Fremdenverkehrsamt
ultimate [ˈʌltɪmət]	vollendet, perfekt
underline [ˌʌndəˈlaɪn]	unterstreichen

Exam Preparation

Unit 11

A

acceleration [əkˌseləˈreɪʃn]	Beschleunigung
anti-lock brake [ˌæntɪˈlɒk breɪk]	Antiblockierbremse
aspect [ˈæspekt]	Aspekt
assembly line [əˈsemblɪ laɪn]	Fließband
automobile [ˈɔːtəməbiːl]	Auto (Am.)

based on [beɪst_ɒn]	basierend, gegründet auf	in the first place [ɪn_ðə_'fɜːst_pleɪs]	zuerst
brake [breɪk]	Bremse	to promote [prə'məʊt]	(be)fördern, Werbung machen für
car maker ['kɑː_ˌmeɪkə]	Automobilhersteller	to recharge [ˌriː'tʃɑːdʒ]	(wieder)aufladen
carbon dioxide [ˌkɑːbən_daɪ'ɒksaɪd]	Kohlendioxyd	scrap heap [skræp_hiːp]	Müll-, Schutt-, Schrotthaufen
(to) challenge ['tʃælɪndʒ]	Herausforderung; herausfordern	zero ['zɪərəʊ]	null
combustion [kəm'bʌstʃn]	Verbrennung	**C**	
concept ['kɒnsept]	Konzept, Entwurf	to accompany [ə'kʌmpəni]	begleiten
to consider [kən'sɪdə]	betrachten, denken (an), berücksichtigen	carburettor [ˌkɑːbə'retə]	Vergaser
contradictory [ˌkɒntrə'dɪktəri]	widersprechend, widersprüchlich	coil [kɔɪl]	(Zünd-)Spule
crush zone ['krʌʃ_zəʊn]	Knautschzone	combustion chamber [kəm'bʌstʃn_'tʃeɪmbə]	Brennkammer
to demonstrate ['demənstreɪt]	demonstrieren	to compress [kəm'pres]	komprimieren
drawing board ['drɔːɪŋ_bɔːd]	Zeichenbrett	compression [kəm'preʃn]	Kompression, Verdichtung
dual ['djuːəl]	Doppel-; doppelt	crankshaft ['kræŋkʃɑːft]	Kurbelwelle
to evolve [ɪ'vɒlv]	(sich) entwickeln	cylinder ['sɪlɪndə]	Zylinder
flair [fleə]	Flair, Gespür, Talent, Begabung	damp [dæmp]	feucht
		to distribute [dɪ'strɪbjuːt]	verteilen
forerunner ['fɔːˌrʌnə]	Vorläufer	distributor [dɪ'strɪbjʊtə]	Verteiler
guideline ['gaɪdlaɪn]	Richtlinie	four-stroke engine ['fɔːstrəʊk_'endʒɪn]	Viertaktmotor
hybrid ['haɪbrɪd]	Hybrid-, Misch-, Kreuzung, Mischung	to ignite [ɪg'naɪt]	zünden
hydrogen ['haɪdrədʒən]	Wasserstoff	ignition [ɪg'nɪʃn]	Zündung
in charge of [ɪn_'tʃɑːdʒ_əv]	verantwortlich für	intake ['ɪnteɪk]	Aufnahme, Ansaugen
		lead [liːd]	Leitungskabel, Zuleitung
to intend [ɪn'tend]	beabsichtigen	lifeless ['laɪfləs]	leblos
internal combustion engine [ɪnˌtɜːnl_kəm'bʌstʃn_'endʒɪn]	Verbrennungsmotor	mixture ['mɪkstʃə]	Mischung
		piston ['pɪstən]	Kolben
kph [ˌkeɪpiː'eɪtʃ] ['kɪləʊˌmiːtəz_pər_'aʊə]	km/h (Kilometer pro Stunde)	piston rod ['pɪstən_rɒd]	Pleuel-/Kolbenstange
		silencer ['saɪlənsə]	Schalldämpfer
litre ['liːtə]	Liter	spark [spɑːk]	(Zünd-)Funke
methane ['miːθeɪn]	Methan(-gas)	spark plug ['spɑːkplʌg]	Zündkerze
mobility [məʊ'bɪləti]	Mobilität	stage [steɪdʒ]	Phase, Stadium, Bühne
rape seed [reɪp_siːd]	Rapssamen	stroke [strəʊk]	Schlag, Hub
regulation [ˌregjʊ'leɪʃn]	Vorschriften, Regelungen	to suck [sʌk]	(an)saugen
seemingly ['siːmɪŋli]	offensichtlich, scheinbar	to turn over [tɜːn_əʊvə]	laufen (Motor)
side impact beam [ˌsaɪd_'ɪmpækt biːm]	Seitenaufprallschutz	voltage ['vəʊltɪdʒ]	elektrische Spannung
spirit ['spɪrɪt]	Geist(eshaltung), Sinn, Einstellung		

Unit 12

A

to standardize ['stændədaɪz]	standardisieren
tough [tʌf]	streng, zäh
unimportant [ˌʌnɪm'pɔːtənt]	unwichtig

B

cheerful ['tʃɪəfʊl]	fröhlich, heiter
to fall asleep [fɔːl_ə'sliːp]	einschlafen
to ignore [ɪg'nɔː]	ignorieren, nicht beachten

action ['ækʃn]	Maßnahme, Handlung
addition [ə'dɪʃn]	Hinzufügen, Ergänzung, Addition
ahead [ə'hed]	vor, voraus
air-conditioning ['eəkənˌdɪʃnɪŋ]	Klimaanlage, Klimatisierung
altogether [ˌɔːltə'geðə]	insgesamt, völlig
anywhere ['eniweə]	überall(hin), wo(hin) auch immer
appearance [ə'pɪərəns]	Erscheinung, Aussehen
beauty ['bjuːti]	Schönheit

blade [bleɪd]	Blatt, Schaufel, Klinge
coal-fired ['kəʊlfaɪəd]	mit Kohle betrieben
conventional [kən'venʃnl]	herkömmlich, konventionell
daffodil ['dæfədɪl]	Narzisse
decibel ['desɪbel]	Dezibel (Maß für Lautstärke)
to disturb [dɪ'stɜːb]	stören
double-glazed [,dʌbl'gleɪzd]	doppelt verglast
to eliminate [ɪ'lɪmɪneɪt]	beseitigen
gear [gɪə]	Getriebe, Gang
geo-thermal [,dʒiːəʊ'θɜːml]	geothermisch (Erdwärme nutzend)
goal [gəʊl]	Ziel, Tor
hydro-electric [,haɪdrəʊɪ'lektrɪk]	hydroelektrisch (Wasserkraft nutzend)
landscape ['lændskeɪp]	Landschaft
mechanism ['mekənɪzm]	Mechanismus
negative ['negətɪv]	negativ
nuclear ['njuːklɪə]	Kern-, Atom-; nuklear
positive ['pɒzətɪv]	positiv
potential [pə'tenʃl]	Potential, Möglichkeiten
to spoil [spɔɪl]	verderben, ruinieren
toxic ['tɒksɪk]	giftig
ugly ['ʌglɪ]	hässlich
unwilling [,ʌn'wɪlɪŋ]	nicht bereit (etwas zu tun), widerwillig
visual ['vɪʒʊəl]	visuell, optisch
to wake (up) [weɪk ʌp]	aufwachen, wecken
wave [weɪv]	Welle
Welsh [welʃ]	walisisch
windy ['wɪndɪ]	windig

B

anyway ['enɪweɪ]	sowieso, wie dem auch sei, jedenfalls
apparent [ə'pærənt]	offensichtlich, offenbar
critic ['krɪtɪk]	Kritiker(in)
fund [fʌnd]	Fond, Fundus, Mittel
furious ['fjʊərɪəs]	wütend, wild, heftig
remote [rɪ'məʊt]	entfernt, abgelegen

C

Central Electricity Generating Board (CEGB) ['sentrəl ɪlek'trɪsətɪ 'dʒenəreɪtɪŋ bɔːd] [,siː,iː,dʒiː'biː]	etwa: Zentrale Energieversorgung (England und Wales)
heavy industry ['hevɪ 'ɪndəstrɪ]	Schwerindustrie
light industry [laɪt 'ɪndəstrɪ]	Leichtindustrie
prime energy [praɪm 'enədʒɪ]	Primärenergie
pylon ['paɪlɒn]	Mast
sub-station ['sʌb,steɪʃn]	Umspannungswerk
transformator [,trænsfə'meɪtə]	Umwandler
transmission cable [trænz'mɪʃn ,keɪbl]	Leitungskabel
various ['veərɪəs]	verschieden, vielfältig

Unit 13

A

air-conditioner ['eəkən,dɪʃnə]	Klimaanlage
ally ['ælaɪ]	Verbündete(r); verbünden
atmosphere ['ætməsfɪə]	Atmosphäre
attempt [ə'tempt]	Versuch
aware [ə'weə]	bewusst
bather ['beɪðə]	Badende(r)
centigrade ['sentɪgreɪd]	Celsius
chemical ['kemɪkl]	chemisch
chlorofluorocarbon CFC [,klɔːrəʊ,flʊərəʊ'kɑːbən] [,siː,ef'siː]	Fluorchlorkohlenwasserstoff (FCKW)
CO_2 [,siː,əʊ'tuː]	Kohlendioxyd
confrontation [,kɒnfrʌn'teɪʃn]	Konfrontation
to confront [kən'frʌnt]	gegenüberstellen, konfrontieren
consequence ['kɒnsɪkwəns]	Folge, Konsequenz
dinosaur ['daɪnəsɔː]	Dinosaurier
English Channel [,ɪŋglɪʃ 'tʃænl]	Ärmelkanal
evolution [,iːvə'luːʃn]	Entwicklung, Evolution
exaggeration [ɪg,zædʒə'reɪʃn]	Übertreibung
extinction [ɪk'stɪŋkʃn]	Aussterben
flame [fleɪm]	Flamme
(to) flood [flʌd]	Flut; überschwemmen
for better or for worse [fə 'betər ə fə 'wɜːs]	zum Besseren oder Schlechteren hin
forest ['fɒrɪst]	Wald
garbage ['gɑːbɪdʒ]	Abfall, Müll
greenhouse effect ['griːnhaʊs ɪ'fekt]	Treibhauseffekt, globale Erwärmung
(to) halt [hɔːlt]	Halt, Pause, Unterbrechung; anhalten
harmful ['hɑːmfʊl]	schädlich
Holy Bible [,həʊlɪ 'baɪbl]	(Heilige) Bibel
huge [hjuːdʒ]	riesig
humanity [hjuː'mænətɪ]	Menschheit, Menschlichkeit
immune system [ɪ'mjuːn ,sɪstəm]	Immunsystem
infertile [ɪn'fɜːtaɪl]	unfruchtbar
irreplaceable [,ɪrɪ'pleɪsəbl]	unersetzlich
lack [læk]	Mangel

massive ['mæsɪv]	massiv, wuchtig, enorm
medical ['medɪkl]	ärztlich, medizinisch
Mediterranean (Sea) [ˌmedɪtəˈreɪnɪən / siː]	Mittelmeer
migration [maɪˈgreɪʃn]	(Ab-)Wanderung
mobilization [ˌməʊbɪlaɪˈzeɪʃn]	Mobilisierung
ordinary ['ɔːdnrɪ]	gewöhnlich
ozone layer ['əʊzəʊn ˌleɪə]	Ozonschicht
to pass away [pɑːs əˈweɪ]	entschlafen, dahinscheiden; Umschreibung für: sterben
to pay attention [peɪ əˈtenʃn]	aufmerksam sein
pesticide ['pestɪsaɪd]	Pestizid
(to) poison ['pɔɪzn]	Gift; vergiften
to release [rɪˈliːs]	freilassen, veröffentlichen
to ruin ['rʊɪn]	ruinieren
sacrifice ['sækrɪfaɪs]	Opfer; opfern
scale [skeɪl]	Maß(-stab)
seal [siːl]	Seehund
sewage ['suːɪdʒ]	Abwasser
smokestack ['sməʊkstæk]	Schornstein
species ['spiːʃiːz]	(Tier-,Pflanzen-)Art, Spezies
stream [striːm]	Bach, Wasserlauf
survival [səˈvaɪvl]	Überleben
threat [θret]	(Be-)Drohung
to threaten [θretn]	(be-)drohen
treatment ['triːtmənt]	Behandlung
tropical ['trɒpɪkl]	tropisch
uninhabitable [ˌʌnɪnˈhæbɪtəbl]	unbewohnbar
unless [ʌnˈles]	wenn ... nicht, es sei denn
warning ['wɔːnɪŋ]	Warnung
wartime ['wɔːtaɪm]	Kriegszeit
to weaken ['wiːkən]	schwächen

B

to convert [kənˈvɜːt]	umwandeln
to establish [ɪˈstæblɪʃ]	schaffen, gründen, errichten
front-page [frʌnt peɪdʒ]	Titelseite
impressive [ɪmˈpresɪv]	beeindruckend
NASA (National Aeronautics and Space Administration) ['næsə] ['nɑːzə] ['næʃnəl ˌeərəˈnɔːtɪks ənd speɪs ədˈmɪnɪstreɪʃn]	Raumfahrtbehörde
power plant ['paʊə plɑːnt]	Kraftwerk
to turn into [tɜːn ˈɪntuː]	umwandeln in
waste-melting [weɪst ˈmeltɪŋ]	"Einschmelzen" von Abfall

C

avoidance [əˈvɔɪdəns]	Vermeidung
cardboard packaging ['kɑːdbɔːd ˈpækɪdʒɪŋ]	Kartonverpackung
incineration [ɪnˌsɪnəˈreɪʃn]	Verbrennung
landfill deposit ['lændfɪl dɪˈpɒzɪt]	Mülldeponie
out-of-date [aʊt əv ˈdeɪt]	veraltet, überholt, altmodisch
physical ['fɪzɪkl]	physikalisch, physisch
soil [sɔɪl]	Boden, Erde
substitution [ˌsʌbstɪˈtjuːʃn]	Ersetzen, Austausch
to treat [triːt]	behandeln

Unit 14

A

accuracy ['ækjʊrəsɪ]	Genauigkeit
aeroplane ['eərəpleɪn]	Flugzeug
airliner ['eəlaɪnə]	Verkehrsflugzeug
brain [breɪn]	Gehirn
brief [briːf]	kurz, knapp, gering
button ['bʌtn]	Knopf
concurrent [ˌkənˈkʌrənt]	gleichzeitig
numerical [njuːˈmerɪkl]	numerisch, zahlenmäßig
to oversee [ˌəʊvəˈsiː]	überwachen, leiten
perfect ['pɜːfɪkt]	vollkommen, perfekt
prototype ['prəʊtəʊtaɪp]	Prototyp
to roll [rəʊl]	rollen
to shorten ['ʃɔːtn]	kürzen
spectacular [spekˈtækjʊlə]	spektakulär
thousandth ['θaʊzənθ]	Tausendstel
to tie [taɪ]	binden, bündeln
twin-engined ['twɪn ˌendʒɪnd]	zweimotorig

B

considerable [kənˈsɪdərəbl]	beträchtlich
(to) debate [dɪˈbeɪt]	Debatte; debattieren, diskutieren
solid ['sɒlɪd]	massiv, verlässlich, ganz
sophisticated [səˈfɪstɪkeɪtɪd]	hochentwickelt, anspruchsvoll, ausgeklügelt

C

acceptable [əkˈseptəbl]	annehmbar, akzeptabel
central ['sentrəl]	zentral
continuous [kənˈtɪnjʊəs]	ununterbrochen, fortlaufend
to implement ['ɪmpləment]	erfüllen, umsetzen, ausführen
plotter ['plɒtə]	Plotter, Kurvenschreiber
scanner ['skænə]	Scanner, Abtaster

Unit 15

A

to affect [əˈfekt]	sich auswirken auf, betreffen
anchorage [ˈæŋkərɪdʒ]	Anker, Verankerung
to attach [əˈtætʃ]	befestigen
beam [biːm]	Balken, Träger, Stütze
belt [belt]	Gürtel, Gurt
to bend [bend]	(sich) biegen
builder [ˈbɪldə]	Erbauer(in), Bauunternehmer(in)
building site [ˈbɪldɪŋ saɪt]	Baustelle
civil engineer [ˈsɪvl ˌendʒɪˈnɪə]	Bauingenieur(in)
cofferdam [ˈkɒfədæm]	Kastendamm, Kofferdamm
concrete [ˈkɒŋkriːt]	Beton
to conserve [kənˈsɜːv]	erhalten, schonen
to construct [kənˈstrʌkt]	bauen, konstruieren
construction [kənˈstrʌkʃn]	Bau, Konstruktion
earthquake [ˈɜːθkweɪk]	Erdbeben
to erect [ɪˈrekt]	errichten, aufbauen
foundation [faʊnˈdeɪʃn]	Gründung, Fundament
helmet [ˈhelmɪt]	Helm
in case of [ɪn ˈkeɪs əv]	im Falle von
itself [ɪtˈself]	selbst
lane [leɪn]	(Fahr-)spur, Landstraße, Weg
misty [ˈmɪstɪ]	neblig, dunstig
net [net]	Netz
(to) pump [pʌmp]	Pumpe; pumpen
rope [rəʊp]	Seil
(to) span [spæn]	Spanne; spannen
suspender [səˈspendə]	Aufhängevorrichtung, Hosenträger
suspension [səˈspenʃn]	Aufhängung, Ausschluss
suspension bridge [səˈspenʃn brɪdʒ]	Hängebrücke
tides [taɪdz]	Gezeiten
unsupported [ˌʌnsəˈpɔːtɪd]	ungestützt, nicht unterstützt

B

besides [bɪˈsaɪdz]	außerdem
to bother [ˈbɒðə]	belästigen, beschäftigen, Sorgen machen
bracket [ˈbrækɪt]	Klammer
to collapse [kəˈlæps]	zusammenbrechen
compact [ˈkɒmpækt]	kompakt, komprimiert
historical [hɪˈstɒrɪkl]	historisch
multi-storey car park [ˈmʌltɪˌstɔːrɪ ˈkɑːpɑːk]	Parkhaus
objective [ɒbˈdʒektɪv]	Ziel
pedestrian [pəˈdestrɪən]	Fußgänger(in)
pedestrian mall [pəˈdestrɪən mɔːl]	Fußgängerzone
pile [paɪl]	Pfeiler, Pfahl, Haufen
to plot [plɒt]	zeichnen, abstecken
preparation [ˌprepəˈreɪʃn]	Vorbereitung
to rot [rɒt]	verrotten
shopper [ˈʃɒpə]	Käufer(in)
to sink [sɪŋk]	sinken
thorough [ˈθʌrə]	gründlich
wooden [ˈwʊdn]	hölzern

C

cemetery [ˈsemətrɪ]	Friedhof
flyover [ˈflaɪˌəʊvə]	Überführung
pavement [ˈpeɪvmənt]	Bürgersteig (Brit.), Straße (Am.)
valley [ˈvælɪ]	Tal

WORD LIST

(alphabetisch)

A

a bit	ein bisschen	to advertise	werben, inserieren	also	auch
a couple of *	ein paar	advertiser	Inserent(in), Auftraggeber(in) von Werbesendungen	alternative	Alternative, Wahl; alternativ
a little	etwas, ein bisschen			although	obwohl
a lot of	viel	advertising	Werbung	altogether	insgesamt, völlig
a number of	einige	advertising campaign	Werbekampagne	always	immer
ability	Fähigkeit			ambition	Ehrgeiz, Ambition
to be able	können	advertising manager	Werbeleiter(in)	Amerasian	amerikanisch-asiatisch
to be about	sich um etwas handeln	advice	Rat(schlag)	among	zwischen, unter
abroad	im/ins Ausland	to advise	(be-)raten	amount	Betrag, Summe
acceleration	Beschleunigung	aeroplane	Flugzeug	amusement arcade	Spielhalle
to accept	annehmen, akzeptieren	to affect	sich auswirken auf, betreffen	anchorage	Anker, Verankerung
acceptable	annehmbar, akzeptabel	affinity	Verbundenheit, Verwandtschaft	anger	Zorn, Wut
				angry	wütend
access	Zugang, Zutritt	to afford	sich leisten	animal	Tier
accident	Unfall	affordable	erschwinglich	to announce	bekanntgeben, ansagen
accommodation	Unterkunft, Zimmer	to be afraid (of)	Angst haben (vor)		
to accompany	begleiten	afternoon	Nachmittag	announcement	Bekanntgabe, Durchsage
according to (him)/(her)	(seiner)/(ihrer) Meinung nach, laut	afterwards	danach		
		again	wieder	another	noch eine(r), ein(e) andere(r)
		again and again	immer wieder		
accountancy	Rechnungswesen	against	gegen	to answer	Antwort; (be)antworten
accuracy	Genauigkeit	age	(Zeit-)Alter		
accurate	genau	aged ...	... Jahre alt	anti-lock brake	Antiblockierbremse
to accuse	beschuldigen, anklagen	aggressive	aggressiv	antonym	Antonym, Wort mit gegensätzlicher Bedeutung
		to agree	einverstanden sein, zustimmen		
(to) ache	Schmerz; schmerzen				
to achieve	erreichen, erzielen	agreement	Übereinstimmung, Übereinkunft	any	irgendeine(-r, -s)
Achilles tendon	Achillessehne			any time	jederzeit
acid rain	saurer Regen	ahead	vor, voraus	anybody	irgend jemand
to acquire	sich aneignen	aid	Hilfe, Hilfsmittel	anyone	irgend jemand
to act	handeln	(to) aim (at)	Ziel; zielen (auf)	anything	irgend etwas
action	Maßnahme, Handlung	air	Luft	anyway	sowieso, wie dem auch sei, jedenfalls
		air-conditioner	Klimaanlage		
active	aktiv	air-conditioning	Klimaanlage, Klimatisierung	anywhere	überall(hin), wo(hin) auch immer
activity	Aktivität				
actual	tatsächlich	airliner	Verkehrsflugzeug	to apologize	sich entschuldigen
to adapt	bearbeiten	airport	Flughafen	apparatus	Gerät
to add	hinzufügen, addieren	airtime	Sendezeit	apparent	offensichtlich, offenbar
		alive	lebend, lebendig, aktiv		
addictive	süchtig machend			to appear	(er-)scheinen
addition	Hinzufügen, Ergänzung, Addition	all	alle(s), ganz	appearance	Erscheinung, Aussehen
		all but	fast		
additional	zusätzlich	all kind(s) of	alle Arten von, alle möglichen	apple	Apfel
address	Adresse			appliance	Gerät
adjective	Adjektiv	all over the world	in der ganzen Welt	applicant	Bewerber(in)
to adjust	einstellen	all-inclusive	alles beinhaltend	application	Anwendung
adult	Erwachsene(r)	to allow	erlauben	to apply (for)	sich bewerben (um)
advanced	fortgeschritten	(to) ally	Verbündete(r); verbünden	to appoint	ernennen, bestimmen
advantage	Vorteil				
adventure	Abenteuer	almost	fast, beinahe	appointment	Verabredung, Termin, Ernennung
advert	Kurzform von "advertisement" = Werbeanzeige	alone	allein		
		along	entlang	approach	Ansatz, Annäherung
		already	schon	approval	Zustimmung

* Der als bekannt vorausgesetzte Grundwortschatz ist kursiv gedruckt.

archbishop	Erzbischof	Austria	Österreich	bedroom	Schlafzimmer
area	Gebiet	author	Autor(in), Verfasser(in)	beer	Bier
to argue	argumentieren, behaupten			before	vorher, ehe
		to automate	automatisieren	to begin, (began, begun)	beginnen
arms	Waffen	automatic	automatisch		
around	herum, um, ungefähr	automobile	Auto (Am.)	beginner	Anfänger(in)
		autumn	Herbst	beginning	Anfang
to arrange	aufstellen, planen, veranlassen	availability	Vorhandensein, Verfügbarkeit	behaviour	Benehmen
				behind	hinter
arrangement	Vereinbarung, Arrangement	available	verfügbar, vorhanden	Belgian	Belgier(in); belgisch
				Belgium	Belgien
(to) arrest	Verhaftung; verhaften	average	Durchschnitt	to believe	glauben
		to avoid	vermeiden	to belong to	gehören
arrival	Ankunft	avoidance	Vermeidung	belt	Gürtel, Gurt
to arrive	ankommen	aware	bewusst	to bend	(sich) biegen
article	Artikel	away	weg	benefit	Zuwendung, soziale Leistung
as	wie, da, als	awful	furchtbar, schrecklich		
as a result	folglich			besides	außerdem
as well	auch, ebensogut			best	am besten
as well as	sowie	**B**		best wishes	alles Gute
ash	Asche	Bachelor of Arts (B.A.)	niedrigster akad. Grad	best-known	bekanntester, -e, -es
Asian	Asiat(in); asiatisch			better	besser
to ask (for)	fragen, bitten (um)	back	Rücken; zurück	between	zwischen
aspect	Aspekt	back-up	Unterstützung	bicycle	Fahrrad
to assemble	zusammenbauen	background	Hintergrund	big	groß
assembly line	Fließband	bad	schlecht, schlimm, böse	bike	Fahrrad (Kurzform)
assertiveness	Selbstbewusstsein			bill	Rechnung
asset	Vermögen(-swert), Besitz	bag	Tüte, Tasche	billion	Billion, (Am.: Milliarde)
		baggage	Gepäck		
assistance	Hilfe	to bake	backen	bird	Vogel
assistant	Assistent(in)	baker	Bäcker(in)	birth	Geburt
to associate	assoziieren, in Verbindung bringen	balcony	Balkon	birthday	Geburtstag
		bank	Bank (Geldinstitut)	biscuit	Keks
at all costs	um jeden Preis	bank holiday	öffentl. Feiertag	bit	Stückchen
at first	anfangs	bar graph	Säulendiagramm	to bite, (bit, bitten)	beißen
at home	zu Hause	base	Basis, Stützpunkt, Ausgangspunkt		
at last	schließlich, endlich			black	schwarz
at least	wenigstens	based on	basierend, gegründet auf	blackboard	(Wand-)Tafel
at once	sofort			blade	Blatt, Schaufel, Klinge
at present	im Augenblick, jetzt	basic	Grund-; grundlegend		
at the moment	jetzt	basket	Korb	to blame (for)	verantwortlich machen (für)
at work	bei der Arbeit	bather	Badende(r)		
atmosphere	Atmosphäre	bathroom	Badezimmer	to blink	blinken
to attach	befestigen	battery	Batterie	block of flats	Wohnblock
to attack	in Angriff nehmen, angreifen	beach	Strand	blood	Blut
		beam	Balken, Träger, Stütze	blue	blau
attempt	Versuch			board	Brett
to attend	(Schule) besuchen	beard	Bart	boat	Boot
attendance	Besuch	beautiful	schön	body	Körper
attention	Aufmerksamkeit	beauty	Schönheit	bog	Moor
attitude	Haltung, Einstellung	to become, (became, become)	werden	to boil	kochen
attraction	Attraktion; Anziehungskraft			boiler room	Kesselraum
		because	weil	bold type	Fettdruck
attractive	reizvoll, anziehend, attraktiv	because of	wegen	bone	Knochen
		bed	Bett	(to) book	Buch; buchen
aunt	Tante	bedsitter	Einzimmerwohnung	booking	Buchung

bookshop	Buchhandlung	to burn,	brennen	career	Beruf, Laufbahn, Karriere
boot	Stiefel	(burnt, burnt)			
border	Grenze	bus pass	Busausweis	careful	sorgfältig
bored	gelangweilt	business	Geschäft	careless	sorglos
boring	langweilig	busy	beschäftigt	cargo	Fracht, Ladung
to borrow	sich ausleihen	but	aber	to carry	tragen
both	beide	butcher	Metzger(in)	to carry out	ausführen
to bother	belästigen, beschäftigen, sich Sorgen machen	button	Knopf	cartridge	Kassette, Patrone
		buyer	Käufer(in)	case	Fall, Koffer, Kiste
		by	durch, bei, neben, bis	cash	Bargeld
bottle	Flasche			cassette	Kassette
bottom	Boden	by far	bei weitem	cat	Katze
to buy, (bought, bought)	kaufen	by rail	mit der Bahn	to catch, (caught, caught)	fangen
		by the way	übrigens		
(to be) bound (to do sth.)	(etwas) bestimmt (tun), verpflichtet, unterwegs	by-product	Nebenprodukt	to cater to	ausgerichtet sein auf
				(to) cause	Ursache; verursachen
		C			
box	Schachtel, Karton, Kiste	cabinet	Kabinett, Schrank	ceiling	(Zimmer-)Decke
		cable TV	Kabelfernsehen	cell	Zelle
boy	Junge	CAD (Computer Aided Design)	Computerunterstützte Zeichnung (Entwurf)	cemetery	Friedhof
(to) boycott	Boykott; boykottieren			centigrade	Celsius
				central	zentral
boyfriend	Freund	cake	Kuchen	Central Electricity Generating Board (CEGB)	etwa: zentrale Energieversorgung (England/Wales)
bracket	Klammer	to calculate	(be-)rechnen		
brain	Gehirn	(to) call	Anruf; (an-)rufen, nennen		
brake	Bremse			centre	Zentrum, Mittelpunkt
brand name	Markenname	to call up	anrufen		
bread	Brot	CAM (Computer Aided Manufacture)	Computerunterstützte Fertigung	century	Jahrhundert
(to) break, (broke, broken)	Pause; (zer-)brechen			certain	sicher
				certificate	Zeugnis
to break down	zusammenbrechen	camera	Kamera	CFC (chlorofluorocarbon	FCKW (Fluorchlorkohlenwasserstoff)
breakfast	Frühstück	(to) camp	Lager; zelten, lagern		
bridge	Brücke	campaign	Kampagne, Werbefeldzug	chain	Kette
brief	kurz, knapp, gering			chair	Stuhl
bright	hell, strahlend	can	Büchse, Dose; können	chalk	Kreide
to bring, (brought, brought)	bringen			(to) challenge	Herausforderung; herausfordern
		can't stand	nicht ausstehen können	(to) change	Wechsel(-geld), Änderung; wechseln, (sich) (ver-)ändern
broadcast, (broadcast, broadcast)	übertragen, senden				
		candidate	Bewerber(in)		
to broaden the mind	den Horizont erweitern	canteen	Kantine		
		capacity	Kapazität, Leistungsfähigkeit	channel	Kanal
brochure	Broschüre, Prospekt			chart	Schaubild, Tabelle, Karte
brother	Bruder	capital	Großbuchstabe, Hauptstadt		
brown	braun				
(to) brush	Bürste; bürsten	car	Auto	cheap	billig
BTEC National Diploma	etwa: Fachhochschulreifeprüfung	car body	Karosserie	(to) check	Kontrolle; kontrollieren
		car maker	Automobilhersteller		
bubble	Blase	car park	Parkplatz	cheerful	fröhlich, heiter
to build, (built, built)	bauen	carbon dioxide	Kohlendioxyd	cheers	Tschüs!, Prost!
		carburettor	Vergaser	cheese	Käse
builder	Erbauer(in)	card	Karte	chemical	chemisch
building	Gebäude	cardboard packaging	Kartonverpackung	chemist	Chemiker(in)
building site	Baustelle			child	Kind
bulb	(Glüh)birne	cardiologist	Herzspezialist(in)	childhood	Kindheit
bumper	Stoßstange	(to) care	Sorge; sorgen	China	China

Chinese	Chinese, Chinesin; chinesisch	college	College, Fach (hoch-)schule	concerned	betroffen, interessiert
chips	Pommes Frites, Kartoffelchips	Colombia	Kolumbien	concrete	Beton
chocolate	Schokolade, Praline	colour	Farbe	concurrent	gleichzeitig
choice	Wahl	(to) comb	Kamm; kämmen	condition	Bedingung
to choose, (chose, chosen)	(aus-)wählen	to combine	verbinden, vereinigen	conference	Konferenz, Tagung
				to confirm	bestätigen
Christmas	Weihnachten	combustion	Verbrennung	to confront	gegenüberstellen, konfrontieren
church	Kirche	combustion chamber	Brennkammer		
cigarette	Zigarette			confrontation	Konfrontation
CIM (Computer Integrated Manufacture)	computerintegrierte Fertigung	to come, (came, come)	kommen	congested	überfüllt, verstopft
				congestion	Stau
		to come into operation	in Kraft treten	to connect	verbinden
cinema	Kino			connection	Verbindung, Zusammenhang
circle	Kreis, Kreislauf	to come true	wahr werden		
citizen	Bürger(in)	comfortable	bequem	connector	Verbinder, Stecker
city	Stadt	(to) comment	Bemerkung, Kommentar; kommentieren	conscious	bewusst
civil engineer	Bauingenieur(in)			consequence	Folge, Konsequenz
civil engineering	Bauwesen			consequently	folglich
civilized	zivilisiert	commercial	Werbespot; kaufmännisch	conservative	konservativ
(to) claim	Anspruch; behaupten, beanspruchen			to conserve	erhalten, schonen
		common	gemeinsam, gewöhnlich, verbreitet	to consider	betrachten, denken (an), berücksichtigen
class	Klasse				
classmate	Klassenkamerad(in)	to communicate	kommunizieren, übermitteln	considerable	beträchtlich
classroom	Klassenzimmer			to consist (of)	bestehen aus
(to) clean	sauber; reinigen	communication	Kommunikation, Übermittlung	constant	ständig, gleichbleibend
(to) clear	klar; säubern, räumen				
		community	Bevölkerungsgruppe, Gemeinde	constituency	Wahlbezirk
clever	klug			to construct	bauen, konstruieren
climate	Klima	compact	kompakt, komprimiert	construction	Bau, Konstruktion
to climb	klettern			to consult	(sich) beraten, zu Rate ziehen
clock	Uhr	company	Gesellschaft, Firma		
(to) close	dicht, nahe; schließen	company car	Firmenwagen	consumer	Verbraucher(in)
		to compare	vergleichen	consumption	Verbrauch
to close down	schließen	competition	Wettbewerb, Konkurrenz	(to) contact	Verbindung, Kontakt; sich in Verbindung setzen mit
clothes	Kleidung				
cloud	Wolke	competitive	wettbewerbsfähig		
CO₂	Kohlendioxyd	competitor	Konkurrent(in), Teilnehmer(in)		
coach	Trainer(in)			to contain	enthalten
coaching days	Postkutschenzeit	(to) complete	vollständig; vervollständigen	container	Behälter
coal	Kohle			continent	Kontinent, Erdteil
coal-fired	mit Kohle betrieben	complex	komplex, kompliziert	continental	kontinental
coast	Küste			to continue	fortsetzen, weitermachen, (-gehen)
coastal	Küsten-	complicated	kompliziert		
coat	Mantel	complication	Komplikation	continuous	ununterbrochen, fortlaufend
coffee	Kaffee	comprehension	Verständnis		
cofferdam	Kastendamm, Kofferdamm	comprehensive school	Gesamtschule	contract	Vertrag
				contradictory	widersprechend, widersprüchlich
coil	(Zünd-)Spule	to compress	komprimieren		
coin	Münze	compression	Kompression, Verdichtung	(to) contrast	Gegensatz; gegenüberstellen
cold	kalt				
to collapse	zusammenbrechen	to concentrate (on)	konzentrieren auf	to contribute	beitragen
colleague	Kollege, Kollegin			contribution	Beitrag
to collect	sammeln, abholen	concentration	Konzentration	control	Kontrolle, hier: Regeltechnik
collection	Sammlung	concept	Konzept, Entwurf		

convenient	günstig, praktisch	critic	Kritiker(in)	(to) debate	Debatte; debattieren, diskutieren
conventional	herkömmlich, konventionell	critical	kritisch		
		to cross	überqueren		
conversation	Unterhaltung, Gespräch	crossing	Kreuzung	decade	Jahrzehnt, Dekade, zehn Jahre
		crossroads	Kreuzung		
to convert	umwandeln	crowd	(Menschen-)Menge	decibel	Dezibel (Maß für Lautstärke)
convinced	überzeugt	crowded	dicht gedrängt, voll		
(to) cook	Koch, Köchin; kochen	crush zone	Knautschzone	to decide	(sich) entscheiden
		(to) cry	Schrei; schreien, weinen	decision	Entscheidung
cooker	Herd			decision-making process	Entscheidungsprozess
cookie	Keks, Plätzchen	Cuba	Kuba		
to cooperate	zusammenarbeiten	cultural shock	Kulturschock	(to) decline	Niedergang, Verschlechterung; sich verschlechtern, sinken
cooperation	Zusammenarbeit	culture	Kultur		
to cope (with)	mit etwas zurechtkommen	cup	Tasse, Pokal		
		curious	neugierig, seltsam		
(to) copy	Kopie, Exemplar; kopieren, abschreiben	currency	Währung	(to) decrease	Abnahme; abnehmen, vermindern
		current	aktuell, gegenwärtig		
		curtain	Vorhang	deep	tief
corn	Getreide, Mais, Korn	customer	Kunde, Kundin	to defend	verteidigen
		customer-orientated	kundenorientiert	defender	Verteidiger(in)
corner	Ecke			definite	eindeutig, bestimmt
corporation	Gesellschaft, Körperschaft	customs	Zoll, Zoll-	degree	akad. Grad, Diplom, Grad (Temperatur)
		(to) cut, (cut, cut)	Schnitt; schneiden		
(to) correct	richtig; korrigieren, verbessern	CV= curriculum vitae	Lebenslauf	(to) delay	Verzögerung, Verspätung; verzögern
		to cycle	Fahrrad fahren	to deliver	liefern, (Rede) halten
correction	Verbesserung, Korrektur	cylinder	Zylinder		
to correspond	entsprechen, übereinstimmen, korrespondieren	**D**		delivery	Lieferung
		daffodil	Narzisse	delivery hall	Auslieferungshalle
		daily	täglich	(to) demand	Nachfrage, verlangen
(to) cost, (cost, cost)	Kosten; kosten	(to) damage	Schaden; beschädigen		
				democracy	Demokratie
cost-efficient	kostengünstig			democrat	Demokrat(in)
cotton	Baumwolle	damp	feucht	democratic	demokratisch
council	(Stadt-, Grafschafts-)Rat	(to) dance	Tanz; tanzen	to demonstrate	demonstrieren
		dancer	Tänzer(in)	Denmark	Dänemark
to count	zählen, ins Gewicht fallen	danger	Gefahr	department	Abteilung
		dangerous	gefährlich	department store	Kaufhaus
counter	Ladentisch, Schalter	dark	dunkel	to depend (on)	abhängen (von)
country	Land	darkness	Dunkelheit	deposit	Lagerstätte, Guthaben
countryside	Landschaft	dashboard	Armaturenbrett		
county	Grafschaft, Bezirk	data	Daten	to describe	beschreiben
couple	(Ehe-)Paar	date	Datum, Zeitpunkt, Verabredung	description	Beschreibung
courage	Mut			(to) design	Entwurf, Muster; entwerfen, konstruieren
course	Kurs, Lauf, Gang, Strecke	date of birth	Geburtsdatum		
		daughter	Tochter		
(to) cover	Abdeckung, Umschlag; (be-)decken	day	Tag	designer	Zeichner(in), Designer(in)
		day by day	Tag für Tag		
cow	Kuh	dead	tot	desk	Schreibtisch
crane	Kran	(to) deal, (dealt, dealt) (in, with)	Geschäft; handeln (mit, von)	desperate	verzweifelt
crankshaft	Kurbelwelle			destination	Reiseziel, Zielort
crazy	verrückt	dealer	Händler(in)	to destroy	zerstören
to create	schaffen, verursachen	dear	lieb	destruction	Zerstörung
		Dear Madam	Sehr geehrte Dame	detail	Einzelheit, Detail
creative	kreativ	Dear Sir	Sehr geehrter Herr	determination	Entschlossenheit, Bestimmung
Crete	Kreta	death	Tod		

to develop	entwickeln
developer	Entwickler(in), Bauunternehmer(in)
developing country	Entwicklungsland
development	Entwicklung
device	Gerät
diagram	Diagramm
to dial	wählen (Telefon)
dialogue	Dialog
diary	Tagebuch, Terminkalender
to dictate	diktieren
dictation	Diktat
dictionary	Wörterbuch
to die	sterben
to differ (from)	sich unterscheiden (von)
difference	Unterschied
different	unterschiedlich
difficult	schwierig
difficulty	Schwierigkeit
to dig, (dug, dug)	graben
dining-room	Esszimmer
dinner	(Mittag-, Abend-)Essen
dinosaur	Dinosaurier
direct speech	direkte Rede
(to) direct (to)	direkt; richten, lenken (auf)
direction	Richtung
director	Leiter(in), Direktor(in), Regisseur(in)
dirty	schmutzig
disadvantage	Nachteil
to disagree (with)	anderer Meinung sein, nicht übereinstimmen mit
disagreement	abweichende Meinung, Meinungsverschiedenheit
disaster	Katastrophe
to discover	entdecken
to discuss	besprechen, diskutieren
discussion	Gespräch, Unterredung, Diskussion
to dislike	nicht mögen
to dismantle	zerlegen, demontieren
disorder	Durcheinander, Funktionsstörung
(to) display	Anzeige; anzeigen
disposal	Beseitigung, Entsorgung
distance	Entfernung, Strecke, Abstand
to distribute	verteilen
distributor	Verteiler
district	Gegend
to disturb	stören
diversion	Umleitung
to divide	teilen
doctor	Arzt, Ärztin
document	Dokument, Unterlage
dog	Hund
domestic	häuslich
to dominate	beherrschen, dominieren
Dominican Republic	Dominikanische Republik
door	Tür
to double	(sich) verdoppeln
double-glazed	doppelt verglast
down	hinunter, unten
down payment	Anzahlung
downstairs	die Treppe hinunter, unten, im Erdgeschoss
(to) draft	Entwurf, Konzept; entwerfen
to draw, (drew, drawn)	zeichnen, ziehen
drawer	Zeichner
drawing	Zeichnung
drawing board	Zeichenbrett
(to) dream	Traum; träumen
(to) dress	Kleid, Kleidung; (sich) anziehen
(to) drink, (drank, drunk)	Getränk; trinken
(to) drive, (drove, driven)	Fahrt; fahren, (an-)treiben
driver	Fahrer(in)
to drop	fallen, fallen lassen
(to) dry	trocken; trocknen
dual	Doppel-; doppelt
due to	aufgrund
(to) dump	Müllkippe; (Müll) abladen
dumping ground	Müllabladeplatz
during	während
dustbin	Mülltonne
Dutch	Niederländer(in); niederländisch
duty	Pflicht, Zoll

E

e.g.	z.B. (zum Beispiel)
each	jede(-r, -s)
each other	einander, sich
ear	Ohr
early	früh
to earn	verdienen
earnings	Einkommen, Verdienst, Ertrag
earth	Erde
earthquake	Erdbeben
east	Osten, Ost-; östlich, ostwärts
eastern	Ost-, östlich
easy	leicht
easy-to-use	einfach zu bedienen
to eat, (ate, eaten)	essen
ecological	ökologisch, umweltfreundlich
ecology	Ökologie
economic	Wirtschafts-; wirtschaftlich
economical	sparsam, wirtschaftlich
economics	Wirtschaft(swissenschaft)
economist	Wirtschaftswissenschaftler(in)
economy	Wirtschaft
ECU (European Currency Unit)*	Europäische Währungseinheit
edge	Kante, Rand, Schneide
edition	Ausgabe
editor	Herausgeber(in), Redakteur(in)
to educate	erziehen
education	Erziehung
(to) effect	Wirkung; durchführen, erzielen, leisten
efficiency	Leistungsfähigkeit
efficient	leistungsfähig
effort	Anstrengung, Mühe, Versuch
egg	Ei
either ... or	entweder ... oder
to eject	auswerfen
to elect	wählen
election	Wahl
electric	elektrisch
electrical engineering	Elektrotechnik
electrically-driven	elektrisch angetrieben

* im Dezember 1995 wurde der ECU in EURO umbenannt

electrician	Elektriker(in)	envelope	Umschlag	to expand	ausdehnen
electricity	Elektrizität	environment	Umwelt	expansion	Ausweitung
electronic	elektronisch	environmental	Umwelt-	to expect	erwarten
electronics	Elektronik	environmentalist	Umweltschützer(in)	expensive	teuer
to eliminate	beseitigen	epilepsy	Epilepsie	experience	Erfahrung
else	sonst	equal	gleich	expert	Experte, Expertin
elsewhere	woanders	to equip	ausrüsten	to explain	erklären
embassy	Botschaft	equipment	Ausrüstung, Ausstattung	explanation	Erklärung
emergency	Notfall			(to) export	Ausfuhr, Export; ausführen, exportieren
to emigrate	auswandern	to erect	errichten, aufbauen		
emigration	Auswanderung	especial	besondere(-r, -s)		
emission	Emission, Ausstoß	essential	wesentlich	export assistant	etwa: Außenhandelskaufmann, -frau
emphasis	Betonung	to establish	schaffen, gründen, errichten		
to emphasize	betonen				
to employ	beschäftigen, einstellen	to estimate	schätzen	exposed	ungeschützt, ausgesetzt
		etc. (et cetera)	und so weiter		
employed	beschäftigt	European Union	Europäische Union (die EC wurde im November 1993 in die EU umbenannt)	(to) express	Schnellzug; als Eilsache; ausdrücken, äußern
employee	Angestellte(r), Arbeitnehmer(in)				
employer	Arbeitgeber(in)			expression	Ausdruck
employment	Beschäftigung, Anstellung, Arbeit	even	sogar, selbst, eben, gleich	extension	(Aus-)Strecken, Verlängerung
empty	leer	evening	Abend	to a great extent	in großem Umfang
to enable (so. to do sth.)	es (jmdm.) möglich machen, (etwas zu tun)	event	Ereignis	extinction	Aussterben
		eventual(ly)	am Ende, schließlich	extra	besonders
		ever	je	extract	Auszug, Extrakt
to enclose	beilegen	every	jede(-r, -s)	extreme	extrem, äußerst, höchst
(to) end	Ende; (be-)enden	everybody	jeder		
energy	Energie, Kraft	everyone	jeder	eye	Auge
engine	Motor, Triebwerk, Lokomotive	everything	alles		
		everywhere	überall	**F**	
engineer	Ingenieur(in), Techniker(in)	evolution	Entwicklung, Evolution	(to) face	Gesicht; konfrontiert sein
engineering	Technik; technisch	to evolve	(sich) entwickeln	facility	Einrichtung, Möglichkeit
English Channel	Ärmelkanal	exact	genau		
to enjoy	genießen, sich freuen an	exaggeration	Übertreibung	fact	Tatsache
		exam(ination)	Prüfung	factor	Faktor
enjoyable	schön, angenehm, unterhaltsam	to examine	untersuchen, überprüfen	factory	Fabrik
				to fade (away)	verblassen, nachlassen, verwelken
enormous	gewaltig, enorm	example	Beispiel		
enough	genug	excellent	ausgezeichnet, hervorragend	to fail	scheitern
to enquire (about)	sich erkundigen (nach), fragen (nach)			fair	Messe, Markt; gerecht, fair
		except	außer		
		exchange	Austausch	fairytale	Märchen
enquiry	Anfrage, Erkundigung, Untersuchung	exchange rate	Wechselkurs	to fall asleep	einschlafen
		excitement	Aufregung, Begeisterung	(to) fall, (fell, fallen)	Fallen, Sturz, (Am.) Herbst; fallen
to enter	eintreten	exciting	aufregend	false	falsch
enthusiasm	Begeisterung, Enthusiasmus	(to) excuse	Entschuldigung; (sich) entschuldigen	family	Familie
				famous	berühmt
enthusiast	Begeisterte(r), Enthusiast(in)			fanatic	fanatisch; Fanatiker(in)
		exercise	Übung		
enthusiastic	begeistert	exhaust pipe	Auspuffrohr	far	weit
entrance	Eintritt, Eingang	to exist	existieren, bestehen	fare	Fahrpreis, Fahrgeld
entry	Einreise, Eingang, Eintritt	existence	Existenz, Dasein	farm	Bauernhof, Farm
		exit	Ausgang, Ausfahrt	farmer	Landwirt(in)

farming	Landwirtschaft	(to) flood	Flut; überschwemmen	to frighten	erschrecken, Angst machen
fascination	Faszination	floor	Boden	*front*	*Vorderseite*
fashionable	modisch	flower	Blume	front-page	Titelseite
fast	*schnell*	(to) fly, (flew, flown)	Fliege; fliegen	*fruit*	*Früchte, Obst*
fat	*Fett; dick*	flyover	Überführung	fuel	Kraftstoff, Brennstoff
father	*Vater*	foam	Schaum	to fulfil	erfüllen, entsprechen
fault	Fehler, Schuld, Mangel	fog	Nebel	*full*	*voll*
favourite	*Lieblings-, Liebling*	*to follow*	*folgen*	full-time	Vollzeit
fear	Furcht	food	Nahrung, Essen	fumes	Rauch, Dämpfe, Abgase
to feed, (fed, fed)	füttern	food stamp	Essensmarke	*fun*	*Spaß*
feedback	Rückmeldung, Feedback	foot	Fuß	function	Funktion, Aufgabe
to feel, (felt, felt)	fühlen	football	Fußball	fund	Fond, Fundus, Mittel
feeling	Gefühl	footballer	Fußballspieler(in)	furious	wütend, wild, heftig
female	weiblich	for better or for worse	zum Besseren oder Schlechteren hin	furnace	Ofen
fertilizer	Dünger	*for example*	*zum Beispiel*	*furniture*	*Möbel*
few	wenige	for instance	beispielsweise	*further*	*weiter*
field	Feld	force	Kraft, Stärke, Gewalt, Macht	furthermore	außerdem
(to) fight, (fought, fought)	Kampf; kämpfen	*foreign*	*ausländisch, fremd*	*future*	*Zukunft; zukünftig*
figure	Zahl, Figur	forerunner	Vorläufer		
to fill	füllen	forest	Wald	**G**	
final	Finale, Endrunde; letzte(-r, -s), endgültig	forever	für immer	gadget	Gerät, Apparat
		to forget, (forgot, forgotten)	vergessen	(to) gain	Gewinn; gewinnen
finance	Finanzwesen			galactic	Weltraum-; galaktisch
financial	finanziell	*fork*	*Gabel*		
to find, (found, found)	finden	(to) form	Form, Formular, Klasse; gestalten	game	Spiel
				garage	Autowerkstatt, Garage
fine	Strafe; fein, gut, schön	former	ehemalig	garbage	Abfall, Müll
(to) finish	Ziel, Vollendung; beenden	formula	Formel	garden	Garten
		fortunate	glücklich	gate	Tor
(to) fire	Feuer; feuern	fortune	Glück, Reichtum	GCSE = General Certificate of Secondary Education	etwa: Fachoberschulreife
firm	Firma; fest, verbindlich	forward(s)	vorwärts		
		fossil fuels	fossile Brennstoffe		
first	erste(-r, -s), zuerst	to found	gründen		
first of all	zuerst, vor allem	foundation	Gründung, Fundament	gear	Getriebe, Gang
(to) fish	Fisch; fischen			gearbox	Getriebe
(to) fit	gesund, in Form, geeignet; (zusammen) passen, einbauen	four-stroke engine	Viertaktmotor	*general*	*allgemein*
		France	Frankreich	general science	allgemeine Naturwissenschaften
		(to) free	frei; befreien	to generate	erzeugen
to fix	befestigen, reparieren, besorgen	freedom	Freiheit	generator	Generator, Lichtmaschine
		freeway	(Am.) Autobahn		
fixed-route	schienengebunden	French	Franzose, Französin; französisch	*gentleman*	*Herr*
flag	Fahne			geo-thermal	geothermisch (Erdwärme nutzend)
flair	Flair, Gespür, Talent, Begabung	*frequent*	*häufig*		
		fresh	*frisch*	geographical	geographisch
flame	Flamme	*fridge*	*Kühlschrank*	to get, (got, got)	bekommen, werden
flat	Wohnung; flach	*friend*	*Freund(in)*	to get married	heiraten
to flee (fled, fled)	fliehen, flüchten	*friendly*	*freundlich*	to get on like a house on fire	sich sehr gut verstehen
flexibility	Flexibilität	Friends of the Earth	Name einer Umweltschutzorganisation		
flexible	flexibel			to get on with	auskommen mit
flight	*Flug*				

to get rid of	loswerden, abschaffen	to greet	grüßen	head of department	hier: Fachbereichsleiter(in)
to get to know	kennenlernen	grey	grau	(to) head off	(hin-) fahren (nach), losfahren
to get up	aufstehen	grid	Versorgungsnetz		
to get used to	sich gewöhnen an	(to) grip	Griff, Halt; (er-)greifen, fesseln	headache	Kopfschmerz
girl	Mädchen	grocer	Lebensmittelhändler(in)	heading	Überschrift
girlfriend	Freundin			headlight	Scheinwerfer
to give, (gave, given)	geben	ground	Boden	headline	Überschrift
		group	Gruppe	health	Gesundheit
to give up	aufgeben	to grow, (grew, grown)	wachsen	healthy	gesund
glad	froh			to hear, (heard, heard)	hören
glass	Glas	to grow up	aufwachsen		
glasses	Brille	grown-up	Erwachsene(r); erwachsen	heart	Herz
global	global, weltweit			heart attack	Herzanfall
global warming	weltweiter Temperaturanstieg	growth	Wachstum	(to) heat	Hitze; heizen
		to guess	erraten	heating	Heizung
glory	Ruhm	guest	Gast	heavy	schwer
glove	Handschuh	guideline	Richtlinie	heavy industry	Schwerindustrie
to go, (went, gone)	gehen	guilty	schuldig	heavy metal	Heavy Metal (harte Rockmusik)
		H		height	Höhe
to go down	untergehen, sinken, fallen	habit	Gewohnheit	hello	Hallo
		hair	Haar	helmet	Helm
to go on	weitergehen, weitermachen	hairdresser	Friseur, Friseurin	(to) help	Hilfe; helfen
		half	Hälfte; halb	helpful	hilfreich
to go on strike	in den Streik treten	hall	Flur, Saal	here	hier
to go shopping	einkaufen	(to) halt	Halt, Pause, Unterbrechung; anhalten	here you are	bitte(schön)!
to go to the greatest lengths	sich die größte Mühe geben			to hesitate	zögern
		ham	Schinken	Hi Tech (High Technology)	Spitzentechnologie
to go up	hinaufgehen, wachsen, steigen	hand side	Seite		
		handbag	Handtasche	to hide, (hid, hidden)	(sich) verstecken
goal	Ziel, Tor	handbook	Handbuch		
good	gut	handful	Handvoll	high	hoch
goodbye	auf Wiedersehen	handkerchief	Taschentuch	high class	hochwertig, erstklassig
goods	Güter, Waren	to hang, (hung, hung)	(auf-)hängen		
to govern	regieren			highway	Landstraße
government	Regierung	to happen	geschehen	hill	Hügel
gradual	allmählich, sanft (ansteigen, abfallen)	happiness	Glück, Heiterkeit, Zufriedenheit	historical	historisch
				history	Geschichte
to graduate	das Studium beenden	happy	glücklich, heiter	to hit, (hit, hit)	Schlag, Treffer, Erfolg; schlagen
		harbour	Hafen		
grandfather	Großvater	hard	hart, schwierig, anstrengend	to hold, (held, held)	halten
grandmother	Großmutter				
grandparents	Großeltern	hard-working	fleißig	hole	Loch
grant	Zuschuss, Bafög	hardly	kaum	holiday	freier Tag, Feiertag, Urlaub
graph	Schaubild, mathematische Kurve	to harm	schädigen		
		harmful	schädlich	holidaymaker	Urlauber(in)
grateful	dankbar	hat	Hut	Holy Bible	(Heilige) Bibel
great	großartig, groß	to hate	hassen	home	Wohnung, Heimat; zu/nach Hause
Greece	Griechenland	to have, (had, had)	haben, lassen		
Greek	Grieche, Griechin; griechisch			home from home	zweites Zuhause
		to have in common	gemeinsam haben	homework	Hausaufgabe
green	grün			honest	ehrlich
greenhouse	Treibhaus, Gewächshaus	to have to	müssen	to hope	Hoffnung; hoffen
		(to) head	Kopf, Leiter; anführen, fahren nach	hopeful	zuversichtlich, vielversprechend
greenhouse effect	Treibhauseffekt, globale Erwärmung				

horse	Pferd	*to imagine*	sich vorstellen	*to induce*	verursachen, herbeiführen
hospital	Krankenhaus	*immediate*	unmittelbar, unverzüglich	industrial	industriell
host	Gastgeber			industrialized	industrialisiert
hot	heiß	*immigrant*	Einwanderer	*industry*	Industrie
hour	Stunde	*to immigrate*	einwandern	infertile	unfruchtbar
hourly	stündlich	immigration	Einwanderung	infinitive	Infinitiv, Grundform
house	Haus	immune system	Immunsystem	inflexible	unflexibel
House of Commons	Unterhaus	to implement	erfüllen, umsetzen, ausführen	*to inform*	informieren
House of Lords	Oberhaus	*(to) import*	Einfuhr, Import; einführen, importieren	informal	informell
household	Haushalt			information sheet	Informationsblatt
housewife	Hausfrau	importance	Wichtigkeit	infra-red	infrarot
housework	Hausarbeit	*important*	wichtig	injury	Verletzung
housing	Unterkunft, Wohnungen	*impossible*	unmöglich	ink	Tinte
		to impress	beeindrucken	ink jet printer	Tintenstrahldrucker
housing estate	Siedlung	impression	Eindruck	inner	Innen-, inner-
how	wie	impressive	beeindruckend	innocence	Unschuld
how are you?	wie geht es dir/Ihnen?	*to improve*	(sich) verbessern	innovation	Neuerung
		improvement	Verbesserung	*inside*	in, innerhalb
however	jedoch	in addition	zusätzlich	to install	einbauen
huge	riesig	in case of	im Falle von	installation	Installation, Anschluss
human	menschlich	in charge of	verantwortlich für		
humanity	Menschheit, Menschlichkeit	in conclusion	abschließend	*instead (of)*	anstatt
		in contrast	im Gegensatz	institute	Institut
hundred	hundert	*in fact*	tatsächlich	*to instruct*	unterrichten, anweisen
Hungary	Ungarn	in favour of	zugunsten von		
hungry	hungrig	*in front of*	vor	instruction	Unterricht, (Gebrauchs-) Anweisung,
(to) hurry	Eile; sich beeilen	in general	im Allgemeinen		
to hurt	verletzen	*in italics*	kursiv		
husband	Ehemann	in my opinion	meiner Meinung nach	instrumentation	Messtechnik
hybrid	Hybrid-, Misch-, Kreuzung, Mischung			to insulate	isolieren
		in my view	meiner Ansicht nach	insulation	Isolierung
		in order to	um zu	*insurance*	Versicherung
hydro	Wasser-	in preference to	unter Bevorzugung (von)	intake	Aufnahme, Ansaugen
hydro-electric	hydroelektrisch (Wasserkraft nutzend)				
		in the end	schließlich	to integrate	integrieren
		in the first place	zuerst	to intend	beabsichtigen
hydrogen	Wasserstoff	in the long run	auf lange Sicht	intercontinental	interkontinental
hypnotic	hypnotisch	*in the meantime*	inzwischen	*interest*	Interesse, Zinsen (Plural)
I		in the mid	in der Mitte von, Mitte der …	to be interested	interessiert sein
ice	Eis			*interesting*	interessant
icecream	Eis(krem)	*in time*	rechtzeitig	interface	Schnittstelle
idea	Idee	inch	Zoll (Maßeinheit)	internal combustion engine	Verbrennungsmotor
to identify	identifizieren	incineration	Verbrennung		
identity	Identität, Übereinstimmung	to be inclined (to do sth.)	dazu neigen, (etwas zu tun)	to be into sth.	Fan von etwas sein
				to introduce	einführen, vorstellen
if	wenn, falls	to include	einschließen		
to ignite	zünden	income	Einkommen	introduction	Einführung, Vorstellung
ignition	Zündung	*(to) increase*	Zunahme; zunehmen, steigen, erhöhen		
to ignore	ignorieren, nicht beachten			introductory	einleitend
				to invent	erfinden
ill	krank	*indeed*	tatsächlich	invention	Erfindung
illegal	illegal, gesetzlich unzulässig	independent	unabhängig	*to invest*	investieren
		India	Indien	investment	Investition, (Kapital-) Anlage
illness	Krankheit	individual	individuell		

invitation	Einladung			to let, (let, let)	lassen
to invite	einladen	**L**		letter	Brief
to involve	beteiligen, verwickeln	labour	Arbeit	level	Stufe, Niveau
		lack	Mangel	to lie, (lay, lain)	liegen
irreplaceable	unersetzlich	ladder	Leiter	to lie, (lied, lied)	lügen
island	Insel	lady	Dame	life	Leben
to isolate	isolieren	lake	See	life peer	Peer auf Lebenszeit
issue	Frage, Angelegenheit, Problem	lamp	Lampe	life-style	Lebensstil
		land	Land	lifeless	leblos
Italy	Italien	landfill deposit	Mülldeponie	(to) lift	Aufzug, Mitfahrgelegenheit; anheben, aufheben
itself	selbst	landlady	Vermieterin, Wirtin		
		landlord	Vermieter, Wirt		
J		landscape	Landschaft	ligament	Band (z.B. am Knie)
jacket	Jacke	lane	(Fahr-)spur, Landstraße, Weg	light	Licht, Lampe; hell, leicht
jam	Marmelade				
jam buster	„Stauknacker"	language	Sprache		
Japanese	Japaner(in); japanisch;	large	groß	light industry	Leichtindustrie
		(to) last	letzte(-r, -s); dauern	to light, (lit, lit)	anzünden, (be-)leuchten
jersey	Trikot	late	spät		
job	Arbeit, Stelle, Aufgabe	later on	später	lighting	Beleuchtung
		latest	neueste(-r, -s)	(to) like	wie; mögen
jobless	arbeitslos	Latin America	Lateinamerika	likely	wahrscheinlich
to join	(sich) anschließen, beitreten	to laugh	lachen	limit	Grenze, Beschränkung
		laughter	Gelächter		
joint	gemeinsam	law	Gesetz	line	Linie, Zeile
journey	Reise	to lay, (laid, laid)	legen	lined with	gesäumt von
juice	Saft	lazy	faul	(to) link	Verbindung; verbinden
(to) jump	Sprung; springen	lead	Leitungskabel, Zuleitung		
just	genau, soeben, nur			to link together	miteinander verbinden
		to lead, (led, led)	führen, leiten		
K		leaflet	(Hand-)Zettel, Flugblatt	lip	Lippe
to keep, (kept, kept)	(be-)halten			(to) list	Liste; aufführen, auflisten
		league	Liga		
key	Schlüssel	lean management	„schlankes" Management	to listen	zuhören
key point	springender Punkt			listener	Zuhörer(in)
to kill	töten	to learn, (learnt, learnt)	lernen	literature	Literatur, Informationsmaterial
kilogram(me)	Kilogramm				
kind	Art, Sorte; freundlich	learner	Lernende(r), Anfänger(in)	litre	Liter
				little	klein, wenig
king	König	least	wenigste(-r, -s), geringste(-r, -s)	(to) live	lebend, direkt, live; leben, wohnen
(to) kiss	Kuss; küssen				
kit	Ausrüstung, Bausatz, Set	to leave, (left, left)	verlassen	living-room	Wohnzimmer
				(to) load	Ladung; laden
kitchen	Küche	left	links	loaded with	beladen mit
knee	Knie	(to feel) left out	(sich) ausgeschlossen (fühlen)	local	lokal, ortsansässig, örtlich
knee-cap	Kniescheibe				
knife	Messer	leg	Bein	Local Education Authority (L.E.A.)	örtliche Schulbehörde
(to) knock	Klopfen; klopfen	legal	legal, gesetzlich zulässig		
to know, (knew, known)	wissen				
		legislation	Gesetzgebung	location	Lage, Standort
knowledge	Wissen	leisure	Freizeit	logical	logisch
kph	km/h (Kilometer pro Stunde)	lemon	Zitrone	logo	Logo, (Firmen-)Emblem
		to lend, (lent, lent)	verleihen		
		length	Länge	long	lang
		less	weniger	long-term	langfristig
		lesson	Unterrichtsstunde	to look	schauen, (aus-)sehen
				to look after	sich kümmern um

to look for	suchen	management	(Geschäfts-)Leitung, Verwaltung, Durchführung	meeting	Treffen
to look forward to	sich freuen auf			megawatt	Megawatt
				to melt	schmelzen
to look into	untersuchen, prüfen	managing director	Geschäftsführer(in)	member	Mitglied
to look like	aussehen wie	mankind	Menschheit	membership	Mitgliedschaft
to look out	aufpassen, hinaussehen	to manufacture	herstellen	memory	Gedächtnis
		manufacturer	Hersteller	to mend	reparieren
to look up	nachschlagen, heraussuchen, aufblicken	manure	Dung	to mention	erwähnen
		many	viele	menu	Speisekarte
		map	(Land-)Karte	message	Mitteilung, Nachricht
to loot	plündern	marital status	Familienstand		
lorry	Lastwagen	mark	Zensur, Note	metal	Metall
to lose, (lost, lost)	verlieren	market	Markt	methane	Methan(-gas)
		market development	Marktentwicklung	method	Methode
loss	Verlust			metre	Meter
lot	Menge, Los	marmalade	(Orangen-)Marmelade	Mexican	Mexikaner(in); mexikanisch
lots of	viel				
loud	laut	married	verheiratet	Mexico	Mexiko
(to) love	Liebe; lieben	to marry	heiraten	microphone	Mikrofon
lovely	hübsch	mass	Masse	microwave	Mikrowelle
low	niedrig	massive	massiv, wuchtig, enorm	middle	Mitte
to lower	senken, herabsetzen			midnight	Mitternacht
luck	Glück, Schicksal	(to) match	Wettkampf, Streichholz; zusammenbringen, passen	might	Gewalt, Macht; könnte(n)
lucky	glücklich (im Sinne von: Glück haben)				
				migration	(Ab-)Wanderung
luggage	Gepäck			migratory habits	Reisegewohnheiten
lunch	Mittagessen	mathematics	Mathematik	mile	Meile
Luxembourg	Luxemburg	(to) matter	Angelegenheit; etwas ausmachen	mileage	Meilen, Meilenstand
				milk	Milch
M		may	dürfen	(to) mind	Meinung, Gedanken, Verstand; etwas ausmachen
machine	Maschine	maybe	vielleicht		
machinery	Maschinen	meal	Mahlzeit		
mad	verrückt	to mean, (meant, meant)	bedeuten, meinen	mine	Bergwerk, Mine
madam	Gnädige Frau			mining	Bergbau
magazine	Zeitschrift	meaning	Bedeutung	minor	kleiner, weniger bedeutend, leicht
mail	Post	means	Mittel, Möglichkeiten		
main	Haupt-			minority	Minderheit
mainly	hauptsächlich	meanwhile	inzwischen	minus	minus, ohne, abzüglich
to maintain	behaupten	measure	Maßnahme		
maintenance	Wartung, Instandhaltung	meat	Fleisch	minute	Minute
		mechanic	Mechaniker(in)	mirror	Spiegel
major	Haupt-; bedeutend	mechanical engineering	Maschinenbau	Miss	Fräulein
majority	Mehrheit			to miss	vermissen, verfehlen, verpassen
to make, (made, made)	machen, herstellen	mechanism	Mechanismus		
		media	Medien	mistake	Fehler
to make sense	einen Sinn ergeben	medical	ärztlich, medizinisch	misty	neblig, dunstig
to make sure	sich überzeugen	medicine	Medizin, Medikament	(to) mix	Mischung; mischen
to make up one's mind	sich entschließen			to mix up	vertauschen
		Mediterranean (Sea)	Mittelmeer	mixture	Mischung
				mobility	Mobilität
maker	Hersteller	medium-sized	mittelgroß	mobilization	Mobilisierung
male	männlich	to meet, (met, met)	(sich) treffen, kennenlernen	modal (auxiliary)	modales Hilfsverb
man	Mann			model	Modell
man-power	Arbeitskräfte	to meet the growing demand	der wachsenden Nachfrage gerecht werden	moment	Augenblick
to manage	zustande bringen, schaffen, leiten, verwalten			money	Geld
				monotonous	eintönig, monoton

month	Monat
moon	Mond
moor	Moor
more	mehr
moreover	überdies, außerdem
morning	Morgen
most	die meisten
mother	Mutter
motorist	Autofahrer(in)
motorway	Autobahn
mountain	Berg
mouth	Mund
to move	bewegen, umziehen
movement	Bewegung
MP (Member of Parliament)	Mitglied des Parlaments
mph (miles per hour)	Meilen pro Stunde
Mr	Herr
Mrs	Frau (verheiratet)
Ms	Frau (verheiratet oder unverheiratet)
much	viel
multi-	Mehr-, Viel-
multi-storey car park	Parkhaus
music	Musik
must	müssen
must not	nicht dürfen

N

(to) name	Name; benennen
namely	nämlich
narrow	eng
NASA (National Aeronautics and Space Administration)	Raumfahrtbehörde
nationality	Nationalität
nationwide	landesweit
native-born	gebürtig
natural	natürlich
nature	Natur
navigation system	Navigationssystem
near	nahe
nearby	nahe gelegen
nearly	fast, beinahe
neat	ordentlich, gelungen, schlau
necessary	notwendig
(to) need	Notwendigkeit; benötigen
negative	negativ
to neglect	vernachlässigen
neighbour	Nachbar(in)
neither ... nor	weder ... noch
net	Netz
Netherlands	Niederlande
network	Netz
never	nie
nevertheless	dennoch
new	neu
news	Nachrichten, Neuigkeit
newspaper	Zeitung
next	nächste(-r, -s)
nice	nett
night	Nacht
no	kein; nein
no longer	nicht mehr
no one	niemand
nobody	niemand
noise	Lärm
noisy	geräuschvoll
non-	Nicht-
non-returnable	Einweg-
noon	Mittag
north	Norden, Nord-; nördlich, nordwärts
nose	Nase
not	nicht
not any more	nicht länger
not either	auch nicht
not even	nicht einmal
not yet	noch nicht
(to) note	Notiz; notieren
nothing	nichts
(to) notice	Aushang, Kenntnis, Beachtung; bemerken
noun	Substantiv
novel	Roman; neu
now	jetzt
nowadays	heutzutage
nowhere	nirgendwo
nuclear	Kern-, Atom-; nuklear
number	Zahl, Nummer, Anzahl
numerical	numerisch, zahlenmäßig
nurse	Krankenschwester

O

o'clock	Uhr (Zeitangabe)
object	Gegenstand
objective	Ziel
obvious	offensichtlich
to occupy	einnehmen, besetzen
to occur	auftreten
ocean	Meer, Ozean
of course	natürlich
off	von ... weg
off-the-grid	nicht an das Versorgungsnetz angeschlossen
(to) offer	Angebot; anbieten
office	Büro, Amt
office skills	Bürofertigkeiten
office worker	Büroangestellter, Büroangestelle
officer	Beamter, Beamtin, Offizier
official	Beamter, Beamtin, Funktionär; offiziell
often	oft
oil	Öl
old	alt
(on the) left-hand	auf der Linken
on the one hand	auf der einen Seite
on the other hand	auf der anderen Seite
(on the) right	auf der Rechten
on the road	auf dem Weg
on time	pünktlich
on top of	zusätzlich zu
on your own	allein
once	einmal
once again	noch einmal
only	nur
(to) open	offen; öffnen
operate	bedienen, verkehren
operator	(Maschinen-)Bediener(in), Telefonvermittler(in)
opinion	Meinung
opportunity	Gelegenheit, Möglichkeit
opposite	Gegensatz; gegensätzlich
or	oder
(to) order	Bestellung, Befehl; bestellen, befehlen
ordinary	gewöhnlich
ore	Erz
organization	Organisation
to organize	organisieren
organizer	Veranstalter(in)
original	ursprünglich, originell
other	andere(-r, -s)
otherwise	sonst, anderenfalls
ought to	sollte(n)
out of town	außerhalb der Stadt
out of work	arbeitslos

out-of-date	veraltet, überholt, altmodisch
to outdo	übertreffen, überbieten
outdoor	draußen, im Freien
output	(Produktions-)Leistung
outside	Außenseite; draußen, außerhalb
outsider	Außenseiter(in)
outstanding	hervorragend, außergewöhnlich
over and over again	immer wieder
overcrowded	überfüllt
to overestimate	überschätzen
overseas	in Übersee
to oversee	überwachen, leiten
over-training	zu häufiges Training
over-use	zu häufiger Gebrauch
(to) own	eigene(-r, -s); besitzen
owner	Eigentümer(in)
ozone hole	Ozonloch
ozone layer	Ozonschicht

P

(to) pack	Packung; packen
package tour	Pauschalreise
packaging	Verpackung
packet	Paket
packing	Verpackung
page	Seite
pain	Schmerz
(to) paint	Farbe; malen
pair	Paar
panel	Schalttafel
paper	Papier
paradise	Paradies
paragraph	Absatz
(to) paraphrase	Umschreibung; umschreiben
parents	Eltern
(to) park	Park; parken
parliament	Parlament
parliamentary	parlamentarisch
part	Teil
part-time	Teilzeit
to participate	teilnehmen
particular	besonderer, -e, -es
to pass	vorbeigehen
to pass away	entschlafen, dahinscheiden; (Umschreibung für: sterben)
passenger	Passagier(in), Fahrgast
passive (voice)	Passiv
passport	Pass
past	Vergangenheit
past tense	Vergangenheitsform
patience	Geduld
pavement	(Brit.) Bürgersteig
to pay attention	aufmerksam sein
(to) pay, (paid, paid)	Bezahlung; (be-)zahlen
payment	Zahlung
peace	Friede
peaceful	friedlich
(to) peak	Spitze, Gipfel, Höhepunkt; seine Spitzenform erreichen
peat	Torf
pedestrian	Fußgänger(in)
pedestrian mall	Fußgängerzone
pen	Füllhalter
pence	Plural von Penny
pencil	Bleistift
penny	Penny (engl. Münze)
people	Leute, Volk
per	pro
per capita	pro Kopf
per cent	Prozent
percentage	prozentualer Anteil
perfect	vollkommen, perfekt
to perform	ausführen, vollbringen
perhaps	vielleicht
period	Periode, Zeitraum, Schulstunde
permanent	(be)ständig, bleibend
permission	Erlaubnis
persecution	Verfolgung
personal	persönlich
personality	Persönlichkeit
personnel	Personal
pesticide	Pestizid
petrol	Benzin
Philippines	Philippinen
(to) phone	Telefon; telefonieren
phone call	Anruf
photograph	Foto
photographer	Fotograf(in)
photovoltaic	fotoelektrisch
phrase	Ausdruck
physical	physikalisch, physisch
to pick	pflücken, wählen
to pick up	nehmen, aufheben
picture	Bild
piece	Stück
pile	Pfeiler, Pfahl, Haufen
pipe	Pfeife, Röhre
piston	Kolben
piston rod	Pleuel-/Kolbenstange
pit	Grube
pitch	Spielfeld
(to) place	Platz; stellen, legen
(to) plan	Plan; planen
plane	Flugzeug
planner	Planer(in)
(to) plant	Pflanze; pflanzen
plastic	Kunststoff, Plastik
plate	Teller
platform	Bahnsteig
(to) play	(Schau-) Spiel; spielen
player	Spieler(in)
playground	Spielplatz
pleasant	angenehm
please	bitte
pleased	zufrieden, erfreut
pleasure	Vergnügen
plentiful	reichlich, häufig
plenty	viel, eine Menge
to plot	zeichnen, abstecken
plotter	Plotter, Kurvenschreiber
to plug	stecken
pocket	Tasche
podiatry	Lehre von den Fußkrankheiten
(to) point	Punkt; zeigen
point of view	Standpunkt
to point out	hinweisen auf
(to) poison	Gift; vergiften
Poland	Polen
Pole	Pole, Polin
police	Polizei
policeman	Polizist
policewoman	Polizistin
Polish	polnisch
polite	höflich
political	politisch
politician	Politiker(in)
politics	Politik
poll	Umfrage, Abstimmung, Wahl
to pollute	verschmutzen
polluted	verschmutzt
pollution	Umweltverschmutzung
poor	arm
popular	beliebt, populär

population	Bevölkerung	to produce	produzieren, herstellen	(to) push	Stoß; schieben, stoßen
port	Hafen	producer	Hersteller(in), Produzent(in)	to put, (put, put)	setzen, stellen, legen
portable	tragbar				
positive	positiv	product	Produkt	to put on	aufsetzen
possession	Besitz	production	Herstellung, Produktion	to put to the test	jdn/etwas auf die Probe stellen
possibility	Möglichkeit				
possible	möglich	production line	Fertigungsstraße, Fließband	to put up	(Hand) heben, bauen, aufstellen
post office	Post				
postcard	Postkarte	productivity	Produktivität, Leistungsfähigkeit	puzzle	Rätsel
postman	Briefträger			pylon	Mast
pot	Topf	professional	beruflich		
potato	Kartoffel	(to) profit	Gewinn; profitieren	**Q**	
potential	Potential, Möglichkeiten	profitable	rentabel, einträglich, lohnend	qualification	Qualifikation, Befähigung
pound	Pfund	*program(me)*	Programm	*quality*	Qualität
pound note	Pfundnote	progress	Fortschritt	*quantity*	Menge
poverty	Armut	project	Projekt	*quarter*	Viertel
power	Kraft	proliferation	Ausbreitung, Umsichgreifen	queen	Königin
power line	(Stark-) Stromleitung			question	Frage
power plant	Kraftwerk	(to) promise	Versprechen; versprechen	quick	schnell
power station	Kraftwerk			quiet	ruhig
powerful	stark, mächtig	to promote	(be)fördern, Werbung machen für	to quit	verlassen, aufhören, aufgeben
practical	praktisch				
practice	Übung	promotion	Werbung, Beförderung	*quite*	ganz, ziemlich
to practise	üben			quotation	Zitat, Kostenvoranschlag
precise	genau	to pronounce	aussprechen		
to predict	vorhersagen	pronounced	ausgeprägt, deutlich		
predictable	vorhersagbar, vorhersehbar	pronunciation	Aussprache	**R**	
		proportion	Verhältnis, Teil, Anteil	racing bicycle	Rennrad
to prefer	vorziehen			rack	Ständer, Regal
prefix	Vorsilbe	proportional representation	Verhältniswahl	rail	Schiene
preparation	Vorbereitung			*railway*	Eisenbahn
to prepare	vorbereiten	prosperous	erfolgreich, florierend	(to) rain	Regen; regnen
(to) present	Geschenk, Gegenwart; anwesend, gegenwärtig; schenken, vorstellen			to raise	(hoch-)heben, erheben
		to protect	schützen	range	Sortiment, Umfang, Reichweite
		protection	Schutz		
		prototype	Prototyp		
(to) press	Presse; drücken, pressen	*proud*	stolz	rape seed	Rapssamen
		to provide	sorgen für, liefern, bereitstellen	rate	Rate, (Prozent-)Satz
pressure	Druck			*rather*	ziemlich
pretty	hübsch	*pub*	Kneipe	raw	Roh-; roh
previous	vorhergehend, früher	*public*	Öffentlichkeit; öffentlich	re-route	Umleitung
				to re-use	wiederverwenden
price	Preis	to publish	veröffentlichen	(to) reach	Reichweite; erreichen
pride	Stolz	to pull	ziehen		
primary school	Grundschule	(to) pump	Pumpe; pumpen	to react	reagieren
prime energy	Primärenergie	(to) punch	Schlag; schlagen	reaction	Reaktion
prime minister	Premierminister(in)	punctual	pünktlich	to read, (read, read)	lesen
principle	Grundsatz, Prinzip	to punish	(be)strafen		
print	drucken	punishing	mörderisch, hart	reader	Leser(in)
printer	Drucker	*pupil*	Schüler(in)	ready	fertig, bereit
private	privat	*purpose*	Zweck, Absicht	real	wirklich
prize	Preis, Gewinn	purpose-built	eigens zu diesem Zweck angefertigt	reality	Wirklichkeit
probable	wahrscheinlich			to realize	erkennen, bemerken
process	Vorgang, Prozess			reason	Grund

165

reasonable	vernünftig, günstig	(to) rent	Miete; mieten, vermieten	rope	Seil
to receive	erhalten, bekommen	(to) repair	Reparatur; reparieren	to rot	verrotten
recent	jüngst, kürzlich			rotation	Drehung
recently	kürzlich	(to) repeat	Wiederholung; wiederholen	round	Runde; rund, herum
reception	Empfang			rubber	(Radier-)Gummi
receptionist	Herr oder Dame am Empfang	repetitive	(sich) wiederholend, eintönig	rubbish	Abfall, Müll
				to ruin	ruinieren
to recharge	wieder aufladen	to replace	ersetzen	(to) rule	Regel, Herrschaft; herrschen
recognition	(Wieder-)Erkennung	(to) reply	Antwort; antworten		
to recognize	(wieder-)erkennen	(to) report	Bericht; berichten	to run on	laufen mit
recommendation	Empfehlung	reported speech	indirekte Rede	to run, (ran, run)	laufen
(to) record	Rekord, Aufnahme; aufnehmen	to require	benötigen, erfordern	to rush	eilen
		requirement	Bedarf, Erfordernis	Russia	Russland
recording	Aufnahme	(to) rescue	Rettung; retten		
to recover	sich erholen	research	Forschung	**S**	
recovery	Erholung	to reset	zurückstellen	(to) sacrifice	Opfer; opfern
rectangular	rechteckig	to resign	zurücktreten	sad	traurig
recyclable	wiederverwertbar	resolution	Auflösung	safe	sicher
to recycle	wiederverwerten	resort	Urlaubsort	safety	Sicherheit
red	rot	resources	Boden-, Naturschätze, Mittel	salary	Gehalt
to reduce	verringern, senken			sale	(Schluss-)Verkauf
reduction	Verminderung	responsibility	Verantwortung	sales (figures)	Verkaufszahlen
to refer to	(sich) beziehen auf	responsible	verantwortlich	sales department	Verkaufsabteilung
reference	Referenz, Bezug	(to) rest	Rest, Ruhe; ruhen	salesman/ woman	Verkäufer(in)
(with) reference to	(mit) Bezug (auf)	(to) result	Ergebnis; resultieren	salt	Salz
to reflect	widerspiegeln	retailer	Einzelhändler(in)	same	gleiche(-r, -s), der-, die-, dasselbe
to refuse	ablehnen, verweigern	(to) return	Rückkehr, Rückgabe; zurückkommen	satisfaction	Zufriedenheit
region	Gebiet, Bezirk	revival	Wiederaufleben, (-aufblühen)	satisfied	zufrieden
to register	registrieren, anmelden,			sausage	Wurst
		to rewind	zurückspulen	to save	retten
regular	regelmäßig	to rewrite	neu schreiben, umschreiben	to say, (said, said)	sagen
regulation	Vorschriften, Regelungen			scale	Maß(-stab)
		Rhodes	Rhodos	scanner	Scanner, Abtaster
related	verwandt	rich	reich	sceptical	skeptisch
relation	Beziehung	(to) ride, (rode, ridden)	Ritt, Fahrt; reiten, fahren	schedule	(Zeit-, Fahr-) Plan, Programm
relative	Verwandte(-r); relativ	right	rechts	scheme	Projekt, Plan, Programm
to relax	(sich) entspannen	(to) ring, (rang, rung)	Ring, Anruf; klingeln, anrufen	school	Schule
to release	freilassen, veröffentlichen			scientist	Wissenschaftler(in)
		riot	Aufruhr, Krawall	(to) score	Spielstand; (Treffer) erzielen
to relocate	(Geschäftssitz) verlegen	(to) rise, (rose, risen)	Aufstieg, Zunahme; (auf-)steigen, zunehmen	scramble	Gerangel, Gedrängel
to remain	bleiben			scrap	Schrott, Fetzen
(to) remark	Bemerkung; bemerken	(to) risk	Risiko; riskieren	scrap heap	Müll-, Schutt-, Schrotthaufen
		river	Fluss		
to remember	sich erinnern an	road	Straße	screen	Bildschirm, Leinwand
to remind (of)	erinnern an	robot	Roboter, vollautomatische Vorrichtung		
reminder	Erinnerung, Mahnung			(to) screw	Schraube; schrauben
		role	Rolle	sea	Meer
remote	entfernt, abgelegen	to roll	rollen	seal	Seehund
remote control	Fernbedienung	romantic	romantisch	seaside resort	Seebad
to remove	entfernen	roof	Dach	seat	Sitz
renewable	erneuerbar	room	Zimmer		

second	Sekunde; zweite (-r, -s)
secret	Geheimnis; geheim
secretary	Sekretär(in)
secure	sicher
to see, (saw, seen)	sehen
to seem	scheinen
seemingly	offensichtlich, scheinbar
self-employed	selbständig
to sell, (sold, sold)	verkaufen
seller	Verkäufer(in)
to send, (sent, sent)	schicken, senden
sensor	Sensor, Fühler
(to) sentence	Satz, Urteil; verurteilen
(to) separate	getrennt; trennen
series	Reihe, Folge
serious	ernst
(to) serve	Aufschlag (Tennis); (be-)dienen, servieren
(to) service	Dienst, Betrieb, (Auto) warten
to set, (set, set)	setzen, stellen, legen
to sever	durchtrennen, abbrechen
several	mehrere
severe	ernst
sewage	Abwasser
to shake (off) (shook, shaken)	(ab)schütteln
shall	sollen
(to) share	Anteil; teilen
sharp	scharf, deutlich, steil
sheet	Blatt, Bogen
shelf	Regal
to shift	verlagern
to shine, (shone, shone)	scheinen, leuchten
(to) ship	Schiff; verschicken
shipbuilding	Schiffbau
shipyard	Werft
shirt	Hemd
shoe	Schuh
shop	Geschäft, Laden
shop floor	Produktionsstätte, -halle
shop-assistant	Verkäufer(in)
shopper	Käufer(in)
shopping	Einkauf(en)
short	kurz
short cut	Abkürzung
short-term	kurzfristig
to shorten	kürzen
should	sollte(n)
shoulder	Schulter
(to) shout	Ruf; rufen
(to) show, (showed, shown)	Ausstellung, Vorstellung; zeigen
shower	Dusche
to shut, (shut, shut)	schließen
sick	krank
sick leave	krankheitsbedingte Abwesenheit
side	Seite
side impact beam	Seitenaufprallschutz
sight	Sicht, Anblick, Sehenswürdigkeit
(to) sign	Zeichen; unterschreiben
significant	bedeutend, bedeutsam
silencer	Schalldämpfer
similar	ähnlich
simple	einfach
simple majority voting system	Mehrheitswahlsystem
to simulate	simulieren
since	seit
since then	seitdem
to sing, (sang, sung)	singen
singer	Sänger(in)
single	einzig, hier: einheitlich
to sink	sinken
sir	Herr (Anrede)
sister	Schwester
to sit, (sat, sat)	sitzen
to sit down	sich hinsetzen
site	Grundstück, Sitz, Standort
size	Größe
skill	Fertigkeit, Fähigkeit, Können
skilled	qualifiziert, ausgebildet
skirt	Rock
sky	Himmel
(to) sleep, (slept, slept)	Schlaf; schlafen
slight	leicht, schwach, gering
slim	schlank
slogan	Slogan, Werbespruch
slow	langsam
to slow down	verlangsamen
small	klein
(to) smell	Geruch; riechen
(to) smile	Lächeln; lächeln
(to) smoke	Rauch; rauchen
smoker	Raucher(in)
smokestack	Schornstein
to snap	einrasten
(to) snow	Schnee; schneien
so far	bisher, bis jetzt
so-called	sogenannt
soap	Seife
to soar	(stark) ansteigen
soccer	Fußball
social	gesellschaftlich, sozial
social studies	Sozialwissenschaften
society	Gesellschaft
sock	Socke
soft	weich
soil	Boden, Erde
solar power	Sonnenenergie
soldier	Soldat(in)
solid	massiv, verlässlich, ganz
solution	Lösung
to solve	lösen
some	einige
somebody	jemand
someone	jemand
something	etwas
sometimes	manchmal
somewhere	irgendwo, ungefähr
son	Sohn
song	Lied
soon	bald
sophisticated	hochentwickelt, anspruchsvoll, ausgeklügelt
sorry	betrübt; tut mir leid!, Entschuldigung!
sort	Art, Sorte
(to) sound	Geräusch; klingen
sound wave	Schallwelle
source	Quelle
south	Süden, Süd-; südlich, südwärts
southern	Süd-; südlich
sovereign	Souverän, Herrscher(in)
Soviet Union	Sowjetunion
space	Platz, Raum, Weltraum
Spain	Spanien
span	Spanne; spannen
spare time	Freizeit

spark	(Zünd-)Funke	to stay	bleiben	sunshine	Sonnenschein
spark plug	Zündkerze	steady	stabil, gleichbleibend	superb	erstklassig
to speak, (spoke, spoken)	*sprechen*	to steal	stehlen	superfast	außerordentlich schnell
speaker	Sprecher(in)	steam	Dampf	*supermarket*	*Supermarkt*
special	*besondere(-r, -s), spezielle(-r, -s)*	steel	Stahl	*supper*	*Abendessen*
		step	Schritt, Stufe	supplier	Lieferant
specialist	Spezialist(in)	*still*	*dennoch, noch*	(to) supply	Versorgung; versorgen, liefern
species	(Tier-,Pflanzen-)Art, Spezies	stone	Stein	(to) support	Unterstützung; unterstützen
spectacular	spektakulär	*(to) stop*	*Halt; (an-)halten*		
speech	*Rede*	storage	Lagerung, Aufbewahrung	to suppose	annehmen, vermuten
(to) speed	*Geschwindigkeit; schnell fahren*	*(to) store*	*(Am.) Laden, Kaufhaus, Lager; lagern*	sure	sicher
to speed up	beschleunigen	storm	Sturm	surface	Oberfläche
speedy	schnell	story	Geschichte	*(to) surprise*	*Überraschung; überraschen*
(to) spell	*Zauber(spruch); buchstabieren*	straight in	(gerade) direkt hinein	surprised	überrascht
to spend, (spent, spent)	*ausgeben, verbringen*	strange	merkwürdig	survey	Überblick, Umfrage
		strap	Riemen, Träger, Bandage	survival	Überleben
spirit	Geist(eshaltung), Sinn, Einstellung	stream	Bach, Wasserlauf	suspender	Aufhängevorrichtung, Hosenträger
to spoil	verderben, ruinieren	*street*	*Straße*	suspension	Aufhängung, Ausschluss
spokesman	Sprecher	*(to) strike*	*Streik; streiken, schlagen*	suspension bridge	Hängebrücke
spoon	*Löffel*	striker	Streikende(r)	suspicious of	misstrauisch gegenüber
sports	*Sport*	stroke	Schlag, Hub		
sportsman	Sportler	*strong*	*stark*	*sweet*	*süß*
sportswoman	Sportlerin	structure	Struktur	*to swim, (swam, swum)*	*schwimmen*
to spray	Spray; sprühen, spritzen, lackieren	studies	Kurs, Studium		
		(to) study	*Studium; studieren*	*(to) switch*	*Schalter; schalten, wechseln*
spring	*Frühling*	style	Stil, Art		
square	Quadrat	sub-station	Umspannungswerk	syndrome	Syndrom
to squeeze	sich drängen, quetschen	subject	Fach, Thema	**T**	
		subject matter	Stoff, Inhalt	*table*	*Tisch, Tabelle*
stable	stabil, dauerhaft	substantial	beträchtlich, erheblich	*to take, (took, taken)*	*nehmen*
staff	*Belegschaft, Kollegium*	(to) substitute	Ersatz-; ersetzen	to take action	etwas unternehmen
staffroom	Lehrerzimmer	substitution	Ersetzen, Austausch	to take away	wegnehmen
stage	Phase, Stadium, Bühne	suburb	Vorort	to take care	aufpassen
		to succeed (in)	Erfolg haben (in, bei)	to take notes	Notizen machen
stamp	*Briefmarke*	success	Erfolg	to take off	abnehmen, starten (Flugzeug)
(to) stand, (stood, stood)	*Stand; stehen, aushalten*	successful	erfolgreich	to take over	übernehmen
		such	*solche(-r, -s)*	*to take part in*	*teilnehmen an*
standard	Niveau, Standard, Maßstab	such as	wie (zum Beispiel)	*to take place*	*stattfinden*
standard of living	Lebensstandard	to suck	(an)saugen	to take the view	der Ansicht sein
to standardize	standardisieren	*sudden*	*plötzliche(-r, -s)*	to take to pieces	zerlegen
standstill	Stillstand	to suffer from	leiden unter	*(to) talk*	*Gespräch; sprechen, reden*
to stare	starren	sugar	Zucker		
(to) start	*Anfang; anfangen*	to suggest	vorschlagen	tall	hoch(gewachsen), groß
to start up (business)	(Geschäft) anfangen	suggestion	Vorschlag		
		(to) suit	*Anzug; passen*	tape	Band, Klebestreifen
(to) state	*Staat, Zustand; erklären, darlegen*	suitable	passend, geeignet	target group	Zielgruppe
		suitcase	Koffer	task	Aufgabe
station	Bahnhof	sum	Summe		
statistics	Statistik	to sum up	zusammenfassen		
		summary	Zusammenfassung		

(to) taste	Geschmack; probieren, schmecken
tasty	lecker
tax	Steuer
tea	Tee
to teach, (taught, taught)	lehren, unterrichten
teacher	Lehrer(in)
team	Mannschaft
technical	technisch
technological	technologisch, technisch
technologist	Technologe, Technologin
technology	Technik, Technologie
telephone	Telefon
television (TV)	Fernsehen
to tell, (told, told)	erzählen
temperature	Temperatur
to tend	tendieren
tense	Zeitform
tension	Spannung
tent	Zelt
term	Ausdruck, Wort
terrible	schrecklich
(to) test	Klassenarbeit, Versuch; untersuchen, testen, überprüfen
textile	Stoff
than	als
(to) thank	Dank; danken
that	dass, jene(-r, -s), welche(-r, -s)
then	dann, damals
theory	Theorie
there	dort
there is/are	es gibt
therefore	deshalb
these	diese
these days	heutzutage
thick	dick
to thicken	dicker werden, dicker machen
thin	dünn
thing	Ding
to think, (thought, thought)	denken
thirsty	durstig
this	diese(-r, -s)
thorough	gründlich
those	jene
though	obwohl, trotzdem
thought	Gedanke
thousand	tausend
thousandth	Tausendstel
threat	(Be-)Drohung
to threaten	(be-)drohen
through	durch
throughout	die ganze Zeit, stets
to throw, (threw, thrown)	werfen
thus	so
ticket	Fahrkarte
tides	Gezeiten
tidy	ordentlich, aufgeräumt
to tie	binden, bündeln
to tighten	(fest) anziehen, verschärfen
till	bis
time	Zeit
times	Mal(e)
tired	müde
title	Titel
(to) transport	Transport; transportieren
tobacco	Tabak
today	heute
toe	Zeh
together	zusammen
toilet	Toilette
tomato	Tomate
tomorrow	morgen
ton(ne)	Tonne
tongue	Zunge
tonight	heute abend
too	auch
tool	Werkzeug
tooth, teeth	Zahn, Zähne
top	Spitze
topic	Thema
total	gesamt
(to) touch	Berührung; berühren
tough	streng, zäh
tour	(Rund-)Reise, Tour
tourism	Tourismus
tourist board	Fremdenverkehrsamt
tourist guide	Fremdenführer(in)
toward(s)	in Richtung
tower	Turm
town	Stadt
town centre	Verkehrsinfarkt
thrombosis	
town hall	Rathaus
toxic	giftig
toy	Spielzeug
(to) trace	Spur; nachgehen, nachspüren
(to) trade (in)	Gewerbe, Handel; handeln (mit)
traditional	traditionell, herkömmlich
traffic	Verkehr
traffic flow	Verkehrsfluss
traffic jam	Verkehrsstau
traffic light(s)	Ampel
(to) train	Zug; ausbilden, eine Ausbildung machen, trainieren
training	Ausbildung, Training
tram	Straßenbahn
tramway	Straßenbahngleis
to transfer	übertragen
transformator	Umwandler
to translate	übersetzen
translation	Übersetzung
transmission	Übertragung
transmission cable	Leitungskabel
to transmit	übermitteln
to travel	reisen, fahren
to treat	behandeln
treatment	Behandlung
treaty	Vertrag
tree	Baum
trillion	Trillion (Am.: Billion)
trip	(Kurz-)Reise
tropical	tropisch
trouble	Schwierigkeit(en)
trousers	Hose
true	wahr, richtig
truth	Wahrheit
(to) try	Versuch; versuchen
turbine	Turbine
to turn	(sich) drehen, wenden
to turn into	umwandeln in
to turn left/right	links/rechts abbiegen
to turn on/off	ein-/ausschalten
to turn over	umdrehen, überschlagen, laufen (Motor)
to turn to	sich zuwenden
turnover	Umsatz
TV set	Fernsehgerät
twice	zweimal
twin-engined	zweimotorig
(to) type	Art, Typ; (Maschine-)schreiben, tippen
typewriter	Schreibmaschine
typical	typisch
typist	Schreibkraft

U		(to) use	Gebrauch; gebrauchen	to wake, (woke, woken) (up)	wecken, aufwachen
ugly	hässlich	used	gebraucht, gewohnt	(to) walk	Spaziergang; gehen
ultimate	vollendet, perfekt	useful	nützlich	wall	Wand, Mauer
umbrella	*Schirm*	useless	nutzlos	to want	wollen
(to be) unable	nicht in der Lage (sein)	user	Benutzer(in)	war	Krieg
unavoidable	unvermeidbar	usual	gewöhnlich	warehouse	Lager
uncle	*Onkel*			(to) warm	warm; wärmen
undemocratic	undemokratisch	**V**		to warn	warnen
underground	Untergrund, U-Bahn	vacancy	freie Stelle	warning	Warnung
to underline	unterstreichen	vacation	Ferien	Warsaw	Warschau
underpaid	unterbezahlt	vacuum-cleaner	Staubsauger	wartime	Kriegszeit
to understand, (understood, understood)	*verstehen*	valley	Tal	to wash	waschen
		value	Wert	washing-machine	Waschmaschine
undesirable	unerwünscht	van	Lieferwagen	(to) waste	Abfall, Verschwendung; verschwenden
unemployed	*arbeitslos*	various	verschieden, vielfältig		
unemployment	*Arbeitslosigkeit*			waste management	Abfallwirtschaft
unemployment benefit	Arbeitslosenunterstützung	to vary	sich ändern, unterschiedlich sein		
				waste-melting	"Einschmelzen" von Abfall
unfortunate	*unglücklich*	vegetable(s)	Gemüse		
unfortunately	*leider*	vehicle	Fahrzeug	wasteful	verschwenderisch
unfriendly	*unfreundlich*	version	Version, Fassung	(to) watch	Uhr; beobachten, sehen
unhappy	*unglücklich*	very	sehr		
unimportant	unwichtig	via	über	water	Wasser
uninhabitable	unbewohnbar	Vienna	Wien	wave	Welle
union	Gewerkschaft	Vietnamese	Vietnamese, Vietnamesin; vietnamesisch	*way*	*Weg, Art und Weise*
unit	Einheit, Gruppe, Kapitel			way of life	Lebensweise
		view	Sicht, Ansicht, Aussicht	weak	schwach
united	vereinigt			to weaken	schwächen
unity	Einheit	viewer	Zuschauer(in)	wealth	Wohlstand, Reichtum
university	*Universität*	viewpoint	Standpunkt		
unknown	unbekannt	*village*	*Dorf*	wealthy	wohlhabend
unless	wenn ... nicht, es sei denn	visa	Visum	to wear, wore, worn	(Kleidung) tragen
		(to) visit	Besuch; besuchen		
unlikely	unwahrscheinlich	visitor	Besucher(in)	weather	Wetter
unlimited (company)	Gesellschaft mit unbeschränkter Haftung	visual	visuell, optisch	wedding	Hochzeit
		vital	lebenswichtig, entscheidend	week	Woche
				weekend	Wochenende
unpopular	unpopulär	*vocabulary*	*Wortschatz, Vokabelverzeichnis*	weight	Gewicht
unreliable	unzuverlässig			(to) welcome	Willkommen, Empfang; willkommen (heißen)
unsuitable	unpassend, ungeeignet	voice	Stimme		
unsupported	ungestützt, nicht unterstützt	voltage	elektrische Spannung	to weld	schweißen
		volume	Lautstärke	welfare	Wohl, Wohlfahrt, Sozialhilfe
until (till)	*bis*	(to) vote	Abstimmung, Stimme; abstimmen, wählen		
unusual	ungewöhnlich			well	gut, gesund; na ja ...
unwilling	nicht bereit (etwas zu tun), widerwillig	voter	Wähler(in)		
		voting system	Wahlsystem	well-known	bekannt
up to	bis zu			well-meaning	wohlmeinend
up to now	bis jetzt	**W**		well-paid	gut bezahlt
up until now	bis jetzt	wage	Lohn	Welsh	walisisch
upon	*auf*	to wait	warten	*west*	*Westen, West-; westlich, westwärts*
upstairs	*(nach) oben, im Obergeschoß*	waiter	Kellner		
		waitress	Kellnerin	western	West-; westlich
(to) urge	Drang; drängen				

wet	nass, feucht	winner	Gewinner(in)	worst	am schlechtesten
what	was	(to) wish	Wunsch; wünschen	worth	wert
what about?	was ist mit?	within	innerhalb	would like	würde(n) gerne
what else	was noch	without	ohne	to write,	schreiben
what for	wofür, wozu	woman	Frau	(wrote, written)	
what … like?	wie …?	(to) wonder	Wunder; sich fragen,	writer	Verfasser(in),
wheel	Rad		sich wundern		Schriftsteller(in)
when	wann	wonderful	wunderbar	wrong	falsch
where	wo	wood	Holz, Wald		
whereas	während	wooden	hölzern	**Y**	
whether	ob	wool	Wolle	year	Jahr
which	welche(-r, -s)	word	Wort	yearly	jährlich
while	während	word-by-word	Wort für Wort	(… years) ago	vor (… Jahren)
white	weiß	(to) work	Arbeit; arbeiten	yellow	gelb
who	wer	to work out	herausfinden, aus-	yesterday	gestern
whole	ganz		arbeiten, lösen	yet	jedoch, schon
whom	wem, wen	worker	Arbeiter(in)	you're welcome	gern geschehen!
whose	wessen	working class	Arbeiterklasse	young	jung
why	warum	working hours	Arbeitszeit	Yours	dein(e)
wide	weit	working week	Arbeitswoche	Yours faithfully	Hochachtungsvoll
wife	Ehefrau	workmate	Kollege, Kollegin	Yours sincerely	Mit freundlichen
will	Wille; werden	workshop	Werkstatt		Grüßen
willing	bereit	world	Welt	youth	Jugend
to win,	gewinnen	worldwide	weltweit		
(won, won)		worried	besorgt	**Z**	
window	Fenster	to worry	sich sorgen, sich	zero	null
windy	windig		beunruhigen	zinc	Zink
wine	Wein	worse	schlechter		

Unit 1

D 1

(An exchange visit)

Mrs Evans: So what are you doing at College this week, John?

John: We're working on the environment project until Thursday, Mum. After that there's a visit to the electronics factory near here and to the power station in Hartlepool. I'm looking forward to it, I think it's really great that we have the chance to see places like that.

Klaus: Oh yes, I'm looking forward to it, too.

Mrs Evans: I'm glad you're enjoying this week, Klaus.

Klaus: Yes, I am. I'm learning such a lot about Britain and the way you do things here.

Mrs Evans: That's why these exchanges are such a good idea in my opinion. You young people have the chance to really get to know each other and that's important.

Klaus: Oh yes, I agree with you, Mrs Evans. I don't think that tourists learn half as much about the people or the country they visit.

John: Exactly. They don't have enough contact with the locals in my view. And when they come back they still think, for example, that all the Germans are serious and work hard.

Klaus: Or that the British are very traditional and drink tea all day!

Mrs Evans: But I suppose it's a bit strange for you, Klaus, living with a foreign family?

Klaus: No, not at all. I mean, you're all so friendly to me. Your house is so comfortable and I love the food. In fact, I feel quite at home already! Even the T.V. programmes are the same as the ones we have at home!

Unit 2

D

(Job advertisements)

Interviewer: Well Miss Long, your CV seems alright. Tell me. What I'd like to know is which subjects did you enjoy most at school?

Miss Long: Ah... I liked foreign languages the most. We did French and German.

Interviewer: And can you speak them well?

Miss Long: Mm, my French isn't so good now, but I think my German is alright. I often spend my holidays in Germany as I have some friends over there and that gives me a chance to practise.

Interviewer: Hm. And why have you applied for this job?

Miss Long: Two main reasons really. First I'd like to travel in Europe more. And secondly, I'm only 22, and I feel it's time for a change. I'd like a more interesting job. As you know, I've worked as a secretary at Hard and Soft for 2 years now in the sales department. They produce machine parts for the car industry. I don't like the work...

Interviewer: Mr Short. I see from your CV that you now work for a large electrical company. Why do you want to change jobs?

Mr Short: Well I'm 30 and I've worked at ElectroMagnum for 5 years. It's time for me to look for something else. I've been a computer operator for 8 years now.

Interviewer: Aren't you happy in your present job?

Mr Short: Well, not really. What I want is a new challenge. And the pay at ElectroMagnum isn't that good.

Interviewer: Well, we can talk about that later. Now, I see from your letter of application that you did a B.Tec course in electrical engineering. What did you like most on that course?

Mr Short: The practical work was the really interesting part of the course, although I also enjoyed learning German. The trouble was I wasn't very good at it.

Interviewer: But you do know that this job involves travelling to Europe a lot and especially to our customers in Germany?

Mr Short: Yes, I know, and I am going to evening classes to improve my German. It's hard work though...

Unit 3

D1

(Voting systems)

((Politician 1)) Brian Taylor:
"Good morning ladies and gentlemen. And welcome to Westminster. My name's Brian Taylor and before I became an MP, I ran my own farm in Scotland and farming is still one of my main interests. In a way, I suppose you could say that I was fortunate to get into Parliament in the first place. You see, I belong to the Liberal Democrats. We're one of the smallest parties in the British Parliament, not because we have the fewest voters, but because of the British voting system. In Great Britain the voters have one vote, which they can use for one particular candidate. The candidate who receives the most votes becomes the Member of Parliament for that con-

stituency. I was lucky in 1992 when I won the election in Perth. But just look at these statistics... "

((Politician 2)) Inge Jensen:
"Hello, I'm Inge Jensen from Copenhagen. Well, we in Denmark have a different voting system to that in Great Britain. Here, the party that wins most of the votes over the whole of Denmark has the most members in our Parliament – which is called the Folketing by the way. This is certainly more democratic because the smaller parties can get into Parliament more easily. Anyway, I expect you'd like to know more about me. Well, I joined the Danish Conservative Party while I was still at school and have been a member ever since. After I left school I got a job as a computer operator. However, politics remained one of my main interests and three years ago I became a member of the Danish Parliament. It has been hard work because I've got two children and a husband to look after as well as my work in Parliament. That's one reason why I'm especially interested in family affairs in politics. But let me go back to our voting system. Now, in my opinion,..."

Unit 4

D1

(Radio advertising)

1.
Keep on running, keep on hiding.
One fine day I'm gonna be the one to make you understand.
With Lukes you're gonna be a man!
Hey, hey, hey everyone is wearing them now. Nearly all the time. Hey, hey, hey your local store is stocking them now. At only £10.99.
Keep on running...

Lukes – the superfast running shoes. Really comfortable and built for speed! Get yours today at Simpson's Sports Store, Penarth Road.

2.
When you order your new car from Wyndham Jones, you can be confident that you're choosing from a world class range. You can be confident that every first-class car is totally safe and engineered to perfection. You can also be sure that at Wyndham Jones you will get excellent service. So whether you want a small or a family-sized car, at Wyndham Jones you know your choice will be the right one! Prices for the 'City' model start at £14,000. Wyndham Jones, Queen Street, Cardiff. Discover the difference!

3.
Shop assistant: Good afternoon sir, can I help you?
Customer: Oh, I'm looking for a personal C.D. player, actually. You know, one that you can carry around.
Shop assistant: I'm sure we can help you there, sir. Here at Sizzle superstore, we have a very large stock. This superb new Williams Mini-master model is very popular.
Customer: Yes, it's not bad, but it hasn't got many functions on it, has it? I mean, it's a bit basic, isn't it? Those Japanese ones, they're very good. Lots of functions on them. My mate at work bought one last week, he thinks it's marvellous.
Shop assistant: Alright sir, but I think you'll find that this Williams model is just as good. It's light and easy to use. It's got twenty functions and it only costs £99.
Customer: 99 pounds! Williams, you say, new company is it? Can't say I've heard of them. But 20 functions for 99 pounds, I'll take it!

Unit 5

D1

(Travel announcements)

1. The train now standing at platform 5 is the 10.20 to Liverpool, calling at Birmingham and Manchester. Passengers for Leeds and Newcastle please change at Birmingham.

2. Flight BA 98 to Dublin is now ready for boarding. Would all passengers please proceed to Gate A6. We apologize for the delay which was due to fog at Dublin Airport. We hope you have a pleasant flight.

3. Travel news ! Trouble again on the M4 motorway near Bristol, where there has been a serious accident. Two lorries are now blocking the westbound section of the motorway and there is a three-mile traffic jam. The police advise motorists to leave the motorway at Exit 19 and to follow the diversion signs.

Unit 6

D1

(Ecology or economics?)

Technologists, working for Zinc UK, a leading British mining company, have just published their plans for North Cornwall. They maintain that they have discovered large deposits of zinc ore in this beautiful part of the country not far from the seaside resorts of St. Agnes and Perranporth. The company believes that this is an extremely interesting commercial project because the ore contains a lot of zinc – up to 24%. And according to Zinc UK there are about 50 million tonnes of the ore only 40 metres below the surface. Furthermore, Zinc UK emphasizes that this project will create about 200 new jobs in North Cornwall. However, not all the people in Cornwall are happy with the news. Local environmentalists and hotel owners have already expressed their fears. They are convinced that the mining project will destroy the area. The environmentalists believe that the beautiful countryside and the wild animals there are in danger. For this reason they have organized a demonstration to take place next week. Some hotel owners have joined the protest action because they fear that the mining company plans to turn the small seaside resorts into big ports for container ships to transport the zinc ore. According to hotel owners this will mean the death of the tourist resorts. So far Zinc UK has refused to make any further comment on this development.

Unit 7

D1

(The Idaho alternative power station)

Chat: Now, this here's where our fuel arrives. The trucks drive straight in and drop the manure into those storage pits way down at the end there.

John: I see. And what about the people who live near here. Do they ever complain about the smell?

Chat: Well, no. We found a kind of neat solution to that problem. You see, the pressure here in the delivery hall is lower, so no fumes can get out. Now do you have your mask? We're going on through to the storage hall.

John: Do many people have to work in here?

Chat: No, there ain't many people here at all. From this point, the plant is fully-automated. Those cranes there for example, which are taking the manure from the storage pits to burn in the furnace, are all computer-controlled.

John: And this furnace produces steam for the turbine, I suppose.

Chat: That's right. It gets real hot in that furnace – up to 800 degrees.

John: And what's your actual output here?

Chat: The generator produces 12.5 megawatts. That's enough electricity for 12,500 homes around here.

John: "Farmphos" – that's your fertilizer, isn't it? I could use some of that for my roses back home.

Chat: Yeah, I was fixing to give you a sack before you left. We produce it from the ash in the furnace. It's a quality product and very good for the environment...

Unit 8

D1

(Sales talk)

Salesman: Good afternoon. Can I help you?

Customer: Well, actually I'm interested in one of your printers. You had an advert in the local paper.

Salesman: Ah, you mean the new laser printer. The Macprint XL7.

Customer: Yes, that's right. Have you still got it in stock?

Salesman: Of course. If you'd like to come over here I can show it to you.

Customer: Hm, nice design.

Salesman: It not only looks good, it's one of the fastest printers on the market at the moment. It can do 20 pages per minute. And the print quality – I'll show you. What do you say to that?

Customer: Yes, it's pretty good.

Salesman: Pretty good? That's the best resolution you can get.

Customer: But what about paper? Can I use different types of paper?

Salesman: Of course. It even does envelopes as well. See this button here. You can decide what size paper you want to print, A4, A3, what you want.

Customer: That sounds good, but what about installing it? Can that be a problem?

Salesman: No, it's really easy. The handbook is so clearly written that even a complete beginner can understand it.

Customer: And what if something goes wrong with the printer?

Salesman: Well, that shouldn't happen. We at Microstore have a very good reputation, as you know. But if you did have a problem, we would come out right away and help you on the same day. You know, these big superstores are a little cheaper, but you don't get the same individual service as we offer.

Customer: Right. How much does one of these cost?

Salesman: It's yours for just £1,499 I think you'll agree that's a fantastic offer. A real bargain. And don't forget our guaranteed good service if anything goes wrong.

Customer: I'll have to think about it first.

Salesman: Yes, of course. May I give you my card?

The name's John Clark. Please ask for me when you come in again.

Customer: Thank you very much.

Salesman: Thank you. May I give you this brochure...

Unit 9

D

(Looking for a new location)

Telephone call 1

Hello there. At the moment I'm here inside the busy shopping centre in Wetherby. Wetherby is a small town only 20 kilometres north west of Leeds, in the north of England. You've probably never heard of it but I can assure you Wetherby is a town which is developing quickly. And I think its success is mainly due to its excellent position. To give you a general idea – it's right next to the A1. And from that main road it's only half an hour's drive down to the M62 motorway which links the big ports of Liverpool and Hull.

As I already said, Wetherby is expanding and the new industrial park just outside the town shows us what opportunities it in fact has. Most of the companies which have their sites there seem to be involved with light industry of one kind or another. The people in the development council I spoke to were very helpful and from my talks with them I found out that the price of land is much lower here than it is in the South of England. Despite the high unemployment rate in the area there's a positive atmosphere about the place. I would say, moreover, that the mixture of modern houses, good roads and clean, modern industry makes Wetherby a pleasant place to live and work. **((fade out))**

Telephone call 2

Hello there. Right now I'm sitting at the railway station here in Wolverhampton. Wolverhampton is about 20 kilometres north west of Birmingham, right in the middle of England.

Wolverhampton is a typical Black Country town, with both heavy and light industries, although most of the steelworks and coal mines have now been closed down. As a result, Wolverhampton still has a rather high unemployment rate. The development council seems to be doing its best, but land still seems difficult to get and is also quite expensive. Most of the people I've spoken to live outside Wolverhampton. They said they prefer living in the new housing estates west of Wolverhampton rather than in the old terraced houses in town. One big advantage for companies here is that Wolverhampton is near the M6 motorway, which is a direct link to London and the Continent. This has attracted a lot of business to the area and has helped Wolverhampton to become a modern industrial centre. The visitor here gets the impression that Wolverhampton is a town which understands how to use the know-how and skills of its manufacturing tradition and at the same time be part of the 21st century.

Unit 10

D1

(The new majority)

1.

I was told by the Russian authorities five or six times that I had no chance to get a visa. You see, back home in Minsk I was a painter. I was married and I had two sons. The only problem was – I was a Russian Jew. In spite of all the difficulties at that time I was reasonably happy, but it was my two sons who wanted to emigrate. In the end we got our visa and arrived here in San Francisco. With all our savings we opened a small fruit and vegetable store. But what I'm really proud of is how my two sons have come to terms with life in America. They are real Americans. I still have a few problems with the language but on the whole I feel happy here. Sometimes I get a little homesick, though.

2.

We came to America ten years ago from Cambodia as refugees. We had no luggage and no money. In Cambodia both my husband and I worked in a restaurant until the Khmer Rouge army took over. We decided to leave our country and made our way to the refugee camps in Thailand. From there we got our visa for America. It was very hard for us at first, but now we've both got jobs near our apartment here in Los Angeles. I work on the production line of a chemical company. The pay is quite good – although it is a 45 hour working week. It's harder for my husband. He's got two part time jobs. In the mornings he works at a training center for Cambodians and the rest of the time he drives a truck for a food-processing company. He does not get home until 11 or 12 o' clock at night. That's not good for the family. The three children only really see him at weekends.

3.

I have been married now for 5 years but I've never met my wife's parents and she has not seen mine. You see, we arrived here from across the border seven years ago as so-called illegal immigrants and we do not dare leave America – we are afraid we will not be able to get across the border again. I have been working as a farm worker here in California and my wife has now got part-time work in a factory not far from our home in San Diego. Life is not easy as an "illegal" but what alternative do we have? You see, in Mexico you cannot find work – that is why we came here in the first place. And I think our daughter has a better future here than back home. Maybe we will get our visa one day.

Quellenverzeichnis

Bilder und Cartoons

Titelseite: ZEFA Zentrale Farbbild Agentur GmbH, Hamburg

S. 9: Sharon: H.-W. Thunig, Winterbach; Garage: B. Boulton, Minehead; Technology Department: IBM Deutschland GmbH; Car Design: IBM Deutschland GmbH; GCSE Certificate: C. Haydon, Stuttgart; BTEC National Diploma: Business & Technology Education Council, London; Kevin: B. Boulton, Minehead; Business Studies Department: H.-W. Thunig, Winterbach; Bachelor of Arts Degree: University of London

S. 11: H.-W. Thunig, Winterbach

S. 12: B. Boulton, Minehead

S. 13: o: B. Boulton, Minehead; u. H.-W. Thunig, Winterbach

S. 14: G. Tucker, Castrop-Rauxel

S. 16: li. Mercedes Benz AG, Sindelfingen; Mi. British Tourist Authority, Frankfurt; re. B. Boulton, Minehead

S. 18–21: H.-W. Thunig, Winterbach

S. 26: B. Boulton, Minehead

S. 29: o: David Shallis, Leonberg; u. Sally Ferries, Ramsgate

S. 30: The European, London

S. 32: B. Boulton, Minehead

S. 36: H.-W. Thunig, Winterbach

S. 37: B. Boulton, Minehead

S. 40: o. E. Feuerbach, Stuttgart; u. Young & Rubicam Ltd., London

S. 41: McLachlan Associates, Leicestershire

S. 42: o. The J. Allan Cash PhotoLibrary, London; u. Panstar Limited, London

S. 43: Trafficmaster Plc, Milton Keynes

S. 45: B. Boulton, Minehead

S. 46: Dr. M. Pabst, München

S. 47: British Rail: Klett-Archiv; Mini-Bus: Klett-Archiv; E-mobil: E-mobil GmbH, Stuttgart; Speed Limit: Klett-Archiv; No Parking: Klett-Archiv

S. 48: City of Wakefield, Metropolitan District Council, Wakefield

S. 49: Dennis Capolongo/Greenpeace, London

S. 51: (1) E. Feuerbach, Stuttgart; (2), (3), (4) Torrobay Ltd., London

S. 53: K. Schickentanz, Stuttgart

S. 54: BMW AG, München

S. 57: OFT Reisen, Ditzingen

S. 61: H.-W. Thunig, Winterbach

S. 62: li. A. Arenz, Twin Falls, Idaho; re. Klett-Archiv

S. 65: o. Ullstein Bilderdienst, Berlin; u. BMW AG, München

S. 68: BMW AG, München

S. 69: H.-W. Thunig, Winterbach

S. 73: Leeds City Council, Leeds

S. 74: J. Krüger, Stuttgart

S. 75: Tyne and Wear Development Corporation, Newcastle upon Tyne

S. 77: H.-W. Thunig, Winterbach

S. 80: Osborne Publicity Services Limited, Derbyshire

S. 81: Obdachloser: ifa, Stuttgart; Freiheitsstatue: Klett-Archiv; Arbeitslose: UPI Bettmann, New York; Segelschiff: Klett-Archiv; Illegaler Einwanderer: Keith Dannemiller – action press, Hamburg; Kubanische Flüchtlinge: Photo AP, Frankfurt

S. 82: o. U.S. Information Service, Bonn; u. © Sarah Lock, HongKong

S. 84: ifa, Stuttgart

S. 85: W. Schickentanz, Hameln

S. 86: U.S. Information Service, Bonn

S. 88: li. M. Görrissen, Ludwigshafen; Mi. Jürgens Photo, Berlin; re. ifa, Stuttgart

S. 89: Heureka-Klett GmbH, Stuttgart

S. 90: action press/allsport photograph, Hamburg

S. 91: Homer Sykes/Impact, London

S. 92: Porsche Kremer Racing, Köln

S. 96: Klett-Archiv

S. 100: Chip Vinai/Greenpeace, Hamburg

S. 104: Boeing Commercial Airplane Group, Frankfurt

S. 107: IBM Deutschland GmbH

S. 108: Klett-Archiv

In einigen Fällen ist es uns trotz intensiver Bemühungen nicht gelungen, die Rechte-Inhaber zu ermitteln.
Wir bitten diese, sich mit dem Verlag in Verbindung zu setzen.